W9-DBV-903

WORLD WAR II IN PICTURES

Volume II

HERMAN C. MORRIS and HARRY B. HENDERSON, Editors

SAM SHAW, Art and Picture Editor

THE WORLD PUBLISHING COMPANY
CLEVELAND AND NEW YORK

Acknowledgements

The editors acknowledge with appreciation the co-operation of the following contributors who have made possible this volume: International News Photos, Inc.; Sovfoto; British Library of Information; British Information Services; Australian News and Information Bureau; Government of India Information Services; Free French Delegation; Pan American Union; French Press and Information Service; United Nations Information Office; Royal Yugoslav Government-in-exile; Netherlands Information Bureau; Polish Government Information Center; Greek Office of Information; Office of Production Management; Office of Emergency Management; Library of Congress; Standard Oil Co. of N. J.; Boeing Airplane Co.; Office of War Information; News of the Day; Press Association; U. S. Air Forces; U. S. Signal Corps; U. S. Navy; U. S. Marines; U. S. Coast Guard; U. S. Maritime Commission; Farm Security Administration; United Service Organization, Inc.; Acme Newspictures, Inc.; British Combine; Brown Brothers; CNS Photos—Paul Guillumette, Inc.; China Film; United China Relief; Three Lions; Phil Stern; Paul Parker Photo; Harrison Forman; and European Picture Service. Maps: PM Daily, The New York Times, British Library of Information, and Richard Edes Harrison.

Detailed picture credits will be given in the final volume.

Parts of the book have been taken from *War in Our Time* under the supervision of William Hendelson and Mary Derieux.

Contents

Roosevelt, Churchill, and aides attending church services during their historic meeting at sea, Aug. 1941.

THE ATLANTIC CHARTER

HITLER had hoped his "crusade" against the Soviets would bring, if not peace with England, at least complacency and no aid to Russia. But Churchill swiftly disillusioned him the very day Russia was invaded, declaring: "Any man or state who fights against Nazism will have our aid. . . . The Russian danger is our danger and the danger of the United States, just as the cause of any Russian fighting for his hearth and home is the cause of free men and free people in every quarter of the globe. . . ." Echoing Churchill's remarks, President Roosevelt paid tribute to the "magnificent" fight of the Red Army and dispatched Harry Hopkins to Moscow to learn what the Russians needed most. On July 12 Britain and Russia signed a pact of mutual assistance. Similar pacts between Russia and the Polish and Czech governments-in-exile followed; Soviet Russia agreed not to recognize her move into Poland in 1939. On Aug. 2 the United States and the Soviets exchanged notes recognizing Nazism as their common enemy. Meanwhile, the R.A.F., in an effort to aid Russia, launched mass daylight raids on Germany and the occupied countries. England and United States were preparing to pool their resources to aid Russia while England faced the task of opening a second front in Europe. On Aug. 12 President Roosevelt and Churchill met secretly at sea aboard the *Prince of Wales* off the coast of Newfoundland to discuss these problems and set up the guiding principles for the peace which was to come when victory had been won. Both countries were fully represented by their military, naval, and supply chiefs, and for three days the discussions went on. The result of this conference, the Atlantic Charter, was announced on August 14. Its chief points pledged no territorial aggrandizement, no territorial changes that were not in accord with the wishes of the peoples concerned, the right of all people to choose their own form of government, free and equal accession to the raw materials and trade of the world by all nations, disarmament after the war. On Aug. 15 Churchill and Roosevelt sent a joint letter to Stalin, who had signified his acceptance of the Atlantic Charter, suggesting a conference in Moscow on increased aid to Russia. Stalin immediately invited delegations. The U.S. sent Harry Hopkins and W. Averell Harriman while Britain sent energetic Lord Beaverbrook.

With each newly liberated country Lend-Lease takes on new significance, the figures involved soar to new astronomical highs. But Lend-Lease is no longer a one-way street. In the beginning, with England reeling under the air-blitz, with Russia's richest food-producing and industrial areas overrun by Nazis or devastated by Soviet scorched-earth policy (or both), it was the U.S. who had to pour food, supplies, munitions across two oceans as fast as ship-builders could keep ahead of the deadly submarine. It was a magnificent achievement, one of which America may well be proud. It helped keep Britain's RAF in the air when they were the world's only barrier across the path of Nazi conquest. It helped Russia, psychologically more than materially, when Hitler's Huns had pushed them back to the very gates of Moscow and Leningrad, dislodging millions of people, sprawling arrogantly over vast reaches of once-productive territory. It brought the first ray of hope to China in her long dark years under the sinister shadow of Japanese aggression. This lend-lease principle—bitterly controversial innovation which has proved itself to be an innovation in the uncrowded field of creative statesmanship—has taken unto itself new and more euphonious names. We speak of it now more often as "Mutual Aid" or "Reciprocal Aid" and that is exactly what it is. When Russia and China joined America and Britain, to girdle the globe with a chain of synchronized activities all directed to one common end, throwing their fighting forces and material resources into the greatest pool of power the world had ever seen, something new had come into man's experience—a faint new hope that someday constructive, co-operative peace might replace the age-old destructive rivalries of war. It was no millennium yet. Disagreements, bickerings, misunderstandings between Allies would still bog down the wheels of action, still furnish aid and comfort to an enemy who could no longer find even their shadow in any other quarter. But a step had been taken, a long step, in the right direction. From the very beginning, America's Allies did their best to supply at least a token of that reverse Lend-Lease which was to grow into a flood of time-saving, life-saving mutual helpfulness from ocean to ocean and continent to continent. Even in those early days, when we furnished Britain with the much-publicized 50 destroyers, they were used in many a convoy which helped keep our own ships sailing on the high seas instead of resting on the ocean bed. From the day when a new AEF landed on British soil in numbers that almost crowded the inhabitants of that "tight little isle" into the sea, the bread we cast upon the waters has indeed been returning to us. Every possible facility in Britain was put at the disposal of U.S. Army Headquarters. Nobody had time to figure the exact cash value of food, supplies, equipment Britain furnished American forces preparing at top speed for invasion of the continent. But at the end of their first year in England the U.S. had spent for supplies for all our forces only about a million dollars—a proportion of 2,500 to 1 as contrasted with AEF figures in World War 1. In the month of December, 1942, with 2,000,000 on the other side of the Atlantic, the U.S. spent $25,000 in cash for their supplies. The British furnished the rest. So it goes, through the list of United Nations, each one contributing as much as possible whenever possible to the common pool, uniting in a system under which goods and services may flow freely to those points at which they will be most effective in the common war effort. In Allied achievements through the closing months of 1944 we have had ample proof that this new principle of mutual international aid in the economic field is important equally with the magnificent pooling of Allied military power which has sealed the fate of the Axis powers in their mad bid for world dominion.

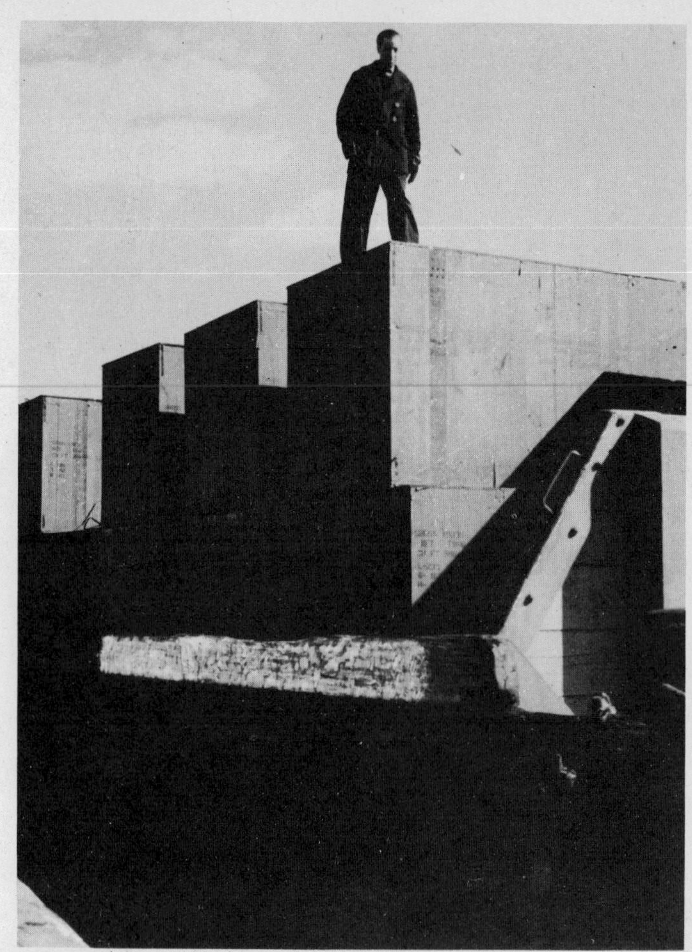

Miniature Dodge trucks, on barges, wait for shipment to Russia.

Lend-Lease creates good will among ill-clad Arabs.

BRITISH-MANNED SHERMAN TANKS follow Lend-Lease into action on Italian front. By 1943 U.S. was shipping everything needed for mechanized war to a hundred battle areas. From Oct. 1941 to Mar. 1944, war supplies and food for Russia alone totaled 9,500,000 tons, included 8,800 planes, 5,200 tanks and tank destroyers, 190,000 trucks. In the same period Britain sent over 5,000 tanks, 6,700 aircraft, many other essentials.

UNDER REVERSE LEND-LEASE, these stoves, made in Scotland to heat U.S. mess-halls, are among thousands of items overflowing U.S. marshalling yards in Britain for distribution to our forces. Huge cranes from Sheffield, bolts from Birmingham, woolens from Yorkshire, food and supplies from every part of the Dominion are turned over, without formality, red-tape, or cash to American Service of Supply.

BOMBS FROM THE U.S. FOR TURKISH PLANES are unloaded at a Turkish port. Lend-Lease—which was extended to Turkey Dec. 3, 1941—became a powerful weapon in Allied hands, helping to offset Axis pressure on neutral countries. In April, 1944 Turkey took a positive stand for the Allies, stopped chrome shipments to Nazis, in June closed the Dardanelles to Nazi war vessels posing as merchantmen.

JAPANESE AMBASSADOR Kichisaburo Nomura, shown entering the White House, initiated talks with the United States at the end of August "to establish a new basis for U. S. relations with Japan," which was spending almost $7,000,000 a year in America on propaganda. Meanwhile, Tokyo began the economic penetration of strategic Thailand, already overrun with Jap 5th columnists.

"SO SORRY..."

Since May, when Vichy France gave Japan economic control of French Indo-China, Japanese-U. S. relations had been under increasing strain as Japan moved toward greater power in the Pacific. With the invasion of Russia by Hitler, the Japanese announced their policy was "immutable." It was expected in many quarters that Japan as the eastern Axis partner would attack Vladivostok. But the eastern Red Banner armies had smashed Japanese troops in two major "border clashes" in 1938 and 1939 and any doubts about the "immutable" Japanese policy were resolved, June 23, 1941, when Vichy accepted Japanese demands for military bases and the right of transit for troops. The new Tokyo move menaced Burma, Malaya, and Singapore, as well as China's Burma Road, the Philippines, and U. S. power in the Pacific. President Roosevelt, who for years had maintained a conciliatory policy toward Japan while, like most Americans, sympathizing with the Chinese people's heroic fight for freedom, made it clear that United States could no longer view Japan's expansion without alarm. On July 25 Britain and the U. S. froze Japanese assets. England canceled her own, Burma's, and India's trade treaties with the Japanese. President Roosevelt ordered the calling up of the military forces of the Philippines under Gen. Douglas MacArthur. On Aug. 1 the President placed an embargo on shipment of aviation gasoline and oil to Japan while the Dutch followed suit in a stern demonstration that the ABCD powers (America, Britian, China, Dutch), were united and meant business.

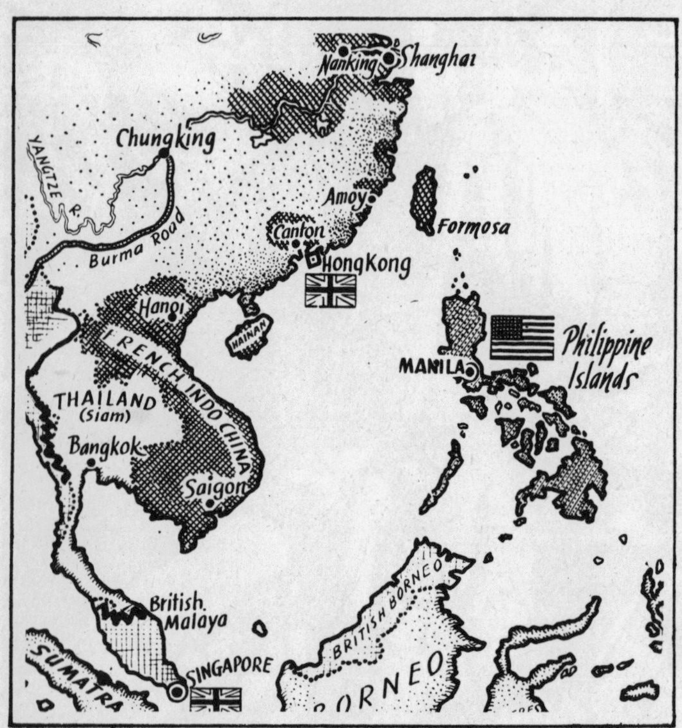

THAILAND OFFERED the Japanese direct access to Burma and British Malaya. The fall of these points would greatly endanger the Philippines. To allay U. S. fears Tokyo released optimistic reports of their belief in peace with the United States and cancelled their intended protests against American shipments of oil to Soviet Russia through the Pacific port of Vladivostok.

BY SEPT. 21 SECRETARY HULL and Nomura found themselves deadlocked. The Japanese demanded U. S. aid to the brave Chinese be stopped and their "new order" be recognized. This the U. S. refused to do. But as negotiations broke down Tokyo announced it was sending Saburo Kurusu to Washington with a new formula to continue negotiations for a peaceful settlement.

NOMURA MET KURUSU on his arrival by plane in Washington on Nov. 15. His dramatic flight brought new optimism to the U. S. although Washington continued to believe there was little hope for peace. Premier Tojo had said, Oct. 26: "Japan must go on and develop in ever-expanding progress—there is no retreat. . . . Nothing can stop us. . . . Wars can be fought with ease." Japanese troop transports flowed steadily southward. Meanwhile, Kurusu began his talks and on Nov. 27 saw President Roosevelt. But by Dec. 3 talks had reached an impasse. Yet the Japanese were not ready to give up negotiations, insisted that they continue, reiterated their desire for peace. They made a new appointment with Secretary Hull for December 7th, 1941.

AT 2:05 P.M. ON DEC. 7 Nomura and Kurusu arrived at the U. S. State Department to see Secretary Hull. Theirs was one of the most treacherous roles in history. Both men probably knew when this picture was made that Japanese planes were bombing Pearl Harbor, the Philippines, and other U. S. Pacific outposts. Note their bland expressions of serenity.

THE PERFIDIOUS JAPANESE AMBASSADORS LEFT Hull's office trying their best to look like martyrs. Just before they talked to Secretary Hull, word had arrived of the surprise attack on Pearl Harbor. But the report was unconfirmed and Hull restrained his angry denunciation of their government to a note they presented which verbally attacked the United States.

At 6:30 A.M. Dec. 7, 1941, a Navy supply ship sighted a Japanese sub off the great U.S. Pacific naval base, Pearl Harbor, at Oahu, Hawaii. Within five minutes the sub had been sunk by a U.S. destroyer and plane. Yet no alert was sounded. At 7:02 A.M. Corp. Joseph Lockard, operating the base's aircraft detection system in voluntary practice, located a large fleet of planes 130 miles northeast of Oahu, but his superiors dismissed them as U.S. planes. No action was taken. At 7:45 a Japanese sub was sighted inside of submarine nets of Pearl Harbor. Ten minutes later a large fleet of Japanese dive bombers dropped out of the skies from all sides, turning the ship-filled harbor and near-by Hickam Field into blazing infernos. Spies had given pilots the exact location of hangars, munitions, anti-aircraft guns, and each plane hurled its death load at a specific objective. U.S. soldiers, sailors, and fliers fought heroically amid flaming wreckage to beat off the attack, but the initial Japanese raiders hit so many of the harbor's defensive weapons that they were able to do little. New waves of raiders struck at 11:29, at 11:59, at 12:22, at 7:15 P.M. and at 9:10 P.M. By the end of the day the Japanese had crippled the striking power of the U.S. Pacific Fleet and

PEARL HARBOR

were free to proceed to the invasion of Malaya, the Philippines, and the Dutch East Indies. The powerful battleship *Arizona*, shown above with her flag still flying, had been sunk along with the *Utah* and the destroyers *Cassir*, *Shaw*, *Downes* while the battleship *Oklahoma* had capsized under the Japanese blows. Also lost were a large number of planes and 2,897 valuable soldiers and sailors. It is a tribute to American ingenuity and naval genius that of all the larger ships lost on that tragic day, only the "Arizona" remained a total loss. The others have all been salvaged and put back into the service of the United States Navy.

THIS WING OFF A DOWNED JAPANESE BOMBER littered a Honolulu lawn. Civilians, thinking Japanese might attempt a landing, armed themselves and prepared to fight to the last man.

THIS ARMY TRUCK SUFFERED A DIRECT HIT just off Hickam Field's parade grounds from the first wave of Japanese planes. Note the burning tire in the foreground.

WAIKIKI RESIDENTS BEGAN CLEANING UP DEBRIS of their bombed-out homes after the attack. Following the same pattern of ruthlessness they had established in China, the Japanese had bombed civilian centers and schools. In Wahaiwa they machine-gunned the streets. Over fifty civilians were killed, many more were wounded.

On Dec. 8 a grim President asked Congress to declare war on the Empire of Japan.

"Remember Pearl Harbor"

OR months before the sneak attack on Pearl Harbor the eople of the United States had been split over President oosevelt's program of aiding the nations fighting the Axis owers. While the President had the solid backing of the ajority of the people, he was under continuous attack by sizable, organized minority called "America First." Its adership, headed by Charles A. Lindbergh, Senators Vheeler, Clark, Walsh, and Nye, scoffed at the President's iterated warning that America was in danger of attack d demanded a program of appeasement. At the news of the eacherous Japanese attack "America First" withered away the pro-Nazis, the anti-Semites, and the Fascist Coughites who had been some of its most aggressive members. t noon on Dec. 8 President Roosevelt, grim, obviously gry yet calm, appeared before a joint session of Congress ask for a declaration of war against Japan. "Yesterday," said, "December 7, 1941—a date which will live in famy—the United States of America was suddenly and liberately attacked by naval and air forces of the Empire Japan." Calling the attack "dastardly and unprovoked," asked for a declaration of war against Japan. "Always ill we remember the character of the onslaught against . . . . We will gain the inevitable triumph." His whole speech took only ten minutes. Within half an hour the Senate had voted for war—82 to 0, and so had the Representatives—338 to 1, the lone dissenter being Jeannette Rankin. As on Dec. 11 the cry "Remember Pearl Harbor" swept America, and as the South American countries moved closer to the U.S. in hemispheric solidarity, the other two nations of the Axis, Germany and Italy, declared war on the United States. Screamed Reichschancellor Adolf Hitler to his heiling Reichstag, "I cannot be insulted by Roosevelt . . . because I consider Roosevelt to be insane. . . . We know, of course, that the eternal Jew is behind all this." Separate declarations of war on Germany and Italy were made by Congress on the next day. On Dec. 13 the Axis satellite nations, except Finland, declared war on the United States. They included Hungary, Rumania, Bulgaria, Manchukuo. Britain had declared war on Japan several hours before the United States. Their vast man power and industrial resources assured the ultimate victory of the anti-Fascist states, although it was certain that there would be defeats for some months to come, particularly in the Pacific. But in Russia the Nazi armies were being bled white and there was no doubt that a second front would be opened at the right time by Britain and the U.S.

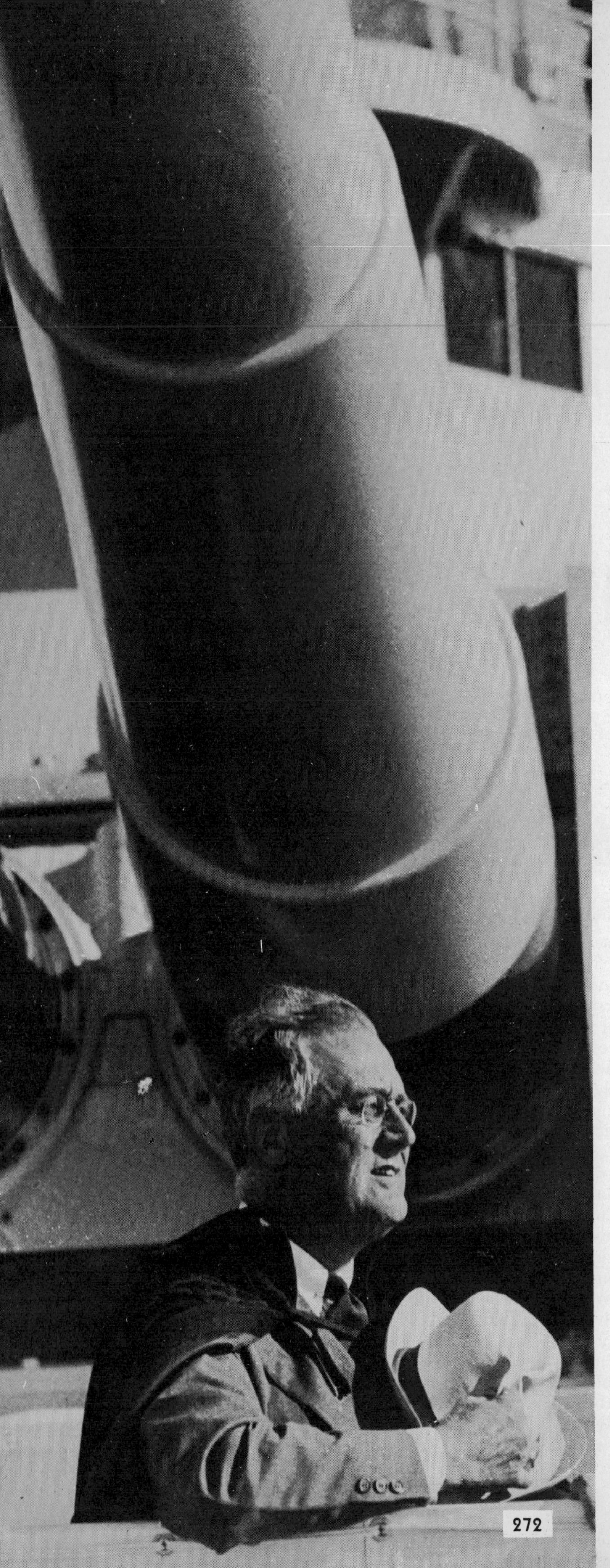

ROOSEVELT: WAR PRESIDENT

FRANKLIN DELANO ROOSEVELT is the seventh President to lead the United States in time of war. That it is the greatest war the world has known assures him of a place in history beside Washington and Lincoln. Yet even if he were not a war President his stature would hardly be less. He is the first President to be elected for more than two terms, the greatest social reformer the Western hemisphere has produced. He is a spectacular President in spectacular times. In 1922 his political career seemed at an end, for he was bedridden and paralyzed. Yet with the determination, confidence, courage few men possess he overcame his affliction. Wealthy, cultured, cosmopolitan, aristocratic, Franklin Roosevelt might well have become a stuffy corporation lawyer. Instead he became the champion of the underdog, the downtrodden, and the oppressed. In 1932 that included nearly everyone. The financial disaster of 1929 was still taking its toll. 15,000,000 were unemployed, banks were failing everywhere, faith in our economic system was shattered. Roosevelt's frank, intimate, confident speeches were in startling contrast to politicians' platitudes. By millions he was hailed as nothing short of a Messiah when he called for a "new deal" for the "forgotten man," bringing to America hope and a richer, fuller concept of what Democracy and Government might be. Few men have had greater ability to inspire great numbers of people. Called a "traitor to his class" by old and wealthy former friends, Roosevelt led the first years of the New Deal with crusading zeal, lessened his pressure for reforms when war overtook the world and threatened America. His reforms, once described as "communist-inspired," have, in less than a decade, been universally accepted as beneficial and necessary and have brought to America a greater appreciation of human life and happiness. A master politician, a dynamic and vigorous humanitarian, buoyant with a fine sense of his own place in history and with an indomitable confidence in himself, he has smashed tradition after tradition without hesitation whenever it seemed necessary for the welfare of the country. He has made few long-range mistakes, has foreseen and prepared for many of the disasters of the war. His "Good Neighbor" policy, bringing to the possessive Monroe Doctrine the same democratic concepts and friendly warmth his New Deal brought to the United States, was begun in 1936, years before most Americans awoke to the vulnerability of our country; its value, in terms of American lives saved, is infinite. His mistakes seem small in historical perspective. Physically and mentally, President Roosevelt has borne the burden of his office far better than past Presidents have, far better than most men could. He likes it.

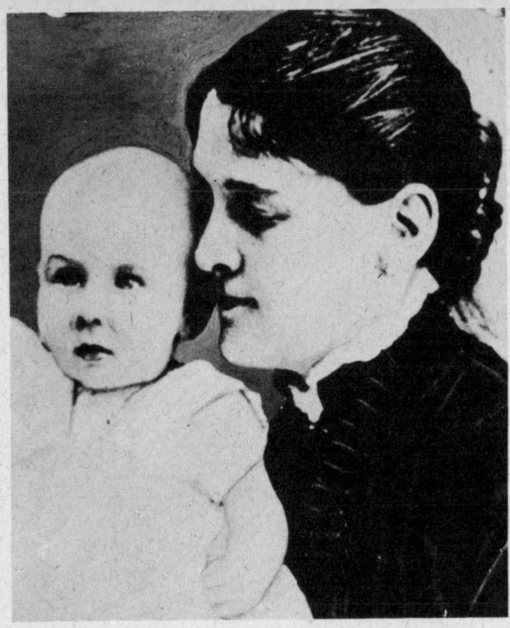

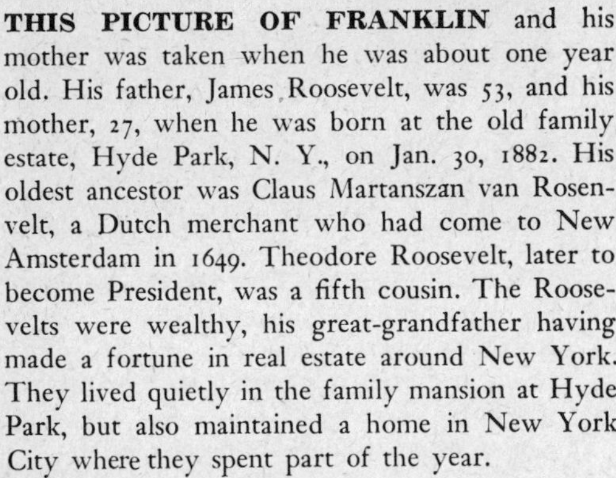

THIS PICTURE OF FRANKLIN and his mother was taken when he was about one year old. His father, James Roosevelt, was 53, and his mother, 27, when he was born at the old family estate, Hyde Park, N. Y., on Jan. 30, 1882. His oldest ancestor was Claus Martanszan van Rosenvelt, a Dutch merchant who had come to New Amsterdam in 1649. Theodore Roosevelt, later to become President, was a fifth cousin. The Roosevelts were wealthy, his great-grandfather having made a fortune in real estate around New York. They lived quietly in the family mansion at Hyde Park, but also maintained a home in New York City where they spent part of the year.

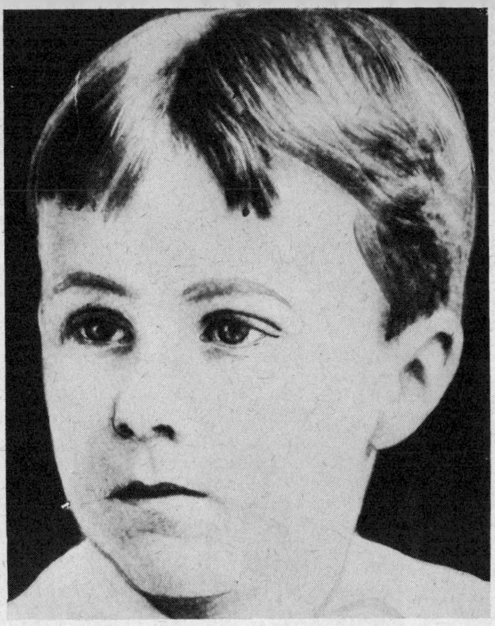

WHEN HE WAS FIVE, Franklin was precocious. He had few playmates, spent most of his time with his father and tutors. The family took him often to Europe. At eleven (right) he was an excellent horseman, owned a pony and a gun, studied bird life with his father. When he visited the White House, Grover Cleveland, who was a friend of his father's, said to him: "I'm making a strange wish for you, little man . . . I hope you'll never be President of the United States." He loved history, memorized most of Admiral Mahan's famous *History of Sea Power*. He liked outdoor life, particularly sailing. One of his few playmates was his cousin Eleanor.

AT 14 HE ENTERED GROTON, an exclusive prep school. He rowed, played football; he is the white-sweatered boy in the center above. A brilliant student, he won the school's Latin prize, finished the six-year course in four with honors, and entered Harvard.

WHILE A HARVARD STUDENT, Franklin posed for this picture with his parents. At Harvard he was a crusading *Crimson* editor, socially popular, and finished his course in three years. Prankish, he swiped a pen from the Kaiser's yacht while vacationing.

HE MARRIED ELEANOR, niece of his fifth cousin President Theodore Roosevelt, in 1905 while a Columbia Law student. He had known her all his life. The President gave away the bride and "stole the show," much to the newlyweds' chagrin.

IN 1910 HE WAS ELECTED state senator after an automobile campaign throughout Dutchess County. It was the first Democratic victory there in 28 years. As Senator he fought against fire traps, child labor. In 1912 he led the N.Y. Wilson forces.

WILSON APPOINTED HIM Assistant Secretary of the U.S. Navy on Mar. 17, 1913. Roosevelt was then only 31 years old. Naval power had been an obsession with him since youth. He owned 9,000 books on sea power, tactics, navies, studied them constantly.

ROOSEVELT, SHOWN HERE WITH SECRETARY DANIELS and Admiral McGowan, had alarmed many stuffy admirals when he entered the Navy by declaring it was overrated, its battleships obsolete and undermanned. Slashing at red tape, he reorganized its yards, supply centers, stimulated construction of modern ships, increased its man power during the war from 78,000 to 500,000.

WITH JAMES M. COX as his Presidential teammate, Roosevelt ran for the Vice-Presidency in 1920. The two candidates (above) were decisively defeated by Harding and Coolidge. Roosevelt, disappointed but not discouraged by the failure of the U.S. to join the World Court and League of Nations, retired from political life to become vice-president of a banking firm.

MEANWHILE, THE ROOSEVELT FAMILY was growing. Shown here with their parents and grandmother, Sara Delano Roosevelt, are: Elliott, John, Franklin Jr., Anna, and James. It was at Campobello in 1921 that Roosevelt was stricken with infantile paralysis. He began his heroic fight to overcome the ailment by learning everything known about the disease.

AFTER THREE YEARS of constant exercise but little improvement Roosevelt went to Warm Springs, Ga., to bathe in its tepid waters. There were immediate benefits. He was able to return to political life, nominating Alfred Smith for President at the 1924 Democratic convention. The picture was made in 1926 when Roosevelt, his handicap overcome, went swimming in Miami.

IN 1928 ROOSEVELT became governor of New York in the same election in which Herbert Hoover defeated Smith for the Presidency. Re-elected in 1930, Roosevelt reformed utility laws, and when the depression hit America he advocated a public-works program to cut unemployment. In 1932 he defeated Smith to win the Democratic Presidential nomination. His theme: "The Forgotten Man."

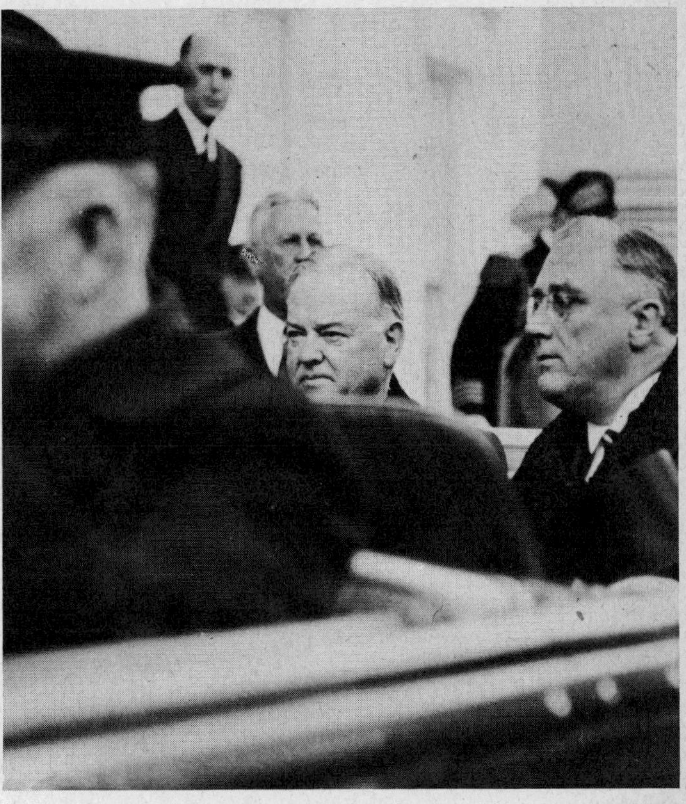

ROOSEVELT DEFEATED PRESIDENT HOOVER in 1932, winning a plurality of over seven million votes and carrying 42 states. Picture above shows President Hoover and President-elect Roosevelt leaving the White House for the inauguration, Mar. 4, 1933. Failure of the Hoover administration was largely attributed to hesitancy in taking steps toward reducing unemployment and extending relief.

FOUR HOURS AFTER HIS INAUGURATION Roosevelt called a special cabinet meeting and decreed a "bank holiday." Banks had been failing at an increasing rate for over a year. The above picture shows a crowd around a closed bank. Over 15 million Americans were unemployed. Relief agencies were unable to cope with the situation. The national income had been cut in half.

THE W.P.A. WAS BEGUN IN 1935 when private industry left ten million still unemployed. Most W.P.A. funds were spent on dams, roads, schools, athletic fields, and later defense work. To three million depression stricken people it meant a job that lifted their families from the doldrums of a meager relief, gave them a chance to maintain their morale, self-respect.

ROOSEVELT'S "GOOD NEIGHBOR" POLICY fostering good will among the American republics proved to be an important step toward uniting the New World in hemisphere defense when a second world war threatened. In the picture above President Roosevelt is shown, in the center, at the opening of the Inter-American Conference for the Maintenance of Peace, Dec. 1, 1936, in Buenos Aires. President Justo of Argentina is at his right, Dr. Carlos Saavedra Lamas, Argentina's Minister of Foreign Affairs, at his left. Fresh from victory at the polls in November—where he had defeated Gov. Alfred N. Landon of Kansas and carried every state but Maine and Vermont—President Roosevelt was the most important figure at this conference of the American republics.

1932

1936

1940

1944

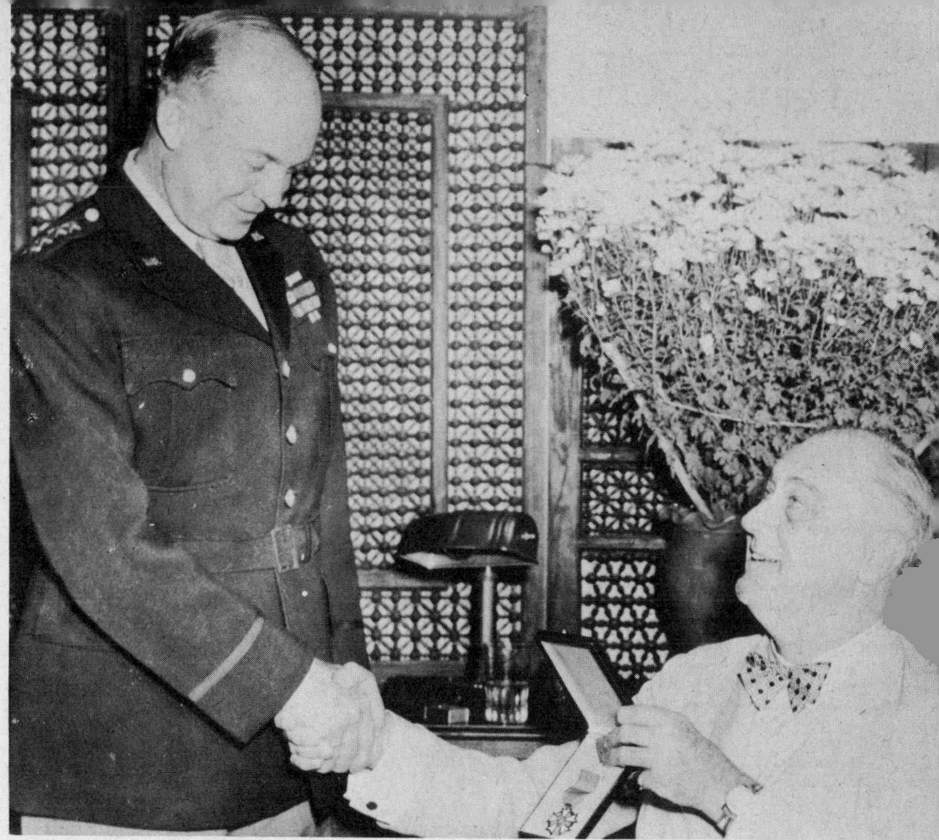

ROOSEVELT HONORED GENERAL EISENHOWER with the Legion of Merit medal during the President's trip to Cairo and Teheran conferences November, 1943. This was the third year since his precedent-breaking election to a third term. In 1940 he had defeated Wendell Willkie, Republican liberal candidate, who had refused to make a campaign issue of his anti-Nazi policy and aid to Britain. When the United States entered the war in Dec., 1941, the country was solidly united behind the President.

THE PRESIDENT VISITED PACIFIC BASES in Aug., 1944. Shown above, in Hawaii, flanked by Gen. MacArthur (left) and Adm. Leahy, he is following with great interest the course of Adm. Nimitz's pointer as it moves over the map toward Tokyo. At the polls in Nov. America endorsed the President's foreign policy and conduct of war by electing him to a fourth term. Thomas E. Dewey, New York Governor, who had not committed himself or his party to a clear-cut course on war and post-war issues, met with decisive defeat.

DECLARATION BY UNITED NATIONS

DECLARATION BY UNITED NATIONS:

A JOINT DECLARATION BY THE UNITED STATES OF AMERICA, THE UNITED KINGDOM OF GREAT BRITAIN AND NORTHERN IRELAND, THE UNION OF SOVIET SOCIALIST REPUBLICS, CHINA, AUSTRALIA, BELGIUM, CANADA, COSTA RICA, CUBA, CZECHOSLOVAKIA, DOMINICAN REPUBLIC, EL SALVADOR, GREECE, GUATEMALA, HAITI, HONDURAS, INDIA, LUXEMBOURG, NETHERLANDS, NEW ZEALAND, NICARAGUA, NORWAY, PANAMA, POLAND, SOUTH AFRICA, YUGOSLAVIA.

The Governments signatory hereto,

Having subscribed to a common program of purposes and principles embodied in the Joint Declaration of the President of the United States of America and the Prime Minister of the United Kingdom of Great Britain and Northern Ireland dated August 14, 1941, known as the Atlantic Charter.

Being convinced that complete victory over their enemies is essential to defend life, liberty, independence and religious freedom, and to preserve human rights and justice in their own lands as well as in other lands, and that they are now engaged in a common struggle against savage and brutal forces seeking to subjugate the world, DECLARE:

(1) Each Government pledges itself to employ its full resources, military or economic, against those members of the Tripartite Pact and its adherents with which such government is at war.

(2) Each Government pledges itself to cooperate with the Governments signatory hereto and not to make a separate armistice or peace with the enemies.

The foregoing declaration may be adhered to by other nations which are, or which may be, rendering material assistance and contributions in the struggle for victory over Hitlerism.

Done at Washington
January First 1942

The United States of America
The United Kingdom of Great Britain & Northern Ireland
On behalf of the Government of the Union of Soviet Socialist Republics
National Government of the Republic of China
The Commonwealth of Australia
The Kingdom of Belgium
Canada
The Republic of Costa Rica
The Republic of Cuba
Czechoslovak Republic
The Dominican Republic
The Republic of El Salvador
The Kingdom of Greece
The Republic of Guatemala
La République d'Haïti
The Republic of Honduras
India
The Grand Duchy of Luxembourg
The Kingdom of the Netherlands
Signed on behalf of the Govt. of the Dominion of New Zealand
The Republic of Nicaragua
The Kingdom of Norway
The Republic of Panamá
The Republic of Poland
The Union of South Africa
The Kingdom of Yugoslavia

THIS "DECLARATION" MADE HISTORY when it was signed by representatives of 26 countries in Washington on Jan. 1, 1942. The nations then at war with one or more Axis powers stated allegiance to the principles of the Atlantic Charter, pledged themselves not to make a separate armistice or peace, and to employ full military or economic resources against the enemy each was fighting. From this pact stemmed many conferences, organizations, important for the political, economic, military co-operation vital to winning the war.

FLAG DAY CEREMONIES IN THE WHITE HOUSE, June 14, 1942, marked ratification of the pact by Mexico and the Philippines. Their delegates are shown here, with President Roosevelt and Secretary of State Hull, surrounded by representatives of the original 26 United Nations. Powers signing later were Ethiopia, Iraq, Brazil, Bolivia, Iran, Colombia, Liberia, Free Denmark, France.

SECRETARY OF STATE CORDELL HULL, UNDER SECRETARY SUMNER WELLES, ably supported the "Good Neighbor" policy. Conferences in Peru, Cuba, Panama decreased Axis influence in Latin-America, led to permanent inter-American advisory committee at Washington. In Jan., 1942, Welles (shown above) represented U. S. at Rio de Janeiro conference where all 21 countries recommended severance of diplomatic relations with Axis. Only Argentina, changing later to a totalitarian government, has failed to support this action.

CHINA IS ONE OF MANY NATIONS TO SHARE in life-giving food, medicine, supplies, distributed through far-flung ministrations of UNRRA. Set up first as "American Relief Activities and Post-War Rehabilitation Abroad," it was reorganized in Nov. 1943 as "United Nations Relief and Rehabilitation Administration." Herbert H. Lehman, originally appointed by Roosevelt, remained as director.

IMMEDIATELY AFTER THE OUTBREAK OF THE WAR air interceptor commands were set up along both our Pacific and Atlantic coasts to head off possible air attacks on U.S. The shelling of the Pacific coast by a Japanese sub and of Aruba by a Nazi sub awoke most Americans to the fact that our coasts might become active war theaters. This picture shows a Pacific patrol receiving instructions before taking off. Note silhouettes of Japanese planes and submarines hanging on the walls of the interceptor command's control room.

THE HOME FRONT

THOUSANDS OF VOLUNTEER firemen and air-raid wardens learned how to extinguish incendiary bombs and render first aid. An air-raid alarm in New York the day after Pearl Harbor, though false, demonstrated how grossly unprepared the United States was and brought thousands of civilian volunteers to defense headquarters.

TO GUARD NEW YORK and other coast cities, interceptor commands such as this worked from control centers modeled after those developed in England. Indeed, our whole Civilian Defense organization profited from Britain's bitter practical experience with the damage done by bombs. All over the country, but particularly along the coasts, civilians sat through the long night hours spotting all airplanes which traveled through the sky, on the lookout for raiding enemy planes. Men and women, old and young, learned to identify friendly and enemy planes.

ANTI-AIRCRAFT GUN EMPLACEMENTS dotted both coasts and ringed the major cities, vital harbors, and industrial plants. Throughout the nation, too, army patrols were set up to guard oil reserves, bridges war factories, and vital roads against saboteurs.

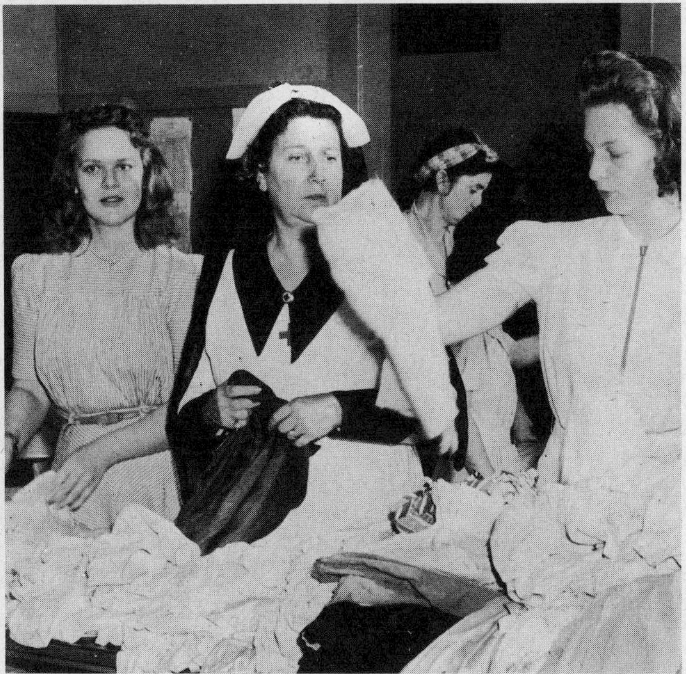

THROUGH THE RED CROSS American women gathered and mended clothes, made bandages, packed medical supplies for use abroad. These Honolulu women are sorting clothes originally intended for Britain to find wearables for Pearl Harbor victims.

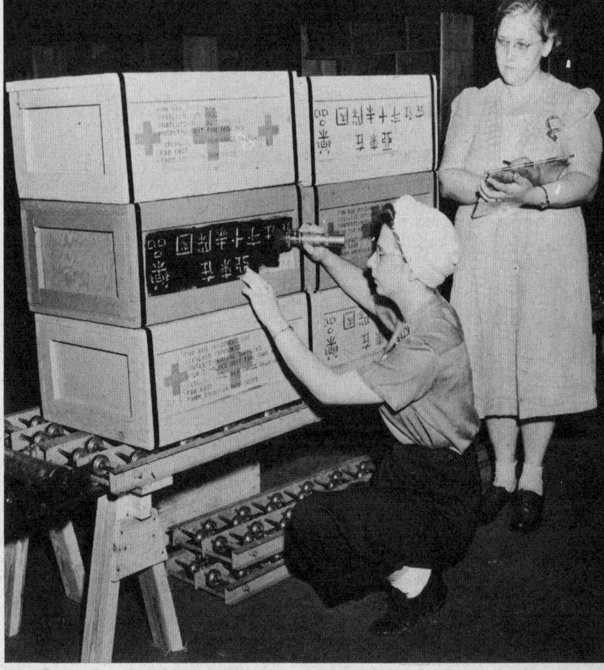

AN 80-POUND PACKAGE which meets shipping limitation and yet fills the needs of disease-racked prisoners in the Fa East has been developed by the Medical Supply Section of the Columbus, Ohio, ASF Depot.

THEY ALSO SERVE . . . Of all the many ways of doing one's part for the war effort, this woman has taken the hardest.

ANOTHER WAY women contributed was to entertain soldiers on leave. USO lounges in every city provided refreshments for the men.

IN THE V-MAIL room, Pentagon Bldg., paper reproductions are developed, fixed, washed, and dried on the continuous processing machine.

JUST A PART of the crowd waiting for one train in the Pennsylvania Station in New York.

MIRACLES OF rehabilitation are worked for disabled service men. They are given new limbs, even new faces, returned to useful lives.

THE BLACK TOM and Kingsland cases have made the public acquainted with the sabotage accomplished by the Germans in World War I. In this war, although the spy system is better organized, chiefly centered in South America, there has been less damage from German-instigated sabotage because the F.B.I. nipped plans in the bud. In 1942 eight trained saboteurs landed on the east coast with $170,000, a store of explosives, maps and plans for a two-year series of accidents in defense plants. The ambulances above are removing the bodies of the six who were tried, found guilty by the American courts and electrocuted for their crimes.

BLACK TOM AND KINGSLAND REMINISCENCE

CALIFORNIA'S 113,000 JAPANESE were rounded up, taken to closely guarded work camps far inland to prevent fifth columnists and spies among them from aiding Japan.

THE MAN STANDING with the earphones is William L. Shirer, for many months a radio commentator stationed in Berlin. He can sniff out a fragment of German propaganda no matter how well it is perfumed. He is listening to a Nazi broadcast, and in a few minutes will go on the air and tell the truth about it. He might be called a debunking specialist.

PLANTS A

WHEN AMERICA awoke,
Dec. 7, 1941, to the st
fact that war was upon her,
dustry accepted the challen
Tens, hundreds, thousands of n
plants sprang up over night
every part of the country. Fr
huge, sprawling new shipbu
ing yards employing thousa
of people, to tiny one-man

ORE PLANTS

-woman factories where there opened to be a lathe in the cel- America went to work. Pro- ction began in new plants be- e the roofs were on. Old ones re doubled, trebled in capac- , doubled again. The answer s a flood of production which lped turn the tide of war on a ndred battle fronts.

Left: The three cat-crackers of the Baton Rouge Refinery in Louisiana.

Above: The day shift lining up in front of the time clocks at the Bethlehem-Fairfield shipyards in Baltimore.

Above: A defense housing project at Erie, Pa. Each trailer can accommodate four people.

Below: The U.S. Government seized plants in any industry affecting the war effort to prevent work stoppage, whether by strikes or management failure to co-operate. Sewell Avery, chairman of the Board of Directors of Montgomery Ward & Co., is shown being forcefully carried out from the general offices in Chicago by U.S. soldiers.

THE SUREST CLUE to black-market meat is slashed points without slashed prices. When the O.P.A. legally cuts points, the price must be lowered too. When you see a sign like the one above, don't buy.

MORE THAN CONSCIENCE should discourage the housewife from buying black-market meat. The black marketer naturally avoids government inspection of the quality of meat and conditions under which it is slaughtered.

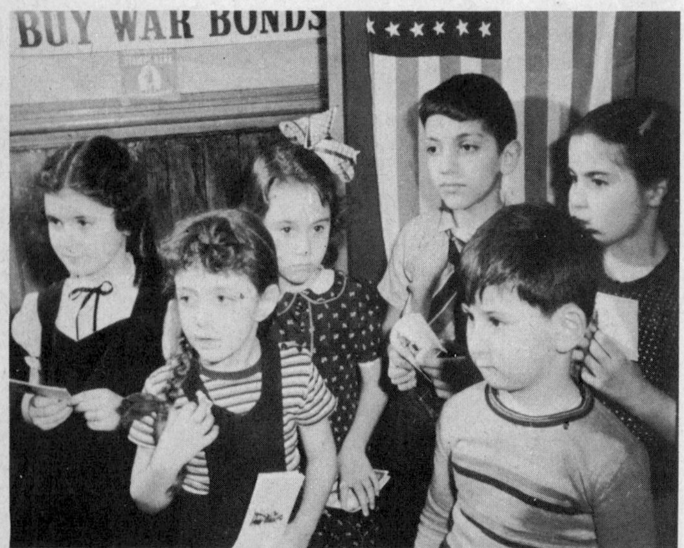

CHILDREN, TOO, do their part. They like to collect tangible possessions, and defense stamps satisfy that desire admirably. Here children in school are waiting in line to buy stamps.

THE LAST WAR taught the U.S. a great deal about the inevitable scarcity of goods for civilian consumption in wartime, and the consequent rise in prices. This time the government, through the Office of Price Administration, has tried to prevent black markets by a system of rationing which would insure equal distribution of necessary goods; and to prevent rise in the cost of living by control of prices, particularly of food and rent. Besides equal distribution of new goods, the government has instituted schemes for salvaging such materials as rubber, paper, aluminum, tin, and iron. The pile of scrap shown above came from a large midwestern tool factory.

TO INCREASE PRODUCTION of aluminum, much needed in aircraft construction, millions of pounds of old aluminum pots, pans, hair curlers, etc., were collected in a nation-wide drive.

V. S. KNUDSEN of General Motors headed OPM, became Nelson's production chief when OPM was replaced by War Production Board.

SIDNEY HILLMAN, ILGWU leader, was appointed to represent labor in OPM, served till poor health forced him to relinquish post.

DONALD M. NELSON, organizer of the WPB, was given cabinet rank in Nov. 1944 as "personal representative" of the President.

TREASURY SECRETARY MORGENTHAU has directed the financing of the War and has helped to put an effective check on inflation of prices.

J. A. KRUG, 36-year-old acting chairman of WPB during Nelson's absence on missions abroad, was appointed chairman of the Board to succeed Nelson.

JAMES F. BYRNES left the Supreme Court to organize and head the Office of War Mobilization, remained as director of War Mobilization and Reconversion.

The Battle of Production

ALTHOUGH the United States had been rearming since May, 1940, the attack on Pearl Harbor found the nation's industrial capacity far from being mobilized for war production, its expanding army without adequate equipment. Before the U. S. could put enough forces in the field to wrest the initiative from the Axis powers, the Battle of Production had to be won. President Roosevelt acted promptly to speed industrial conversion in a country at war, to mobilize fully national resources, man power, economy. He created the War Production Board and put vigorous, far-sighted, hard-working Sears Roebuck executive, Donald M. Nelson, in charge on Jan. 18, 1942. The President's Victory quotas called for 60,000 planes, 45,000 tanks, 8,000,000 tons of shipping, all to be completed in 1942, and more than double those figures in 1943. To a country which in 1940 had produced only 5,480 planes, no tanks at all, other war essentials on a proportionate scale, these figures seemed hopelessly visionary. But America went to work. Philip Murray and William Green, leaders of AFL and CIO, announced labor would sacrifice its right to strike voluntarily, and supported Nelson's plan for joint labor-management boards to increase production in each plant. Industry labored night and day to expand facilities, developed new technological methods for speed, overcame shortages in essentials such as machine tools, rubber and steel, surpassed all previous achievements in mass production. By June, 1942, the War Production Board had won its battle. The President's figures no longer seemed visionary. During the following year they became really spectacular. In Sept. 1943, he reported to Congress that from May, 1940, U. S. output had been 123,000 airplanes, 349,000 airplane engines, 53,000 tanks, 15,000 artillery weapons, 9,500,000 small arms (rifles, carbines, machine guns), 1,233,000 trucks, 2,380 ships, 15,000 landing vessels, and all other needed equipment—the greatest amount of war production in the history of the world. A few days later Donald Nelson stated America would soon be turning out one completed plane every five minutes round the clock every day in the month, American war production in 1943 would be over one and a half times the combined production of Germany and Japan, in 1944 twice the Axis output. By that summer of 1943, when U. S. war production reached its peak, approximately two thirds of the country's industry was engaged in war activity. Pictured above are a few of the many men who played important parts in mobilizing America's magnificent industrial strength for a world-wide offensive.

DEVELOPMENT OF THE HEAVY BOMBER was an outstanding feature of plane construction in World War II. Like a huge dragonfly ready to take flight the B-29 Superfortress above stands at the last station of a final assembly line in a Boeing factory at Wichita, Kansas. Rolling off assembly lines in one of the largest production programs ever conceived for a single weapon of war, these B-29s carry a heavier bomb load faster, higher, and farther than any other bomber ever built. Below, left, are rows of dorsal fins soon to be winging toward Tokyo. At right, the size of bomb bays in the giant bombers is graphically depicted.

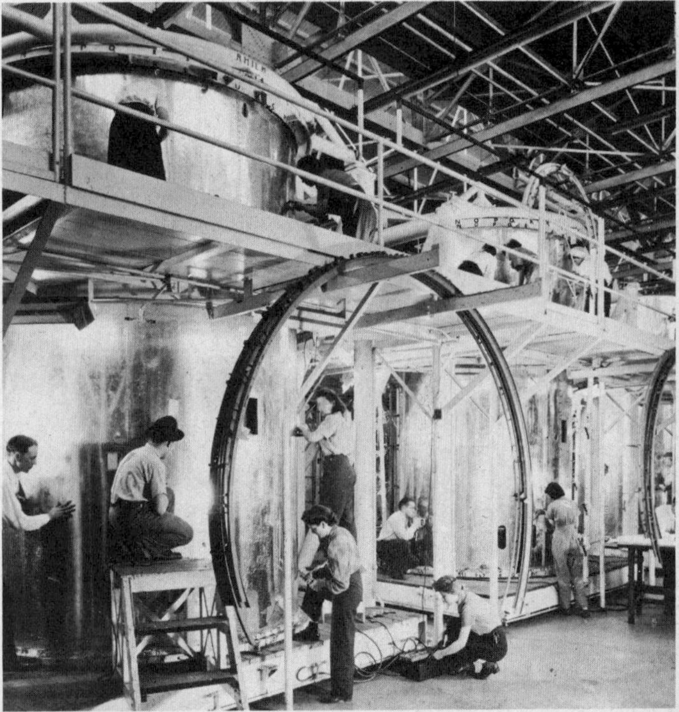

ARMY AND NAVY TOGETHER had in 1940 some 500 planes fit for battle, no plans for mass production, no balanced program. Yet between March 1941 and March 1944 the U. S. had turned out for combat purposes over 175,000 planes, now proving themselves in battle equal or superior to any. Bombers, fighters, interceptors, scouters, transport—all are able to meet the best the enemy has produced.

When the U. S. began to rearm in May, 1940, the Army had 446 tanks, not more than 50 fit for battle. In great automobile factories dies had to be junked, conveyor belts torn down, to make way for new belts and dies before a flood of tanks could roll from assembly lines. Yet by Sept. 1943 U. S. industry had turned out 53,000 tanks. Mass production of medium tanks (M-3s, or "General Grants") had begun late in 1941, but monster 60-ton tanks were not under way until 1942. The need shown in Libyan desert fighting for a large tank with fire power to match the German Mark IV was responsible for new model M-4s fitted with 105 mm. howitzers. These new "General Shermans" helped give the British Eighth Army in Africa battleship strength in tanks, contributed materially to driving back Rommel's forces in the fall of 1942, paved the way for American invasion. By 1944 American tanks were performing valiant service on battlefields of every front.

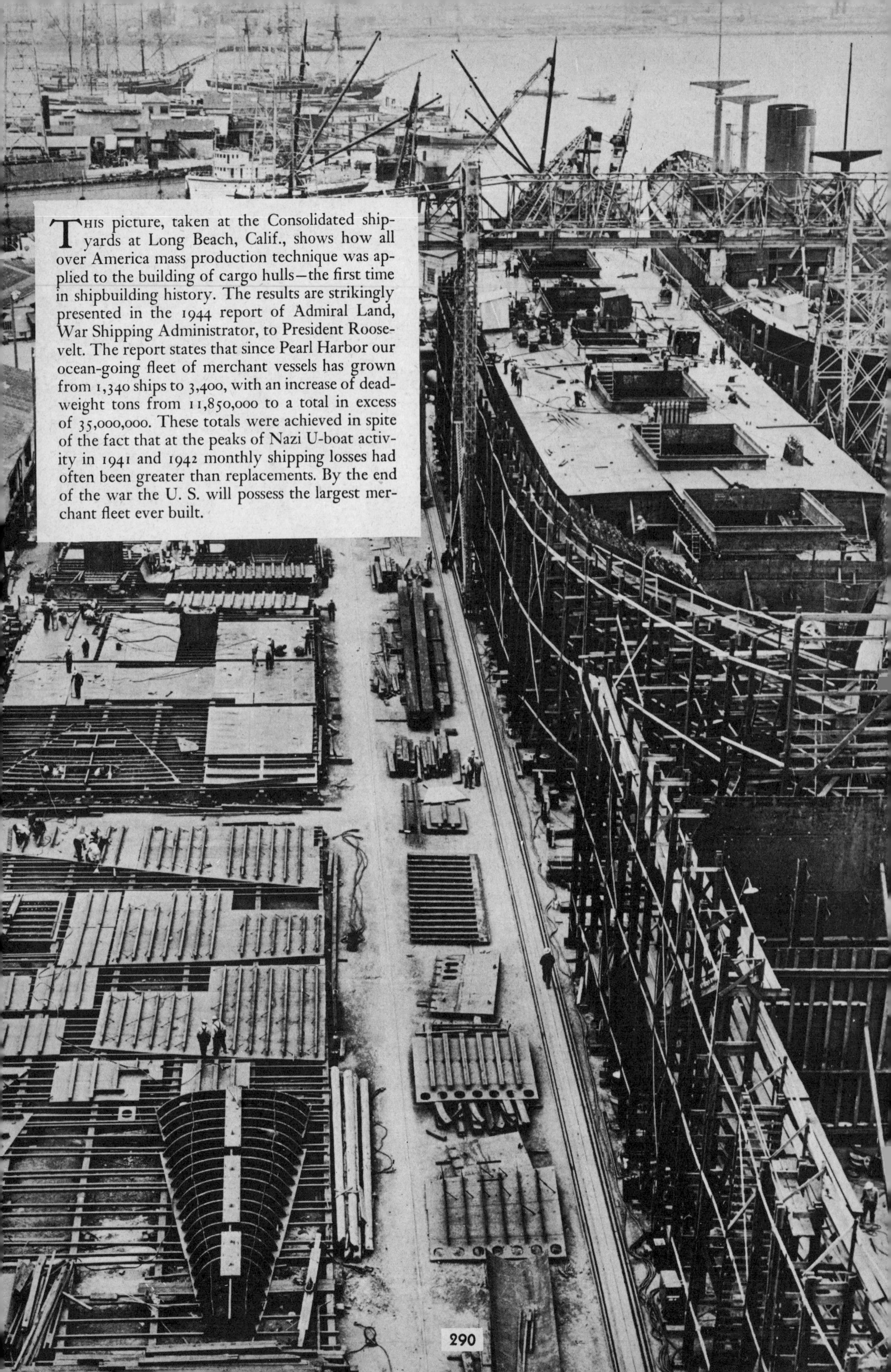

This picture, taken at the Consolidated shipyards at Long Beach, Calif., shows how all over America mass production technique was applied to the building of cargo hulls—the first time in shipbuilding history. The results are strikingly presented in the 1944 report of Admiral Land, War Shipping Administrator, to President Roosevelt. The report states that since Pearl Harbor our ocean-going fleet of merchant vessels has grown from 1,340 ships to 3,400, with an increase of deadweight tons from 11,850,000 to a total in excess of 35,000,000. These totals were achieved in spite of the fact that at the peaks of Nazi U-boat activity in 1941 and 1942 monthly shipping losses had often been greater than replacements. By the end of the war the U. S. will possess the largest merchant fleet ever built.

Merchant Shipping

FACED with the problem of getting supplies to our own fighting forces abroad as well as our Allies, WSA went to work to fulfill the goals set by President Roosevelt in Jan. 1942. Rear Admiral Vickery, vice-chairman of the U. S. Maritime Commission, was placed in charge. Before the war, when Vickery had wanted to build 50 ships a year, it had been flatly declared impossible by the experts. Under the impact of U-boat war on shipping twice 50 had been turned out in 1939. But there was only one way to achieve the President's 1942 goal of 8,000,000 tons in a country short of shipyards, materials, trained men—to cut in half the 210 days then required to complete a ship. This meant mass production, utilization of prefabrication. Vickery brought Henry J. Kaiser, builder of the Grand Coulee dam, into the picture. By summer, 1942, ships were being launched in 156 days—but Kaiser out in Oregon had turned out a 10,000 ton cargo boat in 60. Before the average production time had dropped in December to 55 days, Kaiser had set a record of 10. New records began to be set in other yards, too. Tankers had never gone down the ways so fast. In the last month of 1943 American yards turned out 208 ships—a dramatic answer to those experts who in 1937 labeled 50 ships a year "impossible."

1500 LIBERTY SHIPS, such as the two above, were the backbone of the new fleet. In 1943 merchant ships came off assembly lines at a rate of 6 a day. 1944 added the Victory ship to the fleet. Larger than the Liberty, powered by a 6,000 instead of a 2,500 h.p. engine, it makes 16 knots to the Liberty's 11. It is safe to say vast supplies will continue to flow to every battle front, the U-boat menace never again threaten Allied victory. Women prove their worth in shipyards (below), other industries.

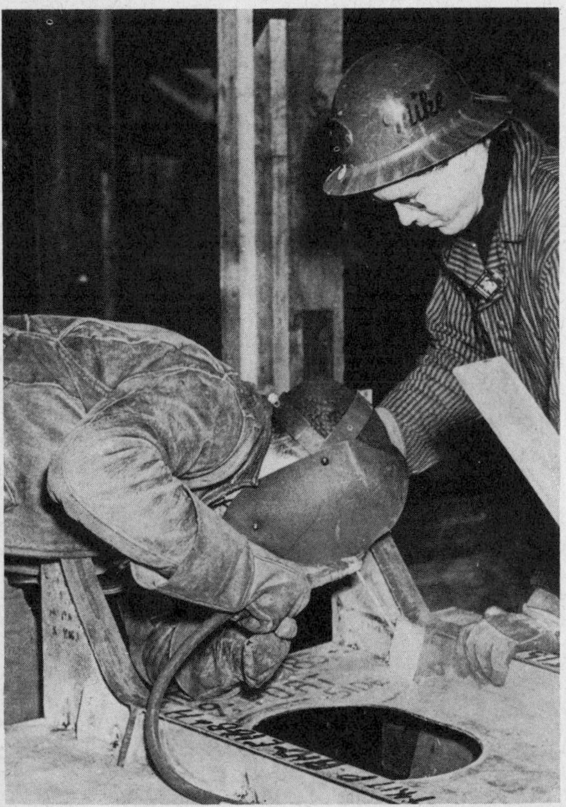

WELDING HELPED SPEED MASS PRODUCTION of ships. Whole sections are welded together, lifted into position by giant cranes. Without rivets, ships are lighter, stronger, faster.

NAVAL CONSTRUCTION

On July 19, 1940, Congress passed a two-ocean Navy bill. France had fallen. The British fleet, faithful guardian of Atlantic waters, was imperiled. Since 1938 U. S. naval expansion had been authorized to the extent of a 20%, later an additional 11%, increase. The bill now passed called for a 70% increase, by construction of 245 combatant ships, including 17 new battleships, 12 new carriers, 48 new cruisers, 166 destroyers, 81 submarines. In charge of this tremendous undertaking the late Secretary of the Navy Knox placed his young assistant, Under Secretary James Forrestal. Forrestal had orders to build a two-ocean Navy. He built it, also the vast armada of special invasion craft for which appropriation after appropriation was passed as D-Day drew closer. He built it in record time, too. Mass production methods working miracles for merchant shipping were applied to more than 200 yards building ships for the Navy. By early 1942 six of the seventeen battleships authorized had been launched. After Pearl Harbor, Dec. 7, 1941, production soared. After Midway, six months later, five monster 60,000 ton battleships planned, but not yet under construction, were converted to carriers. Thirty-five cruisers and merchant ships were also converted to carriers, giving the U. S. Navy some 80 of these new modern weapons of war. U-boats were added to the fleet —long range underseas boats, capable of cruising thousands of miles, unleashed in a war to the death against Axis submarine aggression. The Navy's story of its growth is dramatic. "In the midst of the war the United States has built its Navy into the greatest sea-air power on earth." This Navy report of Sept. 1943, states further that no naval construction program of comparable size and speed has ever been accomplished by any other nation. "Ability to build this huge new naval force—and to continue to build at the present rate—is one of the foundation stones of our military strategy. It underlies our amphibious attacks in the Pacific, the Atlantic, and the Mediterranean." Summarizing the amazing rate of expansion, the report compares the status of July 1940 with that of June 1943, just three years later. In those three years the Navy built 2,200,000 tons of ships. It added to its air arm 23,000 planes. It completed $6,500,000,000 worth of shore facilities. Three years ago the Navy had a fleet of 1,076 vessels—383 of them warships—and 1744 planes. Despite numerous losses, transfers, conversions, the figures now read, 14,072 vessels in the fleet—613 of them warships—and 18,269 planes. "The rise in naval ship completions is without parallel . . . the number of vessels completed in the single month of June, 1943, for example, approximates the number completed in the first 18 months of the World War II defense program." So it has grown—in three short years—the U. S. Navy, greater now than the combined navies of the world.

DEATH AT TWENTY MILES roars from the guns of this U.S. battleship of the S. Dakota class.

THE *RADFORD*, U.S. DESTROYER, camouflaged for its grim job, hunting down enemy submarines.

U.S. CARRIER *ENTERPRISE*, snapped from a plane which has just left its "flat-top" home.

MASS PRODUCTION COMES TO THE NAVY, when four destroyers slide down the ways in a quadruple launching at the Federal Shipbuilding and Dry Dock yards at Kearny, New Jersey. Named in honor of Naval heroes, they are, left to right, the "Kidd," the "Turner," the "Thorn" and the "Bullard." By 1942 building time for destroyers had been cut from 28 months to 8.

A MILLION AND ONE

Two years after America's entry into the war millions of men and women were involved in war production; by 1944 still more had flocked to war plants. They made planes, tanks, guns, warships, also the thousand and one other things needed by armies and navies, such as surgical instruments, blankets, flashlights, needles, canteens, goggles, screw drivers, shoelaces, insulation for wiring, shovels, toothbrushes, lantern wicks. To make the huge multitude of things in this latter classification, the battle of production was fought just as hard, if not as spectacularly, as it was in the basic war industries. Subcontracts on all types of equipment went to all kinds of plants, from tiny cellar machine shops to prison shops. Old industrial prejudices were shattered by the nation's need, and new sources of manpower assured America that the hands needed to meet the tremendous production goals would be available.

SPRAWLING RAILROAD SHOPS turned out new wheels, ready to be fitted to thousands of new freight cars.

FARM PRODUCTION, already high in 1941, increased rapidly as U. S. prepared to feed the world.

UNIFORMS FOR AN ARMY OF 10,000,000 soldiers and for every climate kept the garment industry working 24 hours a day.

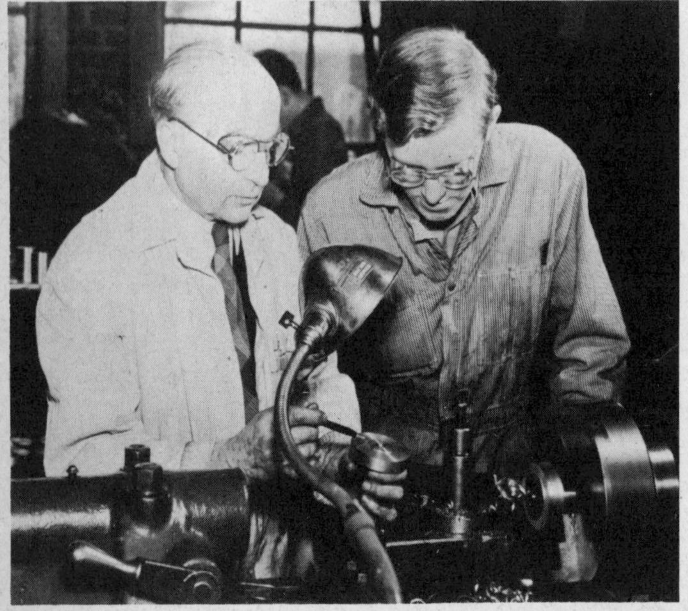

UNIVERSITY MACHINE SHOPS, like those of many schools and colleges, were converted to war production.

PRODUCTION OF MACHINE guns, bazookas, rifles, carbines, small arms, reached the 10,000,000 mark in two years.

IN ORDER TO SERVICE PLANES, more motors were needed than planes, but motor production easily kept ahead of schedule.

MILLIONS OF GAS MASKS WERE MADE to equip the Army, Navy and Marines, preparing for possibility of gas warfare.

MOST OF THE SOLE LEATHER produced in the U.S. was required to make the millions of pairs of shoes needed for soldiers.

MUNITIONS PLANTS, BUILT IN 1941, sent the munitions production rate soaring after Pearl Harbor. These are 155 mm. shells.

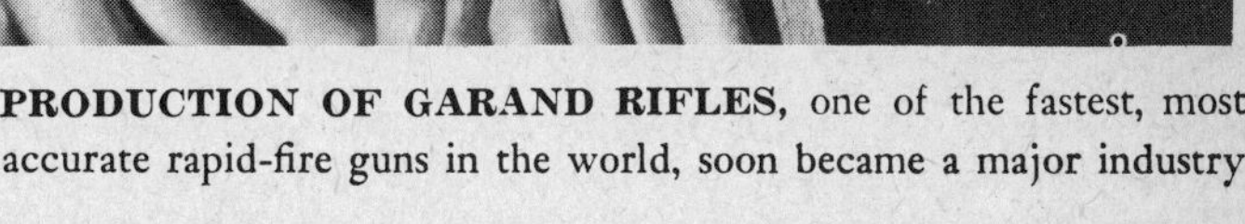

PRODUCTION OF GARAND RIFLES, one of the fastest, most accurate rapid-fire guns in the world, soon became a major industry.

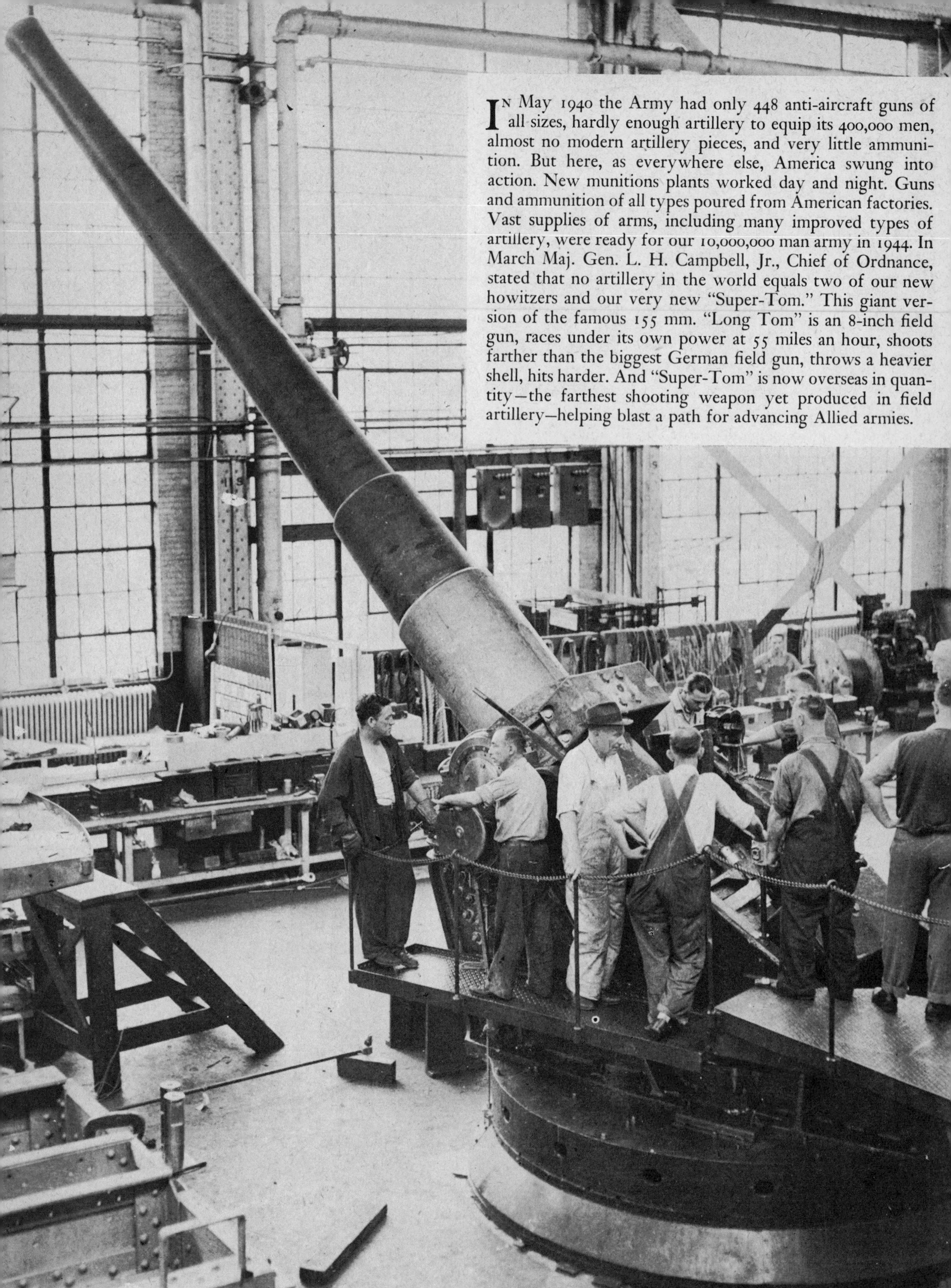

IN May 1940 the Army had only 448 anti-aircraft guns of all sizes, hardly enough artillery to equip its 400,000 men, almost no modern artillery pieces, and very little ammunition. But here, as everywhere else, America swung into action. New munitions plants worked day and night. Guns and ammunition of all types poured from American factories. Vast supplies of arms, including many improved types of artillery, were ready for our 10,000,000 man army in 1944. In March Maj. Gen. L. H. Campbell, Jr., Chief of Ordnance, stated that no artillery in the world equals two of our new howitzers and our very new "Super-Tom." This giant version of the famous 155 mm. "Long Tom" is an 8-inch field gun, races under its own power at 55 miles an hour, shoots farther than the biggest German field gun, throws a heavier shell, hits harder. And "Super-Tom" is now overseas in quantity—the farthest shooting weapon yet produced in field artillery—helping blast a path for advancing Allied armies.

PRODUCTION OF HUGE RAILROAD GUNS took much time because none had been built since 1918 and such guns require delicate balance. Above, balance and recoil mechanisms are being checked inside the plant. After completion of the first one in 1941 production mounted rapidly. Self-propelled anti-tank and anti-aircraft guns, great naval weapons, every kind of infantry artillery—all kept the pace.

Drafted men in Britain's coal mines keep production fires burning.

BRITISH PRODUCTION

When Churchill hurled his challenge at the enemy, "We shall fight on beaches, landing grounds, in fields, in streets, and on the hills," the Battle of Britain became the Battle of Production. By 1944 industrial mobilization for war included over 69% of civilians, men and women, from 14 years up. The average working week had increased from 48 hours to 54. Spectacular production figures tell the rest of the story. In heavy bombers, for example, the yearly rate of 41 turned out in 1940 had jumped to 5,800 in 1944. Between 1940 and 1943 total munitions production had increased 300%. Meanwhile 600,000 acres had been lost to agriculture by industrial expansion, but millions of new acres had been plowed up—park and reclaimed waste land, school yard and village green, even bomb craters yawning in city blocks. A painstaking survey to find new acreage was often helped by reference to the *Domesday Book* of William the Conqueror. In many cases its 900-year-old record pages furnished exactly the information necessary for such a farm survey in 1941. In this ancient British landscape, mechanization of farms was a new note, as was the Women's Land Army, 80,000 strong. But both were vital to a victorious "battle in the fields." By 1943 Britain was producing 70% of her food as against 1/3 in 1939. Thus ship after ship was being freed from food cargoes to carry more Allied soldiers, more munitions, more supplies, for an ever-widening offensive. Britain's swelling flood of war production is even more amazing in the light of the tremendous obstacles her workers have faced and overcome, from endless air raids to rains of deadly robot bombs, disrupting all normal living, destroying tons of irreplaceable tools and machinery. More and more, industry had to be regimented, geared to high production. In 1942 the coal mines were "drafted" into the war. When shortages became acute in fuel which meant war production, the government granted priorities putting that industry in the same bracket as the armed services, allowing 2500 draftees each month to draw service in the coal pits of England instead of the fox holes of Libya—which explains the young faces of the obviously able-bodied men in the picture.

Modern tractors on Britain's ancient farms help to keep her ships free for vital war-time cargoes.

WOMEN PLAY AN IMPORTANT PART in Russia's war effort. In many factories three-fourths of the workers are women, gladly toiling long hours, working at night to help harvest crops, freely choosing a Spartan existence, thinking production, living production, achieving production. There are girls of 18 whose pride is in doing the work of two men at drop press or forge. There is Tsareva, shown above, who regularly fulfills 300% of her daily quota, manufacturing arms to teach the Nazis the real meaning of "total war."

DURING AIR RAIDS AND SHELL FIRE beleaguered Russian workers still produce the sinews of war. Like Gen. de Gaulle in France, Soviet military men foresaw the coming war, the mechanization it would bring. But the Soviet government did something about it. From their transplanted war plants behind the Urals rolled the great self-propelled guns which were to add a new mobility to the "blitzkrieg" technique, send the invaders reeling back from Stalingrad, liberate thousands of miles of scorched Russian earth.

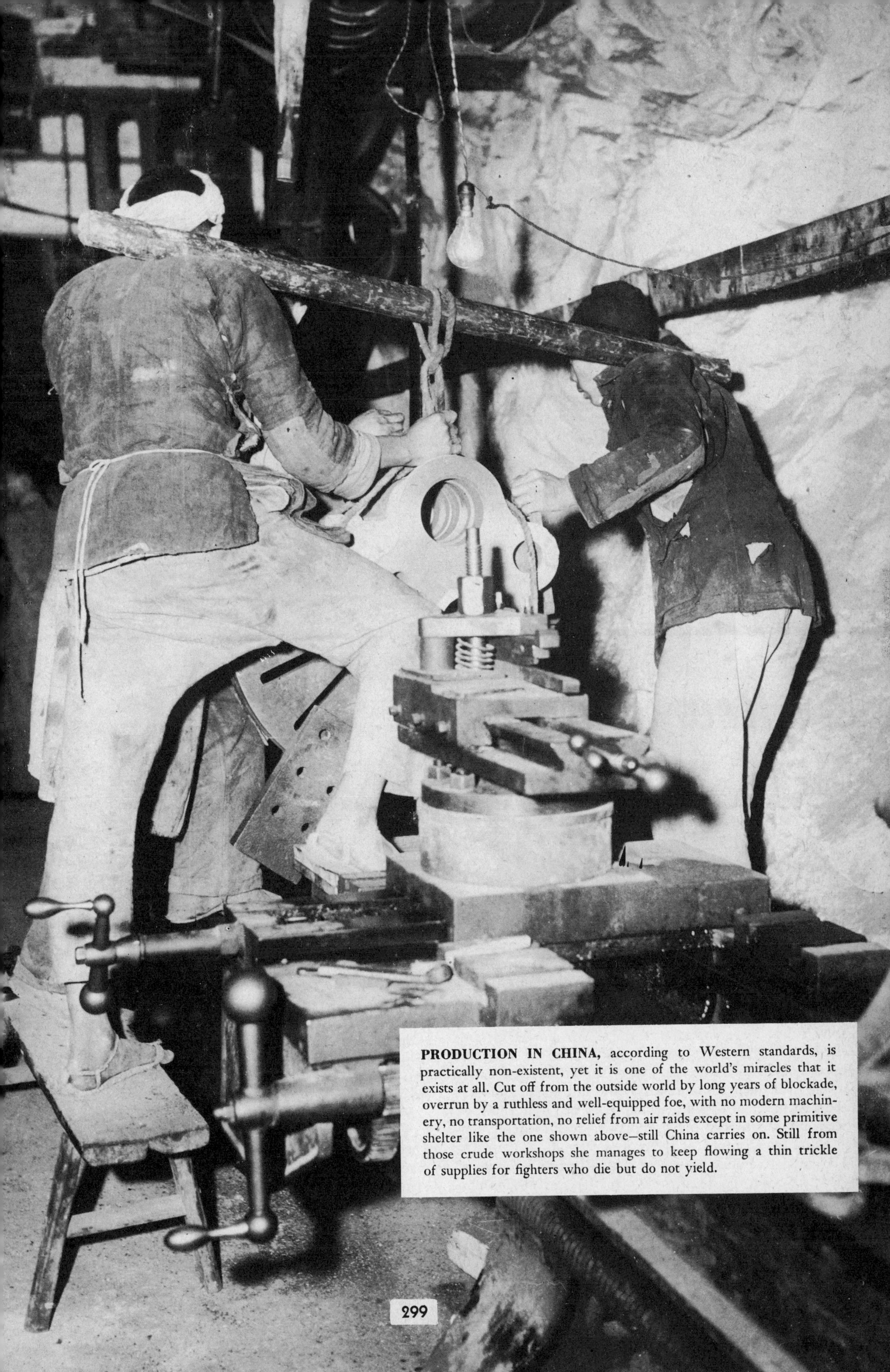

PRODUCTION IN CHINA, according to Western standards, is practically non-existent, yet it is one of the world's miracles that it exists at all. Cut off from the outside world by long years of blockade, overrun by a ruthless and well-equipped foe, with no modern machinery, no transportation, no relief from air raids except in some primitive shelter like the one shown above—still China carries on. Still from those crude workshops she manages to keep flowing a thin trickle of supplies for fighters who die but do not yield.

This striking picture was made of the top commanders of the army early in Mar., 1942, after the reorganization of the army.

The Reorganization of the U.S. Army

By the end of 1941 United States' military power had reached a stage where its rapid development was in danger of being strangled by over a century's accumulation of finely spun red tape and bureaucracy. On March 2, 1942, an executive order effected a sweeping reorganization of U.S. military administration, slashing away mountains of red tape. Numerous cumbersome and conflicting bureaus were dissolved into three supreme sections: Air Force, Ground Force, and Supply. Ever since 1939, when the President jumped young, brilliant, non-West-Pointer George Catlett Marshall over the heads of 20 major and 14 brigadier generals to the post of Chief of Staff, such a move had been rumored. Indeed, months before the President's order General Marshall had effected much of the reorganization.

The new streamlined high command, pictured above, included: Lt. Gen. H. H. Arnold, chief of the autonomous Air Force, who is showing his colleagues something on the map; Gen. Marshall, Chief of Staff, the late Gen. McNair, chief of the Ground Force, including all infantry, cavalry, and armored divisions; standing, right, Major Gen. Brehon B. Somervell, chief of supply; right, Maj. Gen. J. T. McNarney, who was then in charge of War Department reorganization.

On these generals fell the burden of directing United States' effort in global war, the brains of the Army. Yet each of them has had many years of practical soldiering. Marshall planned and organized the Meuse-Argonne offensive in World War I. Arnold, a pupil of the late Gen. Billy Mitchell, directed the training of the air corps in 1917, foresaw the coming of air power, planned for and organized the world's largest air force for the U.S. McNair was an infantry officer since 1904, fought with Pershing in Mexico, Funston in Vera Cruz, won fame in France with the first A.E.F. Somervell is one of the great organizing geniuses of the Army, solved Mississippi River Commission problems for Hoover, WPA problems for Franklin Roosevelt. McNair, an organizer like Somervell, revamped the War Department's outmoded procedures, streamlined its necessary red tape. It is the high command's job to decide strategy, where U.S. forces shall be sent, how many, how to keep them supplied, pick commanders. It is a formidable task.

Yet by May 1942 there were hundreds of thousands of U.S. troops serving in every part of the globe, and the High Command was still building an army which would ultimately reach the 12,000,000 mark. U.S. striking power, which was virtually non-existent two years before, was well on the way to be overwhelming. Over 1,800,000 of America's troops had had over a year's training. The battles of Production and Preparation had been won and opening phase of offensive actions against the Axis had begun.

OUR ARMED FORCES

December 1944 marked the end of three years of war for the most consistently peace-minded nation in the world. Putting behind us our hatred of war, we have piled up figures difficult to believe even when officially reported. The Navy has grown from 50,000 men to more than 2,000,000. It has lost some 230 combat ships, but replacements have made our balanced fleet today probably larger than the other navies of the world combined. While 42,000 planes were being lost in three years, 240,000 new aircraft were being built. Total of our merchant shipping swept from the seas is almost 4,000,000 gross tons, but our warship-building program has turned out 42,000,000 deadweight tons. Our million-and-a-half Army has grown to 12,000,000 men, almost half of them already overseas, together with 74,000,000 ship tons of supplies. There is nothing in our history comparable to this, but it is still not the whole story. We have quality to offer our Allies as well as quantity. The increasing effectiveness of our weapons, our armor, our fighting forces no one can question. The achievements of General Marshall in this respect are as spectacular as our production indices, and his handicaps have probably been even greater than those of industry. From the hundreds of thousands of men sifted out by Selective Service —men of every race, nationality, creed and color—have been shaped an Army and Navy trained and equipped to fight every type of war. Mistakes in training, inevitable when an "amateur" nation in the field of war attempts to become professional over night, have been checked by experience and corrected at the source. Meanwhile the health and welfare of the men in our training camps have been given unparalleled care and protection. Between the Surgeon General's office and the office of the Quartermaster, everything the men wear, use, and consume is tested and retested. The Veterinary Service of the Medical Corps must pass on every pound of meat served to them and they are given every vaccine known to science to prevent epidemic diseases. One result of all this is that in the Armed Forces the disease and death rate from illness is cut to a fraction of the rate among civilians of the same age groups. Science is constantly being called in to serve some new need, or to improve upon something already in use. Many of the amazing developments in health protection, in synthetics, in machines, are still military secrets not to be revealed until peace is here once more. But it is no secret that because of the marvelous work of modern medical research and biochemistry the death rate among the wounded has dropped from the last war's rate of 8 out of 100 to 3 out of 100, and it is the hope of the Surgeon General's office to bring that rate down to 1 out of 100. Our vast training centers for the destructive arts of war may well prove to have served also as laboratories for the greatest advances yet made in constructive living. Meanwhile, the work of turning peace-loving men into warriors goes on. Into a few months of training must be packed the whole body of knowledge necessary for fighting a mechanized war so that wherever American forces go they may be a credit to their "basic training," and to the democracy they represent before the world.

A U.S. ARMY DOUGHBOY must have looked something like this to incredulous Japanese soldiers on Guadalcanal, assured by war lords of the "Son of Heaven" that "decadent" Americans would be "soft."

CAMP LIFE

HUMAN nature having remained pretty much what it was in World War I, while the mechanics of fighting and equipment were undergoing their complete revision, the psychological problems of daily life in camp can often be submitted to that previous experience for solution. In this way many of the earlier mistakes have been avoided. Perhaps the greatest improvement of all is in co-ordination of all activities of various organizations, Y.M.C.A., Salvation Army, Travelers' Aid, etc., into the USO. Expensive duplication of effort is avoided. An overall program insures aid and comfort

REVEILLE — AND TAPS! Immortalized by Irving Berlin, the Arm bugler is the core of Army camp life, symbol to the new soldier of h break with civilian ties.

A NEW "MAIN STREET" COMES TO AMERICA. From one end of the country to the other barrack and tent cities mushroomed into being to house the men Selective Service began sending in.

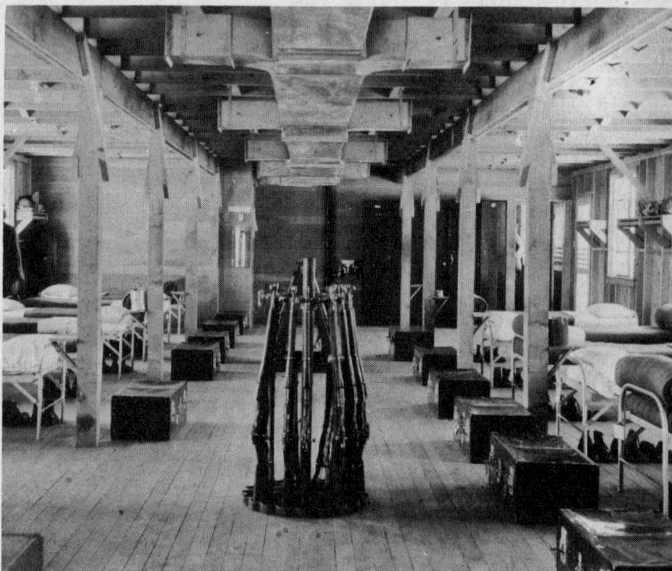

THIS IS SOMETIME BETWEEN REVEILLE AND TAPS, in typical barracks. Military precision saves lives in battle, so it must b made a habit even in rolling of a blanket, placing of shoes under a bed

NO GUESS WORK IN THE ARMY – every scrap of material is tested, in laboratories, and in use. Here samples of cloth spend several days outdoors to see how sun, rain will affect clothes made from them.

THIS ASTONISHING ARRAY OF EQUIPMENT, stowed away in a pack, weighs in at 55 pounds. It all goes with the marching soldier, not by truck, not by mule, but on his back, no matter what the terrain

NAPOLEON'S FAMOUS DICTUM, "An army travels on its stomach," is taken literally and seriously by U.S. dietitians. Never in history have fighting men been fed with such attention to variety, taste-appeal, nutrition.

AND RECREATIONS

to service men no matter where they may be. Mobile units take volunteer USO workers to the loneliest outlying posts. Camp shows introduce the most brilliant talent of Broadway and Hollywood to G.I. Joes as far away as New Guinea jungles or the heart of China. And USO and Red Cross bring the warming influence of home into every training center in the U.S.A. At every possible point of need they extend a helping hand. As for the rest, the camp routines are lightened by excellent food, well prepared, and an extensive educational program designed for better adjustment to army life, and preparation for knowing and understanding our Allies.

EMERGENCY FINDS THIS SOLDIER RISING TO THE OCCASION. Just returned to field quarters from very muddy maneuvers, he decides not to wait for Army laundry service but do a little washing on his own.

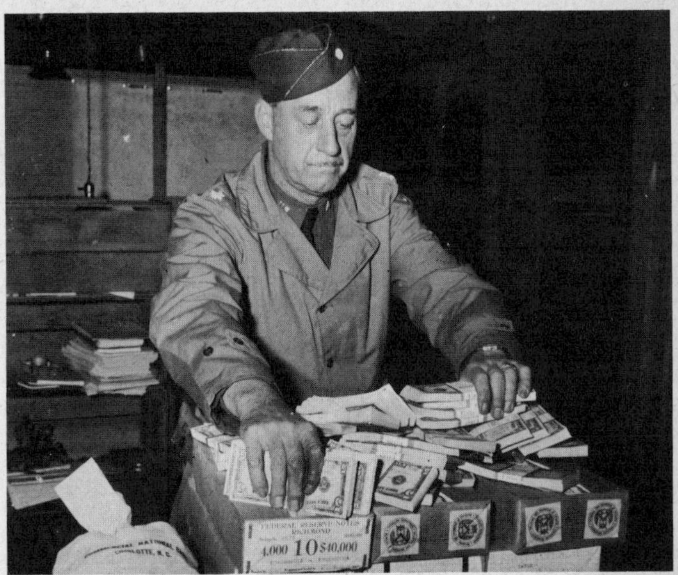

IT WAS A SHAM BATTLE the 6th Army Corps was fighting, on maneuvers in the south, but it is real money their Finance Officer is looking at, half a million dollars of it, to supply the payroll for the Corps.

THE USO WAS ORGANIZED in Feb. 1941 to prevent overlapping which had lessened effectiveness of various war services in World War I. Their canteens and shows carry cheer to service men all over the world.

"THIS IS THE ARMY," by Irving Berlin, is one of the world's all-time hit shows. Opening in New York July 4, 1942, its entire cast soldiers (300), it has piled up a tremendous fund for Army Emergency Relief.

Men of the infantry must know how to swarm over walls.

Army nurses practice foiling snipers by keeping silhouettes low.

WE LEARN TO FIGHT

MILITARY discipline, essential to successful training, is much more difficult in a peace-loving democracy than in a war-minded country or a dictatorship. Add to that the lack of enough trained officer personnel for an army suddenly expanded to undreamed of figures and the problem becomes acute. In the early days of our training program troops sometimes resented having to drill with wooden sticks for guns, live in unfinished barracks, take orders from half-trained platoon and company commanders and non-coms. But democratic resistance to regimentation began to vanish after enough men and officers had found out in the battle zones that the end result of discipline in training camps is the saving of lives on battle fronts. With establishment of the Army-Navy College a new level was reached in training of Army, Navy and Air officers for commands in new types of warfare requiring combined operations. As more and more units were shipped overseas, their experiences were reflected in improved training methods at home. Against a background

This new camouflage suit should help make life difficult for snipers.

From his camouflaged tank, GI Joe aims his 45 cal. automatic.

A smoke screen conceals the water trap, to make going tougher.

of physical fitness unequalled in any army, the Armed Forces of the country were gradually given a professional expertness which paid dividends when they went under fire. No previous army-training in history had been comparable in complexity with that required by this modern "total war." Never before had the training program been required to include techniques and equipment especially adapted to jungle fighting on the one hand, Arctic convoy on the other. And never before had "combined operations," by land, sea and air, made it necessary for each branch of the armed forces to know more than "just a little" about operations of all other branches.

Air gunners gain accuracy by shooting straight, on the ground.

A soldier on maneuvers advancing through a smoke screen

PRIMED FOR BATTLE

THE VASTNESS and complexity of mechanized war, conducted on a global scale, is almost as impossible for the average person to visualize as the Solar System or the national debt. Yet the men in charge of our war effort had to visualize it quickly and every training camp in the country was keyed to this necessity. Good-natured, easy-going men had to be made hard, tough and primed for battle. They were put through realistic reproductions of every known situation they might meet. They were acclimated to a new world of cruelty, of struggle for survival. Women, too, were oriented to war as in the Army and Navy Nurse Corps. Heroic reports of the Nurse Corps in action on battlefields from the Solomons to the Western Front bear witness to the thorough pre-combat training they received, side by side with the men they would minister to.

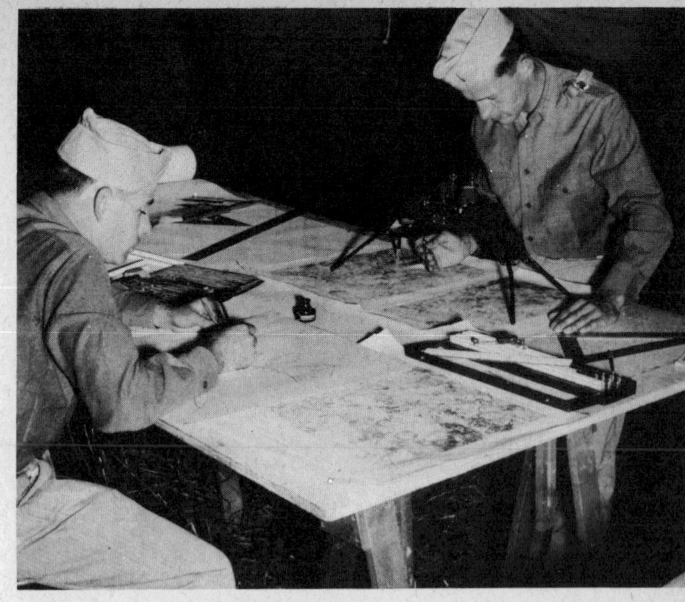

MODERN MECHANIZED WARFARE calls for a vast amount of paper work. These Army draftsmen use Army surveyors' data.

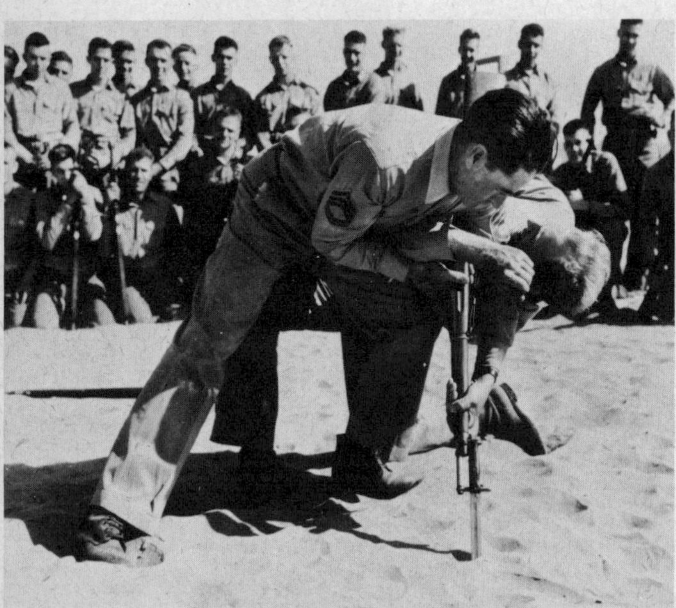

THE ANCIENT ART of hand-to-hand fighting is still part of war. This Marine demonstrates effectiveness of jujitsu in disarming assailant.

ACRES OF CAMOUFLAGE NETTING conceal the location of guns waiting for the moment when they will go into action against the enemy

FIELD NURSES must learn soldiers' protective technique. They hug the ground while debris rains down, live bullets whiz overhead.

RIN TIN TIN III is one of many dogs trained for Red Cross work. At the front these canine heroes make thrilling rescues.

THE TARGET WAS A NAZI FLAG, the explosion, a direct hit. Men run toward it, just as they would if it were an enemy pill box.

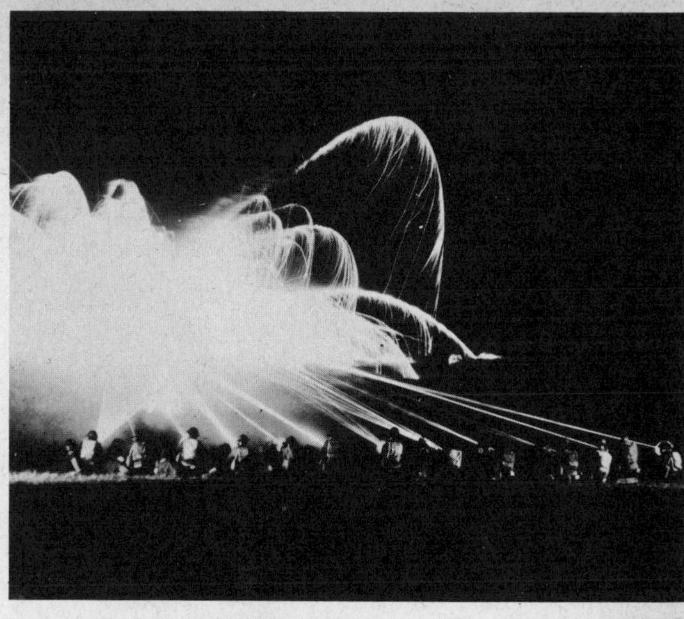

IT IS AN AWESOME SPECTACLE when tracer bullets, phosphorescent shells trace fire patterns against the sky, as in night maneuvers.

A GERMAN VILLAGE WAS BUILT especially to be taken by "trainees," using ball ammunition, in street fighting from house to house. This training prepared them for Cassino, or Aachen, saved many an American boy from snipers' bullets.

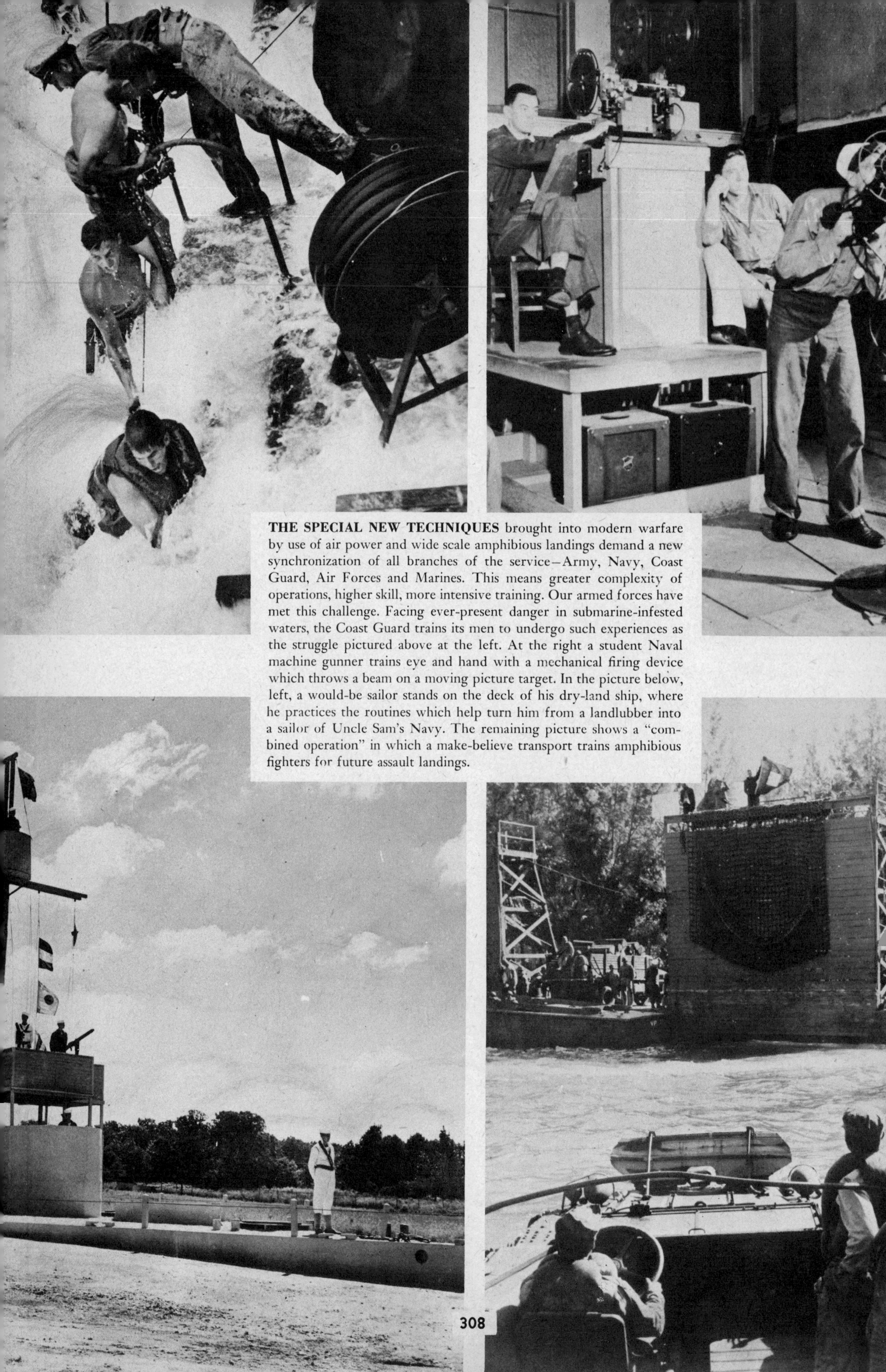

THE SPECIAL NEW TECHNIQUES brought into modern warfare by use of air power and wide scale amphibious landings demand a new synchronization of all branches of the service—Army, Navy, Coast Guard, Air Forces and Marines. This means greater complexity of operations, higher skill, more intensive training. Our armed forces have met this challenge. Facing ever-present danger in submarine-infested waters, the Coast Guard trains its men to undergo such experiences as the struggle pictured above at the left. At the right a student Naval machine gunner trains eye and hand with a mechanical firing device which throws a beam on a moving picture target. In the picture below, left, a would-be sailor stands on the deck of his dry-land ship, where he practices the routines which help turn him from a landlubber into a sailor of Uncle Sam's Navy. The remaining picture shows a "combined operation" in which a make-believe transport trains amphibious fighters for future assault landings.

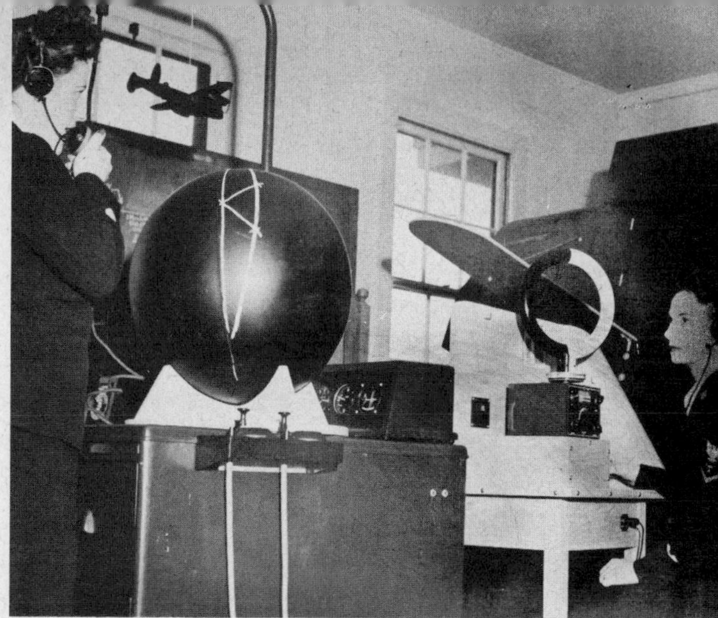

WOMEN GO TO WAR

The Women's Army Auxiliary Corps, organized in the spring of 1942, was the first of its kind in American military history, and like all "firsts" was regarded in many quarters with dread suspicion. Under Col. Oveta Culp Hobby, the WAACS soon became the WACS, Women's Army Corps, part of the U.S. Army in the fullest sense of the word. The only one of the women's divisions to serve abroad, the WACS in North Africa were pronounced "fine soldiers" by General Eisenhower, and their work on other fronts has received equally enthusiastic acclaim. With more than 92,000 enlisted, the WACS now are performing 239 out of 625 Army jobs. One of the most important duties women in all branches of service have taken on is teaching men, even in such unfeminine fields as gunnery. The WAC shown above is acting as gunnery instructor at an Army training camp. In the upper right picture are two SPAR Link Trainer Specialists who instruct men students in instrument and "blind" flying at a Coast Guard Air Station. The SPARS take their name from the Coast Guard motto, *Semper Paratus* (always ready), and they live up to it. Organized in Nov. 1942, under Lt. Com. Dorothy C. Stratton, as the Woman's Reserve of the Coast Guard Reserve, they are filling shore billets from Pensacola to Puget Sound. The Navy's WAVES—Women Accepted for Volunteer Emergency Service—also dating from Nov. 1942—commanded by Capt. Mildred H. McAfee, have released enough fighting men already to make up a good-sized task force. Nearly every naval activity in the Continental U.S. now has its quota of WAVES. From pharmacist's mate to aviation machinist mate—the WAVES have made good. In the lower left picture a WAVE is shown engraving a negative of ocean depths in the Navy Hydrographic Office in Maryland. The U.S. Marine Corps Women's Reserve was the latest of the divisions to be organized, in Feb. 1943, under Maj. Ruth Cheney Streeter, but already it is filling more than 125 different types of jobs. "Hitch your bomber to a star . . ." That's the advice given to bomber fighters and pilots by the Marine Corporal below (*right*) who is shown demonstrating the use of the astro-compass to set a straight course.

TANKS—BATTLESHIPS OF THE ARMY

WHEN the Nazis' *blitzkrieg* sent panzer forces roaring across Europe, they were planting a seed of destruction in their garden of victory. But Americans understood the motor and the machine. It took a little time to divert their vast industrial potential and inventive genius to war, but once on their way nothing could stop them. Most American men had grown up driving automobiles. The tank to them was an old familiar friend—rather larger and heavier, but still a motor vehicle they knew how to handle. Too light at first to meet the heavy Nazi Mark IVs, the U.S. went to work. Today powerful American monster tanks, spearheading drives on Nazis and Japanese on ever-expanding fronts, are being driven into battle by men who know how to drive them, maneuver them, service them. Tank warfare has become a boomerang released by the Nazis to defeat only themselves in the end.

THE YOUNG LIEUTENANT is at the business end of a 50 cal. machine gun in the turret of a medium tank.

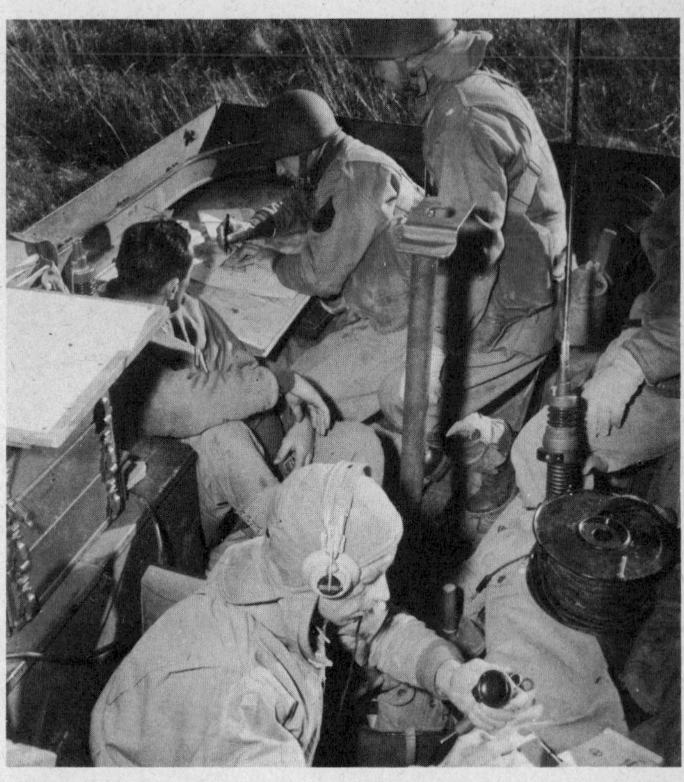

FIRING A BATTERY is not a simple matter. The officer and three men are operating "Battery Fire Direction Control."

NEW TYPE ARMOR calls for new weapons. This sticky grenade will cling to an enemy tank, explode, wipe out the tank.

AN ARMORED TANK LOOMS threateningly over the horizon, with men above and below alert for any sign of enemy approach.

PLANES AND TANKS — spearhead of American attack — clash in simulated battle somewhere in the badlands of the Southwest. Airplanes of the Army Air Forces team up with tanks in these desert maneuvers to work out the timing that means victory in battle. Tank commanders man anti-aircraft guns while the armored fleet drives through blinding heat and choking dust to its objective. Overhead, planes of the Ground-Air Support clear the way with bombs and machine gun fire, fight opposing planes which plaster the tanks with sacks of flour in lieu of bombs. The same combination is constantly being tried in other parts of the U.S., in jungle-like swamps, over roughly wooded hills, across snowy plains in preparation for every kind of climate, every type of terrain. Night maneuvers are carried out, too, testing the men's resourcefulness in varied and difficult situations in a hundred different ways.

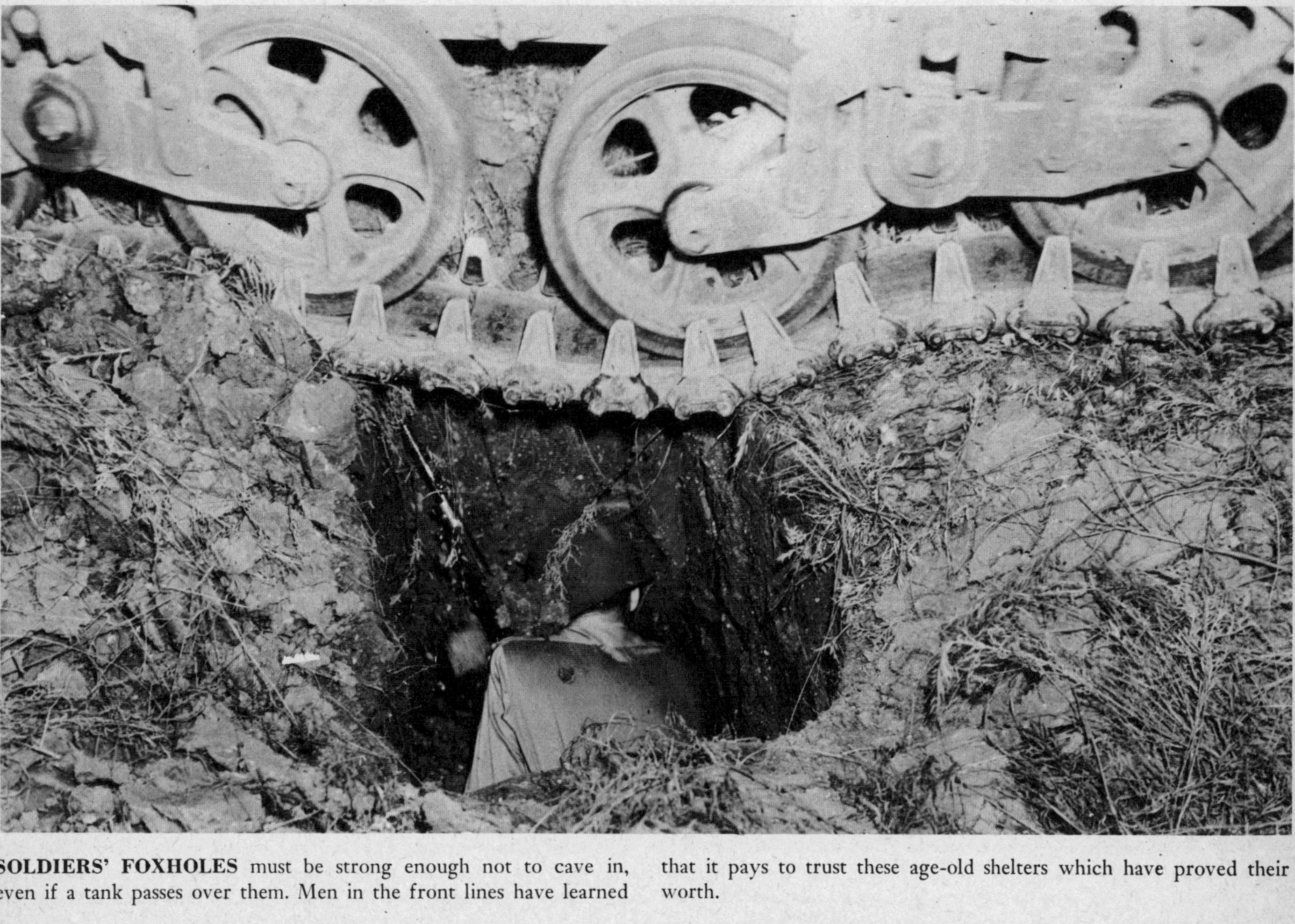

SOLDIERS' FOXHOLES must be strong enough not to cave in, even if a tank passes over them. Men in the front lines have learned that it pays to trust these age-old shelters which have proved their worth.

EAGLETS GE

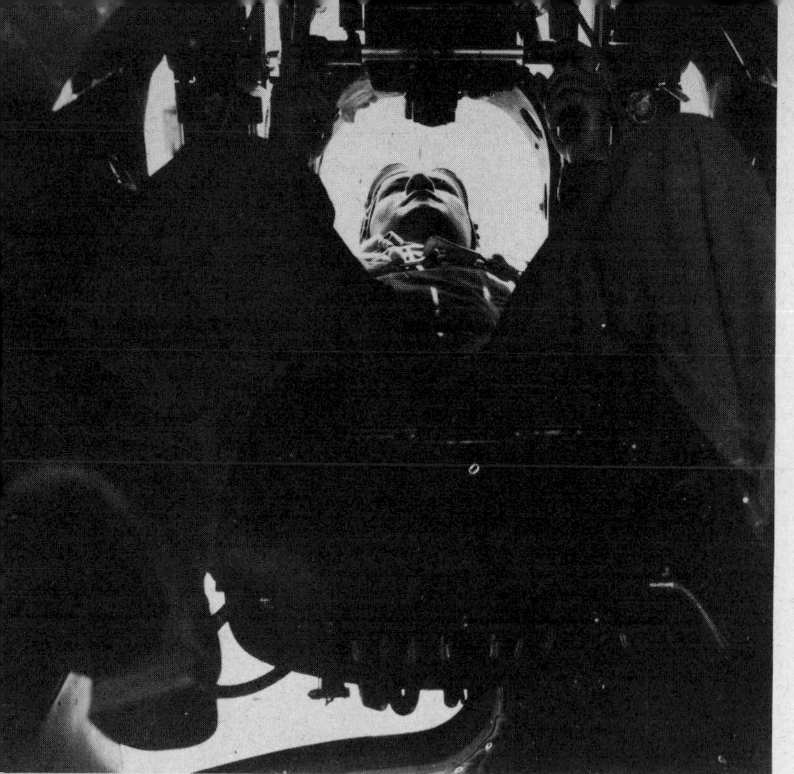

This top turret gunner was trained in a hard school.

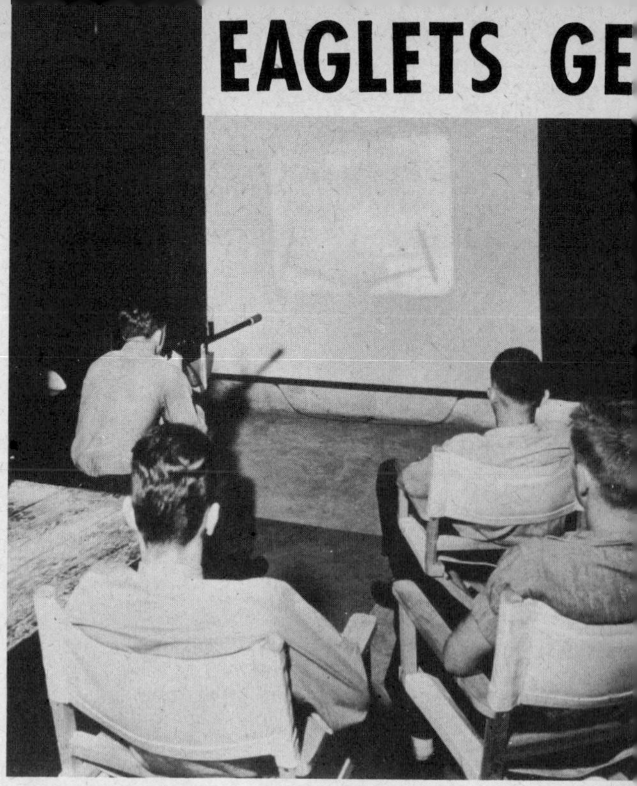

Gunnery lessons give cadets real "battle practice."

"OK, TAKE her up!" These are thrilling words to a fledgling Navy pilot when his instructor in Primary School gives him the signal for his first solo flight in a naval training plane. It takes long months to turn a cadet into a combat flier. There is ground school first, then elementary flight training by the Civil Aeronautics Authority, then "Pre-Flight" to toughen him up. "Primary" is next, with his first military flying, then "Intermediate" where specialized tr ing is given, then at last "Operational," where final polis is done. The Pre-Flight cadet learns rope-climbing tricks, trick of blowing up his trousers to make a life-buoy in water. He studies navigation, radio, aerology, other esse subjects, and undergoes physical training almost as sti Commando routines.

AT THIS GREAT INTERMEDIATE TRAINING CENTER at Corpus Christi, Texas, prospective Navy fliers learn military and formation flying, receive their wings of gold. Aprons and runways, seen from the control tower, are covered with yellow training pla very safe, but dubbed by experienced pilots "Yellow Peril" whe student flier takes one up "solo" with no instructor in the front s

HEIR WINGS

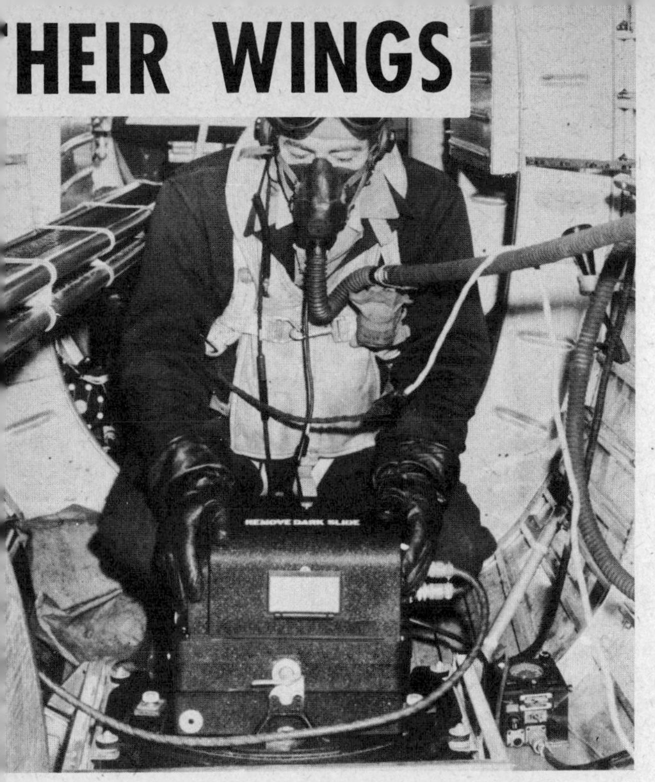

Aerial photography is vital to combat flying.

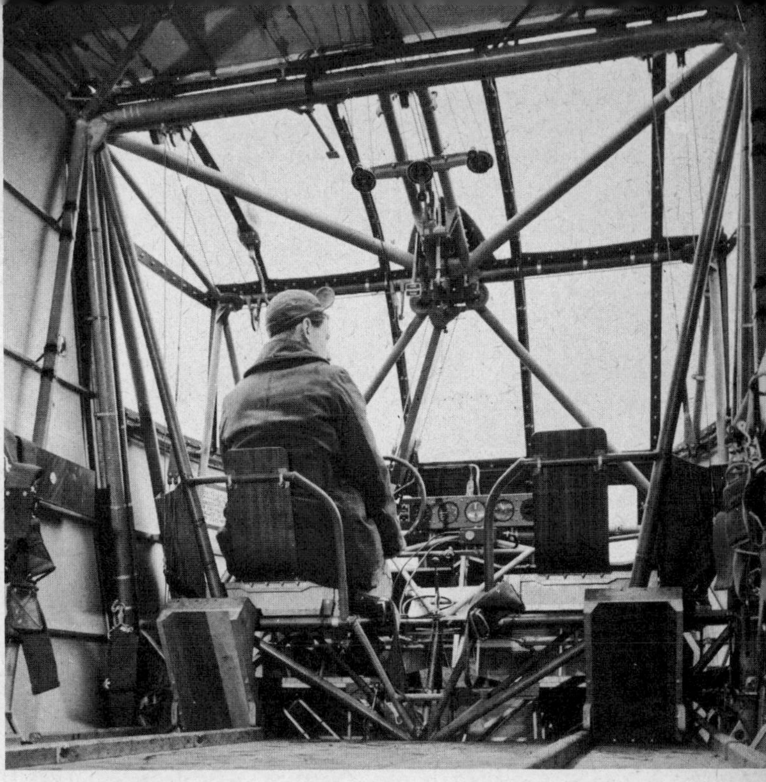

Special glider techniques must be mastered by students.

YOU WILL be the hardest, toughest, and physically the most durable fighters in the sky." Those words of 1. Walter W. Weaver, spoken 2 years ago to young ts in his new aviation cadet training program, have been le good. The Army Air Force sends a cadet through -Flight School, then through primary, basic, advanced ng courses and highly specialized training. When the young pilot, bombardier, or navigator takes his place in a battle zone he has been made ready in every way for combat conditions. Army physical training for flying cadets is based on experiments in which a cadet did a "Lord Godiva" by "riding" his plane, without benefit of clothing while the reaction of each muscle used in flying was analyzed. Those Army-trained cadets do really come out "durable"!

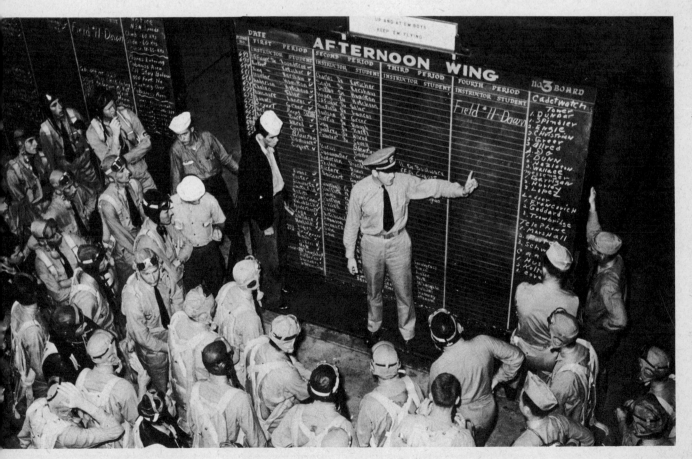

ST MINUTE INSTRUCTIONS are given to students gathered und the schedule board before they take off on a training "mission" ich will reproduce as nearly as possible actual flying conditions they will meet against the enemy. In anticipation of having to bail out they are drilled in the arts of falling, opening a 'chute, rolling on the ground to ease a rough landing.

This map was drawn, at the time of the Cairo Conference, late November, 1943; the grey shadow of Japan had as yet been lifted

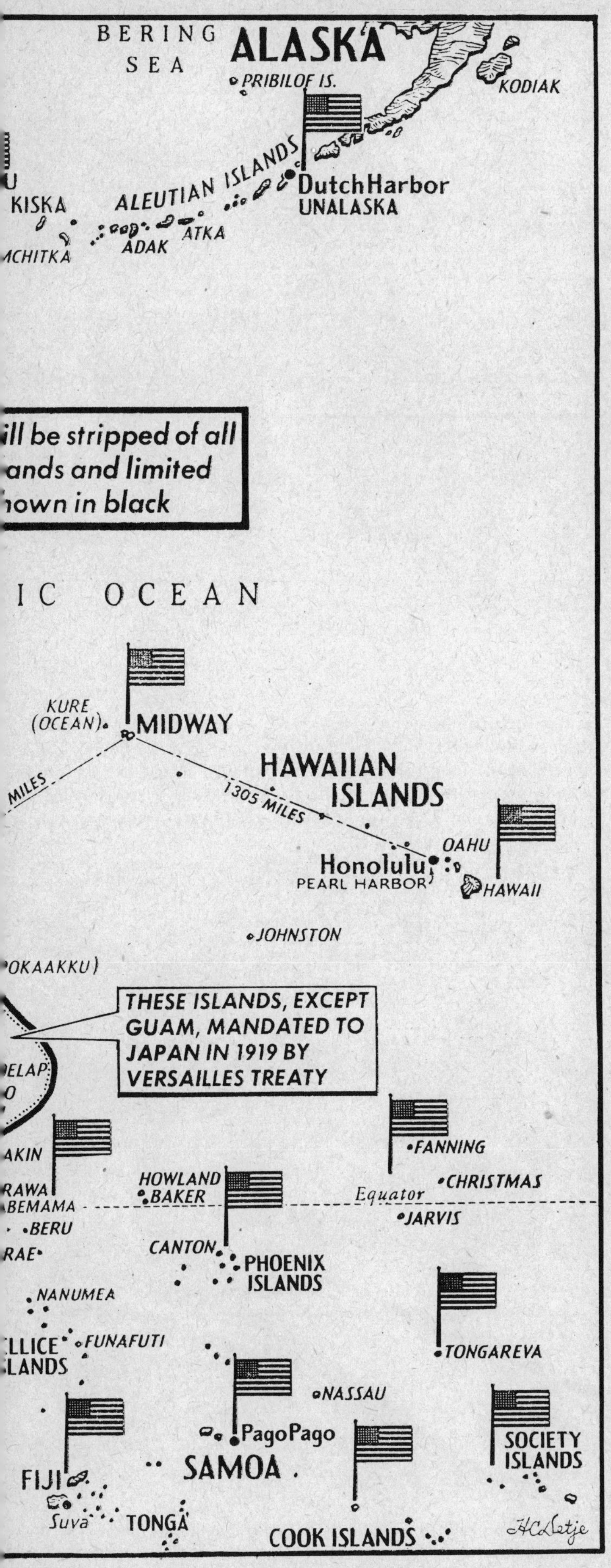

JAPAN'S DRIVE INTO THE SOUTH PACIFIC

YEARS before her treacherous blow at Pearl Harbor, Japan had cunningly acquired control of some 1,500 little-known Pacific islands. Looking at the map, the whole world can see too late what Japan saw long ago. In the location of those tiny scattered islands a design emerges which in the hands of a nation bent upon aggression would make it the strategic key to control of the Pacific. Like fringe on the edge of an open fan, tiny islands and groups of islands extend from Palau, only 600 miles east of the Philippines, through Yap, the Carolines, Truk, Ponape, to the Marshalls—and so within striking distance of Hawaii, thence of the American coast. From the Japanese coast a line of stepping-stone islands leads south to the Carolines. Dots as all these islands are on the map, in the sea their coral reefs sweep in huge circles about many a harbor large enough to shelter a fleet. Ignoring the League of Nations provision forbidding fortification of their mandates, Japan had secretly toiled to convert key islands into powerful bases for use as springboards of attack against the rich island world stretching in a wide arc from Borneo and the Philippines to Hawaii. Along that arc, invasion forces could advance from island to island until they had gained the whole archipelago, cut off Burma, threatened India, dominated the Dutch East Indies, put Australia in desperate peril. Striking their first blow at Pearl Harbor on Dec. 7, 1941, Japanese naval forces also swooped down upon Guam, Wake, and Midway, lone U.S. Pacific outposts. Guam, center of a veritable hornet's nest of Japanese bases in the Marianas, fell on Dec. 12. Wake and Midway, in lines of approach converging upon Hawaii from the Marianas and the Marshalls, resisted strongly. At Wake, heroic U.S. Marines and Seabees held out against repeated Japanese assaults until Dec. 24. Midway alone was able to keep the U.S. flag flying. Taking Manila on Jan. 2, 1942, the Japanese also occupied Sarawak in Borneo, then the port of Tarakan on the other side of the island. The invaders made no attempt to conquer the inland areas of these islands, from which guerrilla bands continued to operate, but instead used the main cities and ports as jumping-off points for the next step leading to their main objectives—Australia, and the Dutch East Indies with their wealth of tin, oil, and rubber. On Jan. 23 enemy forces landed in the Solomons and in Papua, at Australia's front door. At the same time the Japanese fleet, assembling in Sarawak and Borneo for invasion of Java, was caught by U.S. and Dutch naval vessels and aircraft in the Macassar strait. A five-day battle ended in defeat for the invaders on Jan. 29, but too late to prevent landings already made at Sumatra. The rich oil fields at Palembang were seized, Feb. 17, and the fate of Sumatra was sealed. United Nations forces, trying desperately to hold Java, were no match for the superior number of Japanese troops which finally occupied Java's northern coast on Feb. 29, only to find themselves cheated of rich, and much needed, spoils of victory. The Dutch had applied the scorched-earth policy to everything of military value in their islands. Japan turned now in deadly earnest to acquisition of the invaluable oil fields of Burma.

land bases in the Solomons, Gilberts and Aleutians. Among the first retaken were Guadalcanal, Tarawa, Makin, Kiska and Attu.

JAPAN HAD BEGUN CONCENTRATING TROOPS IN INDO-CHINA in June, 1941, after she had bludgeoned that territory away from weak-kneed Vichy France. On Dec. 7, the same day she struck at Pearl Harbor, she launched drives from Indo-China against the British in Burma and Malaya. On Dec. 8 forces landed at the mouth of the Kalentan River in Malaya, and on Dec. 9 along Thailand's Malayan border. Taking Kota Bharu, they split into two columns, one moving south along the Malayan coast toward Singapore, the other pushing northward across the Kra isthmus, taking Victoria Point in South Burma on Dec. 15, heading then toward Rangoon.

FROM SINGAPORE TO RANGOON JAPANESE BOMBERS were hammering cities held by the British. Fires raged through grass-roofed native quarters, despite the work of hastily organized, ill-equipped civilian firemen. With 450 planes, the Japanese controlled the air. Under command of fat, gruff Gen. Yamashita, well-trained, well-armed troops, with a new jungle-fighting technique, moved across Thailand from Indo-China, pushed along the coasts, swarmed over Malay and Burma, struck toward two main objectives. They laid siege to Singapore; at the same time drove against the Burma Road to cut off China's supplies, to end her stubborn resistance, and threaten India.

SINKING OF THE *PRINCE OF WALES*, powerful new British battleship, and the new cruiser *Repulse*, by Japanese torpedo planes off Malaya Dec. 10, 1941, was a naval disaster which experts claim led to the fall of Malaya and Singapore. Without adequate sea protection, battered by bombs, overwhelmed by superior numbers, the British garrison at Hong Kong surrendered to the Japanese Dec. 25.

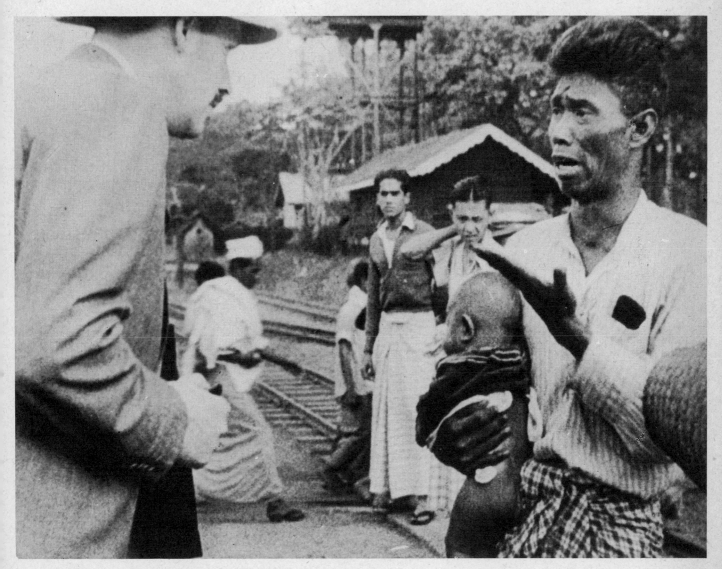

IN JANUARY, JAPANESE TROOPS WERE ADVANCING RAPIDLY toward Rangoon, port of entry for the Burma Road, while their air force bombed it unmercifully. In the picture above a terror-stricken native tells his story to Burma Governor, Sir Reginald Borman-Smith. The Japanese, adept in jungle warfare, had little real opposition from the few poorly trained Burmese and Indian troops opposing them. Veteran Chinese forces, sent by Chiang Kai-shek to help the British defend Burma, were not acceptable to Burmese ministers, and had to be immobilized in the north while the Japanese took Rangoon on Mar. 8, then moved on toward Lashio to cut the Burma Road.

A Japanese bomb has just killed this grief-stricken Singapore mother's child, whose body lies on the right.

SINGAPORE, at the tip of Malaya, one of the world's greatest naval bases, squarely blocked the gateway to direct assault upon the Dutch East Indies from Japanese bases on the coast of Asia. Under never-ending bombardment, Singapore's defense was desperately brave, but futile. The failure of the British commander, Brooke-Popham, to take the Japanese threat seriously in the beginning, his reluctance to mobilize the native population, had laid the foundation for the fall of the city. On Dec. 26 he was replaced by Gen. Pownall, but by now the Japanese moving down both Malayan coasts were within 200 miles of the city. Adept at jungle warfare, naked, grease-covered Japanese slithered through underbrush trap British units bogged down with useless artillery. Jan. 26 the Japanese had taken Batu Pahat, western anchor Malaya's defense line, and two days later they were neari Kalui, only 18 miles from British Singapore. By Jan. 31 t British were forced to evacuate the city proper on Malayan mainland and retreat to Singapore Island where naval base was located. They had never counted on assa from .he mainland, had never believed tanks could negoti flooded rice-fields, had never expected naval protection to weakened by sinking of two mighty battleships on almost

Bomb fragments have hit the other woman in the leg. This is one of the most remarkable pictures of the war.

rst day of invasion. Now only the shallow half mile of water 1 the Johore Strait separated the troops on Singapore Island rom the gathering forces of Gen. Yamashita on the mainind. On that 14-by-16-mile island were packed 750,000 ungry, thirsty people, of virtually every race and national-y in the world. On Feb. 8 the Japanese captured the stoutly efended Singapore airport to end what little air protection ıe base had. Repeated attempts to land on the island were ırown back, until Feb. 13 when the Japanese captured the ingapore reservoir, shutting off the meager water supplies of the defenders. Three powerful drives, by 100,000 Japanese, crossed to the island, and on Feb. 15 Gen. Percival, commander of the base, found it impossible to continue resistance and surrendered. In far away Australia, on Feb. 16, Premier John Curtin stated that the fall of Singapore marked the opening of the "Battle of Australia," upon whose outcome "hinges in large measure the fate of the British-speaking world." On Feb. 22 President Roosevelt ordered Gen. MacArthur to leave the Philippines and take command of making Australia into a great military base.

The Defense of the Philippines

THIS REMARKABLE PICTURE, SHOWING JAPANESE LANDING barges approaching Luzon on Dec. 9, was developed from film found on the body of a dead Japanese on the beach.

THE blow which devastated Pearl Harbor did not have the same effect in the Philippines where Gen. Douglas MacArthur, former U.S. Chief of Staff, had been preparing the islands' defenses since 1935. And it was on the Philippines that the brunt of the Japanese drive fell. Regardless of the Japanese advances in Malaya, the Philippines offered a jumping-off point for attacks on Japanese communications and simultaneously immobilized Japanese naval and army forces badly needed elsewhere. The Japanese attack, Dec. 7, 1941, attempted to knock out Manila's great naval base, Cavite, and near-by Nichols Field. The next day Japanese transports appeared off Vigan and northern Luzon to attempt landings. But these were driven off by hard-fighting Filipino troops, and not until Dec. 9 were superior Japanese forces, at a frightful cost, able to seize beach heads. MacArthur's forces totaled less than 100,000 men, including reservists, only 10,000 regular U.S. troops. Lack of planes and tanks made it doubtful if they could hold out long. Nichols Field and other Philippine air bases were under almost continuous attack as more Japanese troops landed in the north and at Lingayan. Meanwhile, other Japanese forces had landed in Malaya and were besieging the British sea base at Hong Kong from its defenseless land approaches. In Malaya the British fell back rapidly. Japanese propaganda that they were waging a war against the "white oppressors" of the yellow race had a powerful effect in Malaya and Burma, and contributed much to the British inability to stem the tide. But this propaganda made no headway in the Philippines, where the people, who had been armed and promised complete independence in 1946, fought furiously against the invaders. But they were unable to prevent a Japanese landing at Legaspi, south of Manila, on Dec. 11, and the invaders now began a drive for Manila from north and south.

COURAGEOUS, WELL-TRAINED FILIPINO TROOPS smashed the first Japanese attempts to land, but by mid-December the Japanese had effected landings at three points in northern Luzon.

FIRST AMERICAN HERO of the war was Capt. Colin Kelly who, on Dec. 11, dived his flaming, bomb-laden Flying Fortress into a Japanese battleship, sinking it immediately.

CIVILIAN MANILA WAS BOMBED SAVAGELY, even after MacArthur declared it an open city and withdrew his troops, largely Filipino. To prevent use of the port of Cavite, MacArthur fired the port. His men retired slowly toward the hills of Bataan peninsula, bitterly contesting every inch. Manila was occupied Jan. 2, 1942, but the Corregidor garrison dug in to keep the bay open at all costs.

THE DEFENDERS OF BATAAN, worn down by endless air and artillery attacks, exhaustion, hunger, disease, cut off from reinforcement, fought on. When fat, able, arrogant Gen. Yamashita arrived with troops fresh from Japanese victories in Singapore, Malaya, Java, it was 200,000 against 37,000. The epic defense of Bataan ended April 9. Only a few thousand troops got away, across the bay to Corregidor.

THE THOUSANDS OF JAPANESE TAKEN PRISONERS by MacArthur's men became a difficult problem as the siege went on, for there was barely enough food for Filipino and U.S. troops.

MacARTHUR ORDERED THE "SCORCHED EARTH" POLICY of Russia and China, to slow Japanese advance. Here, with help of loyal Filipinos, his men prepare to dynamite an already damaged bridge.

MacARTHUR TURNED OVER PHILIPPINE DEFENSE TO LT. GEN. JONATHAN M. WAINWRIGHT when President Roosevelt ordered him to assume command of the A.E.F. now landing in force in Australia. Spirited from Luzon, under the very eyes of the Japanese, MacArthur and his party escaped in three small PT boats commanded by Lt. John Bulkley who had made himself and his boats famous by torpedoing a Japanese cruiser and several transports. Completing the perilous 2,000 mile journey to Australia by plane, MacArthur received command of all the United Forces in the Southwest Pacific, pledging rescue to the Philippines with these historic words: "I came through and I shall return."

EXHAUSTED DEFENDERS OF CORREGIDOR'S ISLAND FORTRESS finally came out of their smoke-filled tunnel on May 6, 1942. They had held out miraculously under bombardment which never ceased, wasted by want, without hope of relief. By their heroic stand they had written a new page in the history of bravery. The last message heard from the "Rock" was tapped out on a radio key by 22-year-old Pvt. Irving Strobing of Brooklyn, N. Y.

Last Message from Corregidor

". . . THEY are not near yet. We a
waiting for God only knows wh
How about a chocolate soda? . . . N
many. Not near yet. Lots of hea
fighting going on. We've only g
about one hour, twenty minutes b
fore . . . We may have to give up
noon. We don't know yet. They a
throwing men and shells at us and
may not be able to stand it. They ha
been shelling us faster than you c
count . . . We've got about fifty-fi
minutes and I feel sick at my stomac
I am really low down. They a
around smashing rifles. They bring
the wounded every minute. We w
be waiting for you guys to help. Tl
is the only thing I guess that can
done . . . General Wainwright is
right guy and we are willing to go
for him, but shells were dropping
night, faster than hell. Too much f
guys to take. Enemy cross-shelling a
bombing. They have got us all arou
and from the skies. . . . From here
looks like firing ceased on both sid
Men here all feeling bad, because
terrific nervous strain of the sieg
Corregidor used to be a nice place b
it's haunted now. Withstood a terri
pounding.

". . . Just made broadcast to Manila
arrange meeting for surrender. Ta
made by General Beebe. I can't s
much. Can't think at all. I can hard
think. Say, I have 60 pesos you c
have for this week end.

". . . The jig is up. Everyone is baw
ing like a baby. They are piling de
and wounded in our tunnel. Arn
weak from pounding key, long hou
no rest, short rations, tired . . .

"I know now how a mouse fee
Caught in a trap waiting for guys
come along and finish it up. Got
treat. Can pineapple. Opening it wi
Signal Corps knife . . . My name
Irving Strobing. Get this to n
mother, Mrs. Minnie Strobing, 6
Barbey Street, Brooklyn, N. Y. Th
are to get along O.K. Get in tou
with them as soon as possible. Me
sage. My love to Pa, Joe, Sue, Ma
Garry, Joy, and Paul. Also to all fa
ily and friends. God bless 'em a
Hope they be there when I co
home. Tell Joe, wherever he is, to gi
'em hell for us. My love to you a
God bless you and keep you. Lov
Sign my name and tell my mother ho
you heard from me . . ."

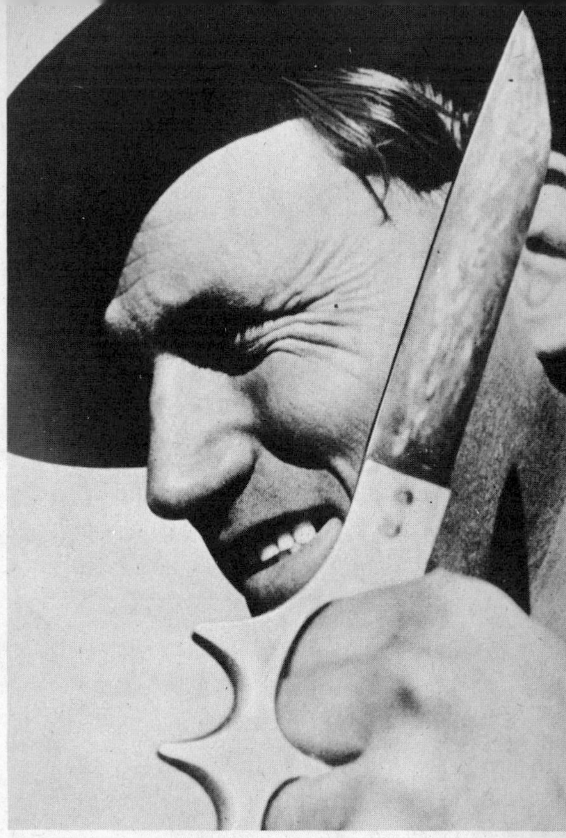

IN AUSTRALIA, IN THE SPRING OF 1942, U.S. P-40 FIGHTER planes and Aussie spitfires, stationed along coasts and near principal cities to intercept bombing, proved more than a match for Japanese Zeros. Many a Zero met the fate of the plane shown above, shot down in one of the frequent raids over Darwin.

AUSSIE COMMANDOS LIKE THE VETERAN shown above used this ugly-looking combination knuckle-buster-dagger as part of their regulation sidearms issue. Australian troops fought magnificently alongside Allies.

BATTLE-HARDENED AUSSIES WERE RECALLED FROM the Middle East to defend their homeland, grimly facing danger of invasion from Japanese forces spread in a great arc from the Solomons to the Dutch East Indies. Thousands of U.S. troops were pouring into Australia, MacArthur was gaining control of the air. When heavy bombers began long-range raids on enemy bases, the tide was turning. Australia would never serve the Japanese as a base for world-wide conquest.

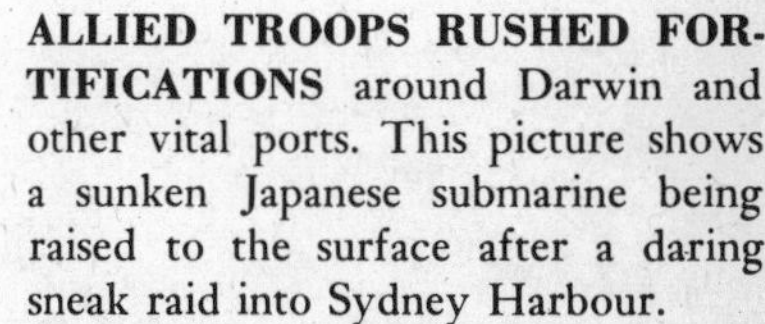

ALLIED TROOPS RUSHED FORTIFICATIONS around Darwin and other vital ports. This picture shows a sunken Japanese submarine being raised to the surface after a daring sneak raid into Sydney Harbour.

TROOPS LIKE THIS SIKH RIFLE SECTION fought magnificently beside American, British and Chinese defenders of Burma. They helped to turn the tide when the Japanese swept across Thailand into Burma on their drive for conquest of India, the Middle East, and the world.

THIS FAITHFUL ELEPHANT helped the war effort by rolling logs at a timber depot in the Burma jungle to make room for fresh supplies. American and British troops found jungle roads not built to carry the hundreds of vehicles needed for a modern army. Rivers, streams, gullies were everywhere, winding between dense undergrowth and towering trees. Elephants proved invaluable in building bridges.

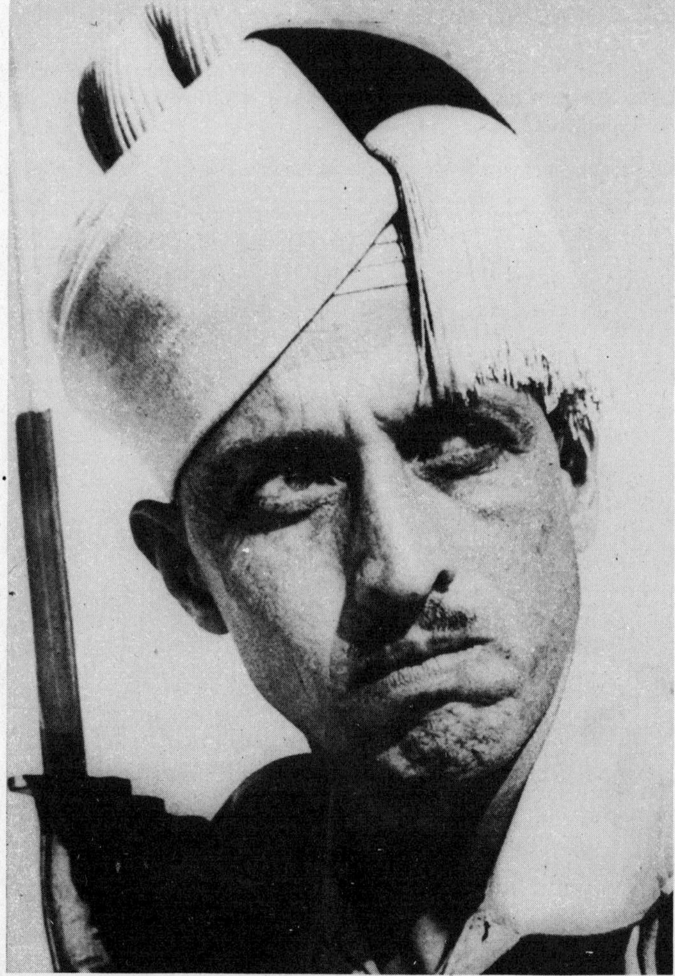

MEN OF INDIA FIGHT for United Nations' ideals in Burma, Malay , Singapore, North Africa, Europe – wherever the line of battle is joined.

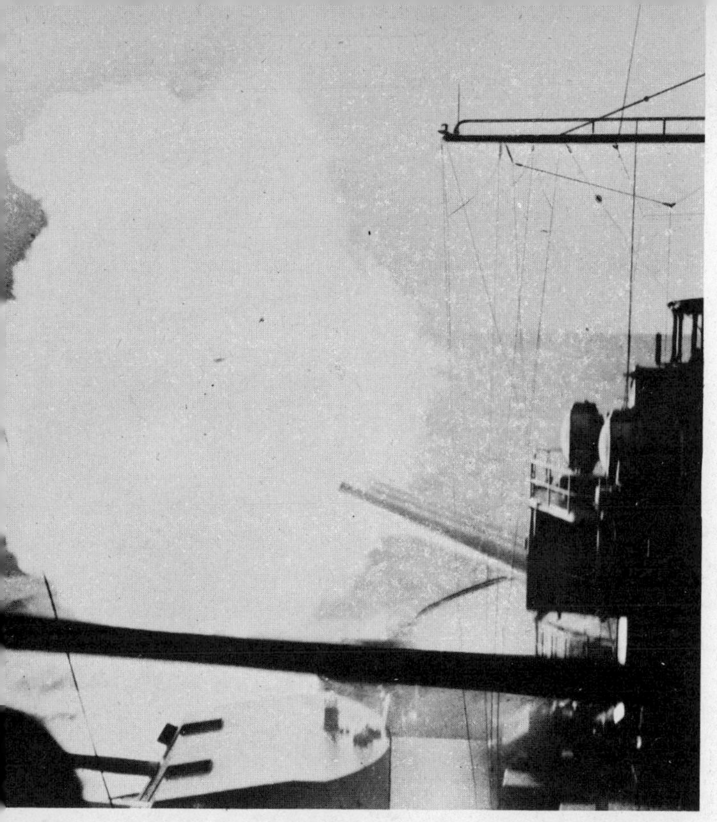

BIG GUNS OF U.S. BATTLEWAGONS soften Japanese in the Aleutians, prepare to take back those bleak, fog-covered stepping stones on the sea-road from Alaska to Tokyo. Seized by Japanese in first summer of war, 1942, they planned to use them as bases for invasion of America.

FIRST ATTACK ON U.S. MAINLAND IN WORLD WAR II was on Feb. 2, 1942. Shell from Japanese submarine, aimed at oil refinery in Santa Barbara, Calif., splintered a few boards of ocean pier. Later, brief shelling, in June, did no damage at all to Fort Stevens, Oregon.

FLYING FROM A MYSTERIOUS BASE — KNOWN ONLY AS the "Shangri-La" until it was revealed as the U.S. carrier *Hornet*—Brig. Gen. James H. Doolittle (see insert) led the first dramatic raid over the Japanese homeland. His squadron of bombers, flying low by daylight, threw Tokyo into a panic of confusion and rage. The Allied world was shocked by Tokyo's boasts that several fliers forced down on Japanese soil had been ruthlessly executed for alleged "desecration" of the sacred person of the emperor. Men from planes landing in occupied China were welcomed, nursed, aided to escape. Chiang Kai-shek later reported revenge killing by the Japanese of every man, woman and child in those areas. Picture shows survivors of the raid being decorated by Gen. Arnold at Bolling Field, June 27, 1942.

For five months after the infamy of Pearl Harbor the sweep of Japanese aggression in the South Pacific area had been practically unchecked, and the territory seized and occupied was a third the size of the U.S. But this was only preparation for conquest of Australia, guardian of vital sea lanes, queen of the Pacific in her own right, made-to-order base for the vast Allied counteroffensive which would break the hold of the Japanese octopus in the Pacific. To meet the gravity of the situation U.S. Pacific naval forces were reorganized under command of Adm. Chester W. Nimitz, on his shoulders the job of fitting a five-ocean strategy to his one-ocean navy. A focus of enemy attention in March, 1942, was Port Moresby, on New Guinea's southern tip, perfect take-off point for invading Australia. Battered by constant air attack, U.S. and other Allied fliers based at Moresby hung on, struck back. On Mar. 10 a Japanese fleet, assembling at Lae and Salamaua on the other side of New Guinea for sea assault on Moresby, was badly mauled by U.S. shore- and carrier-based planes. Losing 20 ships, they gave up the attempt. It was two months before U.S. scout planes sighted a new invasion fleet, moving southeastward along fringes of the Coral Sea. At dawn on May 4 American planes from two carriers found part of a task force in the harbor of Tulagi, capital of the Solomon Islands, another launching point for assault upon Australia. Taken completely by surprise, Japanese anti-aircraft guns got into action too late. Every U.S. flier had been assigned a specific target. Within a few minutes the tiny harbor was littered with hulks of Japanese ships, heavy and light cruisers, destroyers, transports. U.S. losses—only three planes! When the main Japanese task force was sighted May 6 by Navy planes, the *Ryukaku*, one of Japan's newest, largest carriers was added to the U.S. score, also a heavy cruiser. May 8 more Japanese ships were heavily damaged. Meanwhile, retaliating planes from a Japanese carrier left the U.S. carrier *Lexington* in such bad shape it had to be abandoned and destroyed. Japan reported her staggering toll of losses in the Battle of the Coral Sea as a "victory." But it was another month before she was ready for further aggressive action, and then Japanese strategy turned in a new direction. Far to the north above Pearl Harbor, half-way between San Francisco and Tokyo, lay tiny Midway Island, held successfully by Marines in December when Guam and Wake fell. In enemy hands, it would be an invaluable base for operations against Hawaii. On June 3, 1942, a Japanese invasion fleet was sighted 700 miles southwest of Midway. An assault fleet, located northwest of the island, brought to 80 the number of ships in the powerful task force heading for Midway.

A U.S. CARRIER, probably the *Yorktown*, stands off a torpedo plane. After this picture was taken the plane was downed.

THE BATTLE OF MIDWAY MARKED THE FIRST REAL check to Japanese aggression in the Pacific. U.S. Army, Navy, and Marine forces participated in the savage battle which raged for three days and three nights. Heavy bombers based on Midway sped to join carrier-based attacks, pursued battered units seeking escape. Japanese rout and disaster ended the fight. Four of their carriers and many planes had been lost, also two heavy cruisers, three destroyers, loaded transports. Nine other war vessels had been damaged, and more transports. U.S. losses were: destroyer *Hamman* sunk, carrier *Yorktown* heavily damaged, several scores of planes destroyed. Over 4,800 Japanese had been killed or drowned, while only 300 U.S. officers and men had lost their lives. Above is shown one of the Japanese heavy cruisers—the stricken *Mogami*—just before it sank, insides burned out by repeated bomb hits, a picture of complete desolation.

U. S. Fleet Wins At Coral Sea and Midway

THE SMASHING VICTORY OF THE U.S. FLEET AT MIDWAY left Japanese naval striking power definitely crippled, though its future potentialities could not yet be predicted. More than that, the Battles of Coral Sea and Midway marked a striking new development in naval warfare, a turning point in sea power history. In the entire course of the engagement no surface ship had come within range or sight of any enemy surface ship. Air power alone had stopped a great fleet, and routed it. The carrier would now become the backbone of the fleet. From this time forth it would bulk large in U.S. construction plans, even though that would mean sacrifice of previously projected super-battleships. But something even more important had emerged from these Pacific battles. In the Japanese fleet of battleships, cruisers, destroyers, submarines, the carrier was the capital ship. Destruction of carriers had sent a Japanese task force reeling homeward, relentlessly pursued by long-range bombers from land bases on Midway. A mighty fleet, built around sea-borne air power, had been routed by air power in a still mightier manifestation. The long-range, heavy-loaded, land-based bomber had come into its own in naval warfare. More significant even than the striking contrast between Japanese and U.S. losses at Midway was the fact that the U.S. would be increasingly able to surpass Japanese output of heavy bombing planes. The problem now would be bases. But with the Battles of Coral Sea and Midway the Pacific pendulum had begun its swing. As the offensive passed from Japanese to Allied hands, the carefully planned "island hopping" strategy of Gen. MacArthur and Adm. Nimitz would begin to move U.S. forces inexorably toward Tokyo.

Gen. Chiang Kai-shek, National China's hero, and leader in the bitter and costly war with Japan.

CHINA FIGHTS ON

SINCE 1937, when the Japanese put full pressure behind their "undeclared" war against China, the Chinese people, under the courageous, stubborn leadership of Gen. Chiang Kai-shek, had waged an epic battle in defense of their country and its freedom. The key to the Generalissimo's policy of "trading space to get time" lay in the geography of the country. In the early days of the invasion, the Chinese, faced with Japanese superiority in tanks, artillery and planes, were unable to do more than retire slowly across wide, open valleys toward the mountains, drawing the invaders ever deeper into the vast country, inflicting what punishment they could. But when they began to feel the hills at their back, resistance stiffened. They devised a new kind of guerrilla-like warfare which enabled them to break up even heavy Japanese offensives supported by tanks, planes and artillery. Sabotaging all roads passable for wheeled vehicles, making a feint of weak resistance, they drew the over-confident Japanese on, closed in and cut them off. Armed only with trench mortars, rifles, or machine guns, they could not hope to stage an offensive on anything more than a local scale—but they could and did immobilize whole Japanese armies which might have been very useful elsewhere. By 1940 they had lost most of their great cities and industries, their entire coast, and 900,000 inland square miles. Their railroads had been destroyed or seized by the Japanese. A solid wall of blockade had been drawn around them, with only the Burma Road to bring in a thin trickle of supplies to Chungking, provisional capital. But in five years they had killed or wounded 1,664,000 Japanese. Their "scorched earth" policy had left little in evacuated territory to aid or comfort the enemy. Behind a front Japan had thought was stabilized, a million partisans had been organized to carry on relentless guerrilla fighting. After three years of intensive warfare, the Japanese were as far from subjugating China as the day they had begun. Their ruthless bombings of China's teeming cities, killing thousands, neither broke her people's hearts nor her determination to fight on. They only gained for China worldwide sympathy and aid, including war materials from the Soviet Union and loans from the U.S. for war equipment. At Changsha, in Oct. 1941, Chinese troops, for the first time, inflicted a real defeat on the Japanese, who lost 30,000 men and much matériel. Two months later, when the Japanese launched their attack on Pearl Harbor and moved into Malaya and Burma, China welcomed powerful Allies.

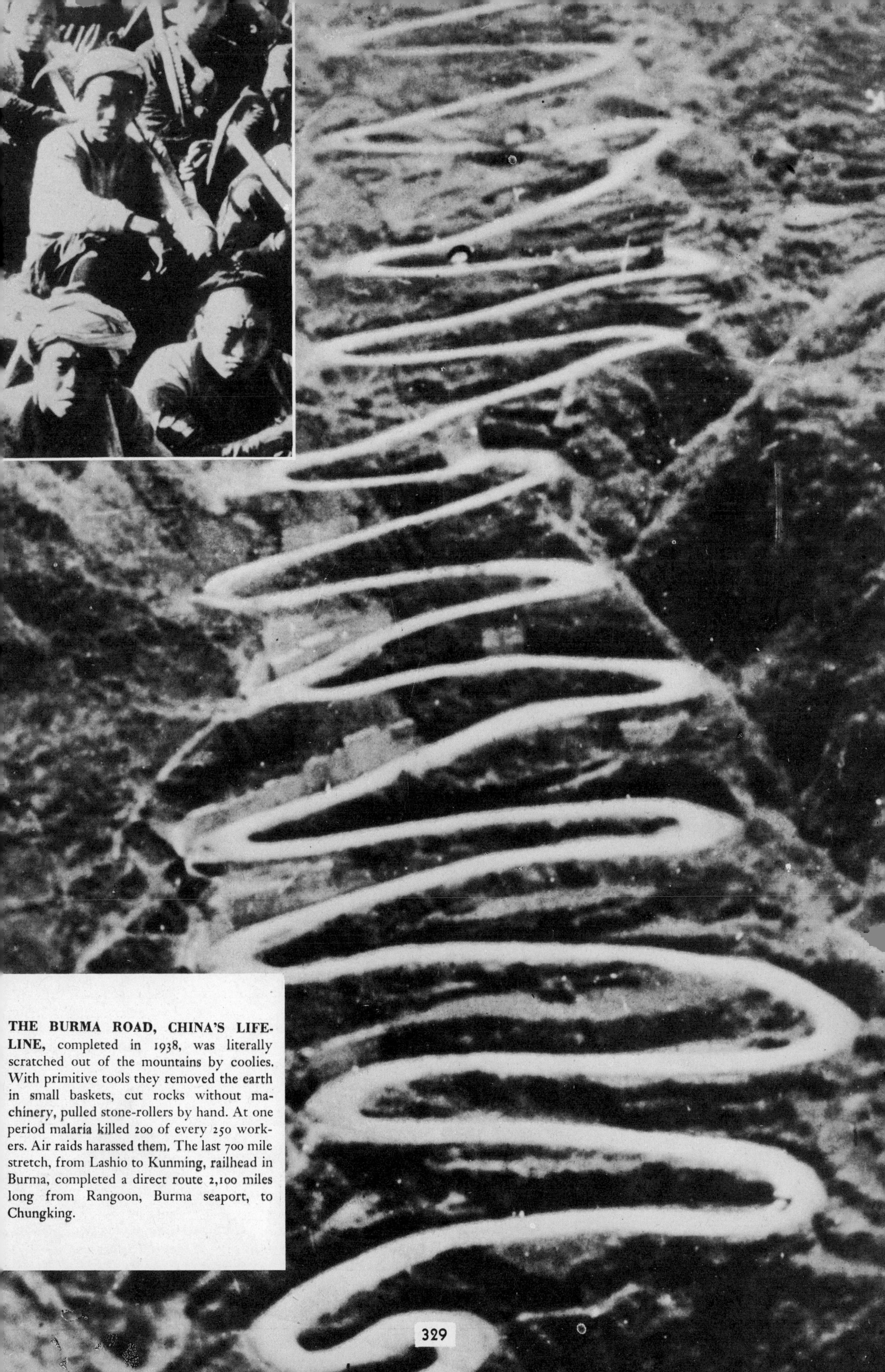

THE BURMA ROAD, CHINA'S LIFE-LINE, completed in 1938, was literally scratched out of the mountains by coolies. With primitive tools they removed the earth in small baskets, cut rocks without machinery, pulled stone-rollers by hand. At one period malaria killed 200 of every 250 workers. Air raids harassed them. The last 700 mile stretch, from Lashio to Kunming, railhead in Burma, completed a direct route 2,100 miles long from Rangoon, Burma seaport, to Chungking.

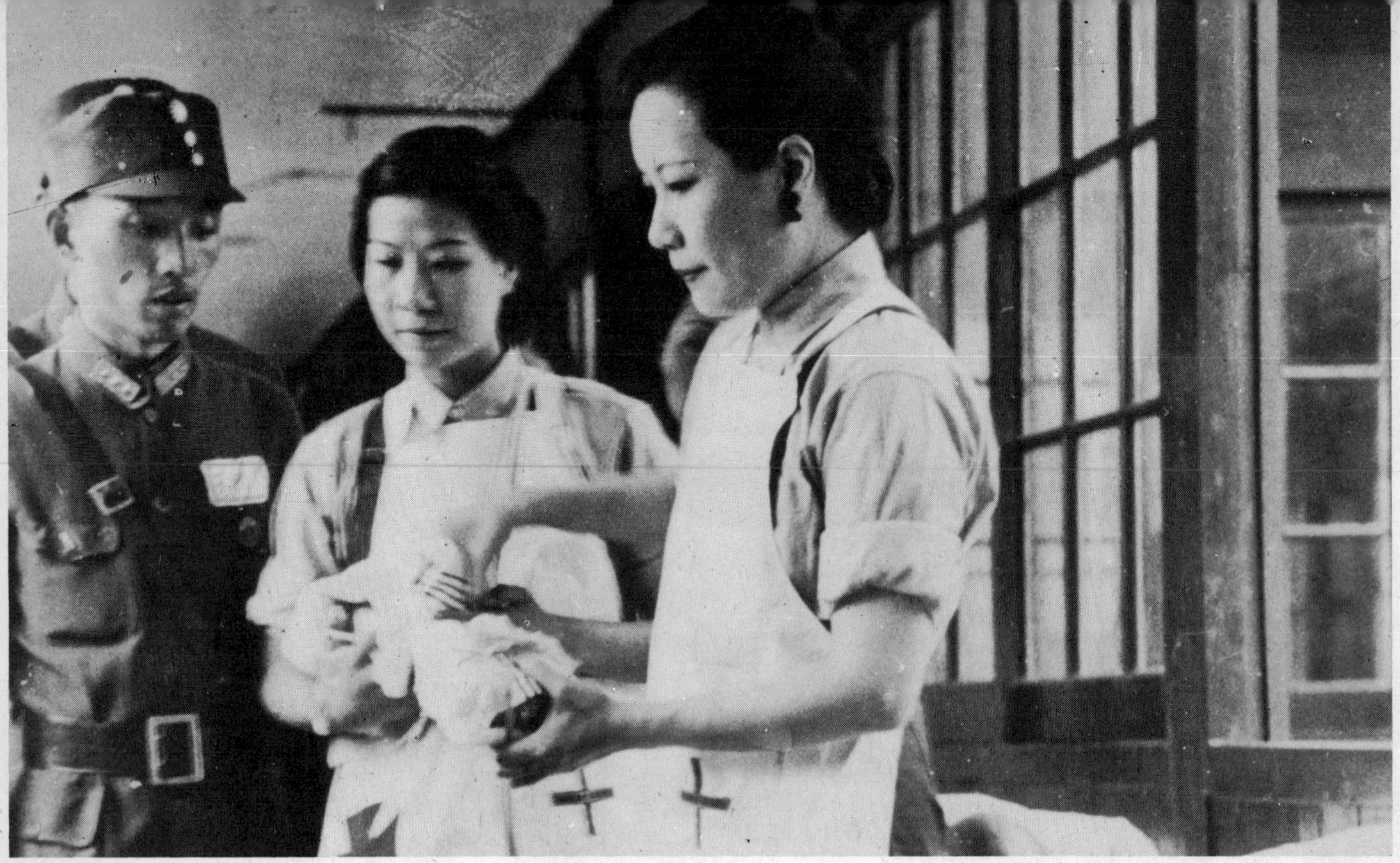

Madame Chiang Kai-shek, better known than her husband to most Americans, distributes medical supplies from U. S.

When the Japanese attacked Burma in Dec., 1941, China's plight was more desperate than at any time in the past five years. But Generalissimo and Mme. Chiang Kai-shek carried on. From America President Roosevelt promised, "ways will be found to deliver airplanes and munitions." China sent 150,000 workmen to hack out a new road across the perilous Himalayans to India, and battle-trained Chinese troops, like those at lower left, played a notable but hopeless part in Burma Road defense. Rangoon's fall, Mar. 8, and lack of road communications with India ended hope of British reinforcements – Chinese equipment was no match for Japanese. When Lashio, Burma Road key, fell on April 28 the fate of Burma was sealed. Mar. 19, tough, wiry U.S. Gen. Joseph Stilwell (below right) who had spent years in China, took command of Chinese troops in the Toungoo area. Outnumbered, surrounded, on foot, he led a small party through 110 miles of dense jungle to India and safety. Meanwhile at Changsha, Chuhsien, and Nanchang the Japanese had opened powerful drives in an attempt to knock China out of the war.

Directed by a skeleton American ground force, nimble Chinese mechanics serviced the A.V.G.'s overworked Tomahawks.

Brightest spot in the disastrous Malayan and Burma campaign was the spectacular work of the "Flying Tiger Sharks," as the Chinese called this American Volunteer Group which had served several years in China's air force under U.S. Gen. Claire L. Chennault (*See insert*). Always outnumbered, flying obsolete P-40 Tomahawks, in 90 days over Burma they destroyed 457 Japanese planes, lost 15. For a while, helped by two British squadrons, they wrenched air control in South Burma from the Japanese. Highly colorful, unique in originality and inventiveness, they smashed Japanese airports with bombs carried in their laps, patched up bullet-riddled planes with tin cans, moved from one makeshift airport to another to keep their bases secret. Returning to serve as regular members of the U.S. Air Force, they upheld tradition by scoring 8 planes to 1 against the Japanese. On July 27, 1942, U.S. planes saved battered Chungking from repetition of a scene like the one pictured below, taken after one of the many air raids when fires swept out entire streets. Now at last the Chinese felt a corner had been turned in their long battle against a pitiless foe.

THIS PICTURE, FAMOUS FOR ITS STATUESQUE QUALITY, shows some of the 700 persons killed when a Japanese bomb hit their jammed air raid shelter. Most of them suffocated. Despite years of horror like this, the Chinese carried on and Japan found herself incapable of decisive victory. By the summer of 1942 China's Allies were working valiantly to make up for loss of the Burma Road by flying supplies and munitions from India into China. By the end of August much ground the Chinese had lost earlier in 1942 was regained. A threat to Changsha was averted. Japanese were dislodged from 100 miles of railway and three important air bases. In December the Chinese stopped a new Japanese drive to cross the Salween River and lay siege to Kunming. The Chinese soldier was proving his ability now to outfight the Japanese, given anything approaching a decent break in equipment and conditions.

In far-away Chungking Allied leaders are honored by the Parade of Flags on United Nations Day, June 14, 1943.

CHINA, already deep in war with Japan, declared war on Germany and Italy the day after Pearl Harbor in 1941, and joined the United Nations on Jan. 1, 1942. Two days later Chiang Kai-shek was made United Nations Commander-in-Chief of all operations in China, Indo-China and Thailand. A year later, on Jan. 11, 1943, China won a political victory when the U. S. and Great Britain formally relinquished extraterritorial rights. In May, Winston Churchill pledged, "We will wage that war [against Japan] side by side with you in accordance with the best strategic employment of our forces, while there is breath in our bodies and blood flows through our veins." On Sept. 13 Chiang Kai-shek was elected "Tsungtsai" (Chief Executive), supreme ruler in military and foreign affairs. China's growing importance in over-all planning for global war, was confirmed when the Generalissimo joined the British and American leaders at the Cairo conference on Nov. 22. Under this agreement Japan was to be stripped of all her ill-gotten gains, — the millions of square miles stolen since the turn of the century.

Generalissimo Chiang Kai-Shek, President Roosevelt, Prime Minister Churchill, Madame Chiang Kai-Shek and their staff at Cairo.

THE YEAR 1943 MARKED REPEATED JAPANESE ATTEMPTS to overrun the fertile regions in the interior known as China's "Rice Bowl." An American army was being built up in India, but the battle against the submarine had to be won and supplies made available before the Allies could bring direct help to China. However, Chinese troops, like those shown, counterattacking constantly in Yangtze River and Lake Tungting areas, held the Japanese all the way from the lake country north of Shanghai to the jungles of Yunnan province in the southwest. In April China was thrilled when Gen. Chennault announced American-trained Chinese pilots had flown their first combat mission, a raid over Burma. By summer U.S. Liberators operating from Chinese bases had helped the Chinese recover several important Yangtze ports. The rest of the year produced no important changes, but the situation generally was not favorable to the invaders, part of whose strength was now being siphoned from the China front to meet growing Allied strength in the South Pacific.

New, hard-hitting Russian bombers which led the Red assault were eventually to drive the *Luftwaffe* from Russian skies.

SOVIET COUNTER-OFFENSIVE

STALIN AND MOLOTOV LOOK ON with interest, while British Ambassador Sir Stafford Cripps signs a mutual assistance pact for Britain.

In Moscow, on July 12, 1941, Britain and Russia had signed a mutual assistance pact, followed by notes exchanged in August between the U.S. and Russia recognizing Nazism as their common enemy. Credits were granted the Soviets, and by September shipments of supplies were arriving at Vladivostok, Murmansk and Persian Gulf ports. Late in November the heavy snows and sub-zero weather set in. The Nazis having confidently expected to be settled in Moscow no later than Sept. 15, had not prepared for this kind of winter. Freezing, they clung close to towns which afforded them shelter, stripped Russian villages bare of clothing, begged Berlin for warm coats. In their fast-moving summer *blitzkrieg* their mechanized equipment had given them a tremendous advantage, but now their guns were jammed, their tanks locked in ice, their planes grounded. They had few skis and fewer skiers. It was the Russians—warmly clothed, on skis, on foot, on horseback, riding in aero-engine sleds, driving "winterized" tanks and motor vehicles, flying special planes—who were ready for the new type of mobile winter warfare which made military history when the offensive was launched before Moscow on Dec. 7, 1941.

THE SOVIET WOMAN SKI PARACHUTIST above, with the tommy gun slung about her neck, has just been decorated for bravery under fire. The Red Army made extensive use of parachutists, depositing troops behind Nazi lines to wreck communications, dropping nurses and doctors for units temporarily cut off. As the Russians seized the initiative along a 2,000-mile front from Finland to the Crimea, hundreds of Nazi-held villages were recaptured. Monster camouflaged Russian tanks, charging through snow in a series of small encircling movements, bit off one square mile after another. Armored ski-sleds, driven by airplane propellors, enabled Red troops to flank Nazi strong-points, make sudden swift raids, while the Nazis with no ski-sleds floundered through the bad roads and bogged down completely with all their equipment in the snow-covered open fields.

FREEZING NAZIS WERE POWERLESS to check the new Russian war-of-movement over wide fronts regardless of snow, ice, weather. By Dec. 17 Kalinin and Klin had been retaken, the deep pocket around Tula was being cleared, Red Army reserves were speeding to the front in huge armored sleds towed by tanks especially designed for use in deep snow. Hundreds of yelling, saber-swinging Red cavalrymen (*below*), charging through raging snow, often shocked demoralized Nazi units into surrender. The drive had reached such proportions that Hitler, acting on "intuition," ousted Field Marshal von Brauchitsch and himself took over command of the Russian front.

ALONG THE WHOLE FRONT THE NEW YEAR SAW Russian attacks hacking at the retreating enemy, threatening the vital centers he still held. With the capture of Mozhaisk on Jan. 20, 1942, the Nazis abandoned the last foot of ground they had won in their November assault on Moscow. They were being pressed back on a line from Rzhev through Vyasma to Briansk, with the railroad already cut by the Russian advance. The little Austrian corporal's dream of a triumphal entry into Moscow was as dead now as Napoleon's. Although the Germans were still holding in the north around Leningrad, their anchor at Schluesselburg on Lake Ladoga was being assailed by Red troops advancing across the ice. During February a determined assault against Nazi siege lines threatened a breach, prevented only by desperate efforts of Nazi parachute shock troops. By Feb. 23 Russian armies, everywhere turning frozen fields into highways, had pushed their way to Dorogobuzh, 50 miles east of Smolensk, while the Nazis floundered in the snows of Vyasma and Zaihov. On Feb. 24, at Staraya Russa, Hitler's entire 16th army was encircled and smashed. By the middle of March, with spring on the way, when mud would replace the solid ice-floor over which Red troops had moved with such amazing success, Russian operations settled down to local thrusts designed to maintain a limited initiative while they gathered strength for supreme efforts still to come.

DEMORALIZED NAZIS SURRENDERED BY THOUSANDS TO RED TROOPS. There was no longer any pretense of the "voluntary withdrawal to prepared lines" announced in December. Between January and March, 1942, Hitler had thrown into his desperate Russian gamble 38 Nazi divisions, totaling 500,000 men, to back up his faltering lines. On March 19 he was forced to recall the generals his intuition had ousted in December. He admitted in April: "Neither the German soldier, the German tank, nor the German locomotive was prepared for the sudden onset of cold." But he did not take back his promise, made while his men froze to death in Russia, that "the Bolsheviks will be annihilatingly defeated by us in the coming summer"—a promise still unfulfilled.

The fleeing Nazis abandoned thousands of heavy guns, troop carriers, trucks, and tanks to escape the advancing Red Army.

ICE-COVERED CONVOYS BRAVED NAZI RAIDS and Arctic weather all winter long on the Murmansk route, bringing in supplies from U.S. and Britain, to help Russia prepare for Hitler's promised spring offensive.

IN SPRING 1942 world attention focused on the sprawling uneven, forever-fluid Soviet front, awaited the much advertised Nazi spring offensive. Until now the Russians had done an incredibly magnificent job, but their losses were enormous. Britain and America rushed all the equipment they could spare to supplement new Russian tanks, planes and mobile guns pouring to the front from great industrial bases in the Urals. To every doubting Thomas in the family of nations, that spring brought a deep upsurge of interest in the vast country to the north. It came as a shock of pained surprise to the Axis peoples when a nation which their leader had written off as a military power after the bungling war against tiny Finland in 1939—with an army which their *Führer* had assured them would tumble like toy soldiers in the conquering path of the *Wehrmacht*—rose like a snow-clad giant from the steppes to lay upon shivering Nazi "Supermen" the icy hand of fear. To the Allies, the shock was one of mingled incredulity and vast relief. For years Russia had withdrawn within her wide borders to prepare grimly, secretly, and alone, for a war which she alone was realistic enough to accept as inevitable, instead of dismissing it as a "war-monger's" phantasy. She alone was ready to fight it. To unprepared England and America that realization was like a five-minute reprieve before a scheduled execution. They united in plans to ensure extension of every possible help to Russia. In May, Soviet Commisar of Foreign Affairs, Viacheslav Molotov, arrived in London. On May 26 Eden and Molotov signed a 20-year military alliance providing for the fullest possible collaboration and assistance in the post-war period. The political sections of the alliance pledged both countries against "territorial aggrandizement" and interference in the affairs of other states. Shortly afterward President Roosevelt announced that Mr. Molotov had been his guest at the White House, and that a master lend-lease agreement had been signed in Washington providing for reciprocal defense aid designed to create a "new and better world" after victory had been won. He added that the U.S. and Russia had reached a full understanding on the "urgent tasks of creating a second front in Europe in 1942." So, in the space of a few short months, that "man in the Kremlin" had gained for his country the fear and hatred of the Axis, the admiration and respect of the Allies.

To ease the strain on their overworked munitions plants, the Russians salvaged much of the equipment won from Nazis.

THE REUNION OF A GUERRILLA FIGHTER and his wife brings happy smiles to the faces of his fellow guerrillas. Scenes like this took place in thousands of villages "liberated from the Nazi yoke." But often there was no happiness. Soldiers and guerrillas frequently found their loved ones had been murdered by the Nazis, had died of privation, or been driven westward to become slave laborers for the Nazi régime. One of the *Führer's* promises seemed on its way to fulfillment. "If our hearts are set on establishing our great German Reich," he said, "we must above all things force out and exterminate the Slavonic nations. Twenty million people must be wiped out. From now on, this will be one of the principal aims of German policy. . . ." Small wonder the Red Army fought with a grim and deadly purpose which drove them on to superhuman feats of courage and endurance. Small wonder their "Slavonic nation" closed ranks solidly behind them.

THE RED ARMY fought with deadly skill and determination whether pursuing a retreating enemy, as in the winter offensive, or carrying out delaying actions, always exacting a grim toll for every foot of ground. In May, 1942 Timoshenko, anticipating the Nazi offensive, struck along a hundred mile arc, centering his attack upon Kharkov. But powerful Nazi counterattacks brought the Kharkov front again to a stalemate, and the Nazis drove down toward the Crimea to put an end to the siege of Sevastopol. Meanwhile they were gathering their strength for their great offensive, which was to subdue Stalingrad, gain control of the Volga River, capture the oil fields of the Caucasus—according to orders, all in three weeks! The main strength of the new drive was directed toward Voronezh, in the Stalingrad sector, with spearheads reaching down toward Rostov and the northern approach to the Caucasus. For this mighty offensive Hitler's generals had gathered a million and a half troops—including Rumanian, Hungarian and Italian contingents—3,000 planes, vast fleets of tanks, every kind of motorized equipment. It was launched on June 28, 1942, east of Kursk, on a 50-mile front, after a terrific bombardment. When by July 5 Nazi shock troops had driven more than 100 miles, almost to Voronezh on the other side of the Don, it began to look as if the three-week schedule might be kept. But Timoshenko, wary of encirclement, knew exactly what he was doing.

THIS CLOSE-UP SHOWS THE CRIMEA AND LOWER DONETS area where Nazi forces were massing in the spring of 1942. Their gathering summer offensive was to cripple the Red Army, overrun the richest part of Soviet territory, free the Nazi Army to meet any invasion from the West. Southern Russia – the Ukraine meant food, supplies. The Caucasus meant precious oil. A breach in Rostov's defenses would make possible a sweeping campaign from Rostov to the Caucasus, putting the Black Sea in Nazi control. The Caucasus would also open the door—by way of Egypt—to vaulting Nazi dreams of conquest in the Middle East, where they would meet the conquering forces of their Japanese ally moving in from India through Persia.

BATTLE FOR THE UKRAINE

WHILE the determined Red Army and the heroic people of Moscow and Leningrad fought for their lives in the north, the fall of 1941 saw equally furious battles raging in the lower Dnieper regions of the Ukraine. The first Nazi blow in force, directed against Rostov by way of the north coast of the Sea of Azov, was supported by terrific concentrations of air power. While the Russians resisted every step of the way, von Kleist's mobile armored forces pushed relentlessly ahead to master Mariupol on Oct. 14, subdue Taganrog, release the full fury of their attack against the important city of Rostov, seaport, rail center, gateway to the Caucasus. Meanwhile Kharkov, rich industrial center farther north in the heart of the Ukraine, was also feeling the full fury of Nazi assault. Pounded by the *Luftwaffe*, stubbornly defended street by street and house by house, Kharkov was a shambles by the time the Nazis finally occupied it on Oct. 25. On Nov. 22 Rostov fell to determined assaults. But on the 29th the battered Russian forces, reorganized by Timoshenko, who had been transferred from Moscow to meet the desperate situation along the southern front, surged back toward the city, throwing von Kleist's troops out, and reoccupying what was left of Rostov. Their failure to hold this key point eliminated Nazi hopes of a major winter campaign against the Caucasus. Also their attention was being diverted elsewhere. The shock of the Red Army's surprise counteroffensive launched in December along the whole front from the Sea of Azov to Leningrad threw the Nazis back on the defensive while they waited for spring to unlock the frozen country and restore mobility to their stalled equipment. The strategically vital city of Kharkov remained in the hands of the despoilers, but its empty shell and the scorched earth around it rendered it of little value to the victors.

NAZIS SLAUGHTERED over 500 civilian men, women, and children from Kerch outside that Crimean city when they found they could not hold the city on Dec. 30, 1941. The woman in the foreground of the picture has just found the body of her murdered husband. The massacre enraged Russia. Molotov spoke for the people when he promised "punishment for all these incredible crimes."

HEROIC SEVASTOPOL

While the Nazis had been battering at Rostov, they had also been thrusting against the heavily defended Russian fortifications on the narrow neck of the Parekop isthmus leading into the Crimea. By Oct. 28 their panzer units had forced a breach and spread out for two separate attacks, one against Kerch at the eastern end of the Crimea, the other against Sevastopol, the great naval base at the southern tip. After Kerch fell on Nov. 16, 1941, the whole fury of the assault centered about embattled Sevastopol. On Dec. 30 the Russians, supported by the Black Sea Fleet, recaptured Kerch, but could not relieve Sevastopol. All winter, while a victorious Russian offensive swept the invaders back on the northern and central fronts, the Nazis hurled themselves against Sevastopol's defenses. But Sevastopol held. On May 8, 1942, the Crimea became the scene of the first major drive in the Nazi spring offensive. Kerch fell on May 16, after grim and bitter fighting, leaving the Nazis once more with only Sevastopol between them and complete control of the Crimea. In June von Mannstein attacked with 250,000 men. "Although the upper stories of Maxim Gorki Fort are in our hands and the battle line has moved some 1,400 yards forward, Soviet soldiers deep underground in the lower stories continue to resist. We have sent negotiators to explain to them that further resistance is useless, but they won't come out. . . ." That was the complaint of an outraged Nazi radio reporter describing the defense of Sevastopol. It had taken the Nazis 130 days to fight their way 300 miles from the Rumanian border to Sevastopol's outer defenses. It took them another 245 days to cover the remaining 35 miles that meant conquest of the city. On July 3 the Red Navy evacuated most of the troops. Two days later the Nazis were in control of the port. The way was cleared for their drive along the coast of the Caucasus toward the coveted oil fields of Maikop, Grozny and Baku.

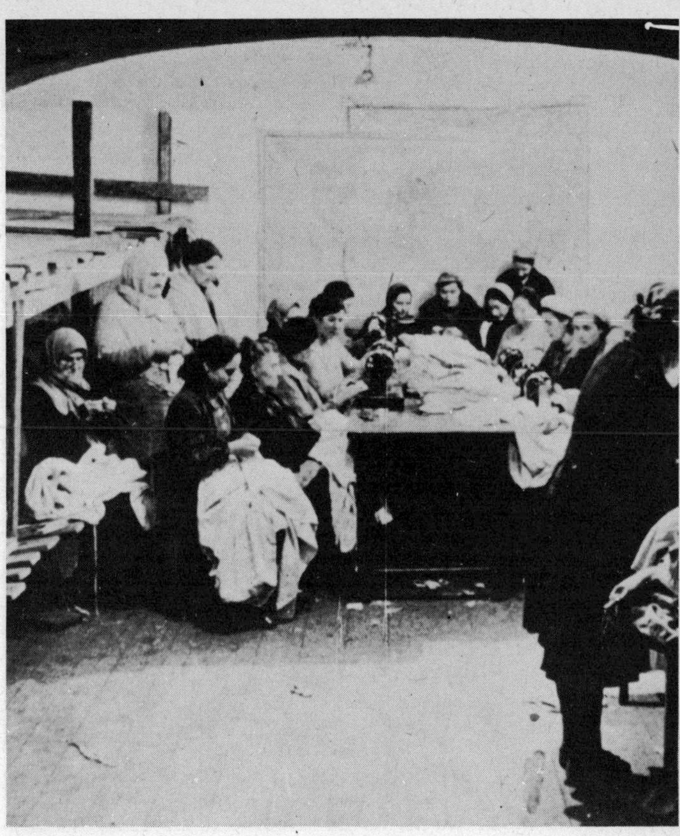

THE FALL OF SEVASTOPOL ON JULY 3, 1942, was hailed by ever-bombastic Nazis as a victory over the "most powerful land and sea fortress in the world." Exaggeration perhaps, but certainly for the Russians the loss of that Crimean port marked a new peak of disaster. The heroic people of Sevastopol had carried on their lives burrowed underground like moles during the long months of siege. Munitions factories had continued production in cellars. Slowly the town was reduced to rubble over its citizens' heads. Still those who had refused evacuation carried on side by side with the soldiers and marines of the Black Sea Fleet, until there was nothing left to fight for or with. The story of Sevastopol is an incredibly magnificent epic of human courage.

THE BLACK SEA FLEET OF THE RED NAVY, based at Sevastopol, had contributed valuable assistance in the historic siege of that city. Deprived of the great port, the fleet was forced to carry on from secret bases in the Caucasus, its free movement greatly restricted by enemy planes operating from the Crimea. The loss of the "home" of the Black Sea Fleet gave the Nazis a base for future naval operations.

THE OIL FIELDS OF THE CAUCASUS were in serious danger of capture when von Bock's victorious Nazis pushed down from Rostov, while other Nazi forces moved along the coast from the Crimea. After violent battles, Novorossisk and other towns fell in August and September. Against stubborn resistance the Nazis continually forced the Russians back to new defense lines, and October found a bitterly contested deadlock in the Caucasus. Eventually Nazis forced their way through to Nalchik, but the Grozny and Mozdok oil fields beyond were still safely in Russian hands. Only the small Maikop field had fallen, and its installations had been ruined. After Nov. 1941 no further advances were claimed by the Nazis in the Caucasus. Above, von Bock's troops are shown crossing the Don River in rubber boats on their way to the Caucasus, while the graphic picture below reveals what happened to any Russian oil field in danger of falling into enemy hands.

SKILLFUL WITHDRAWAL

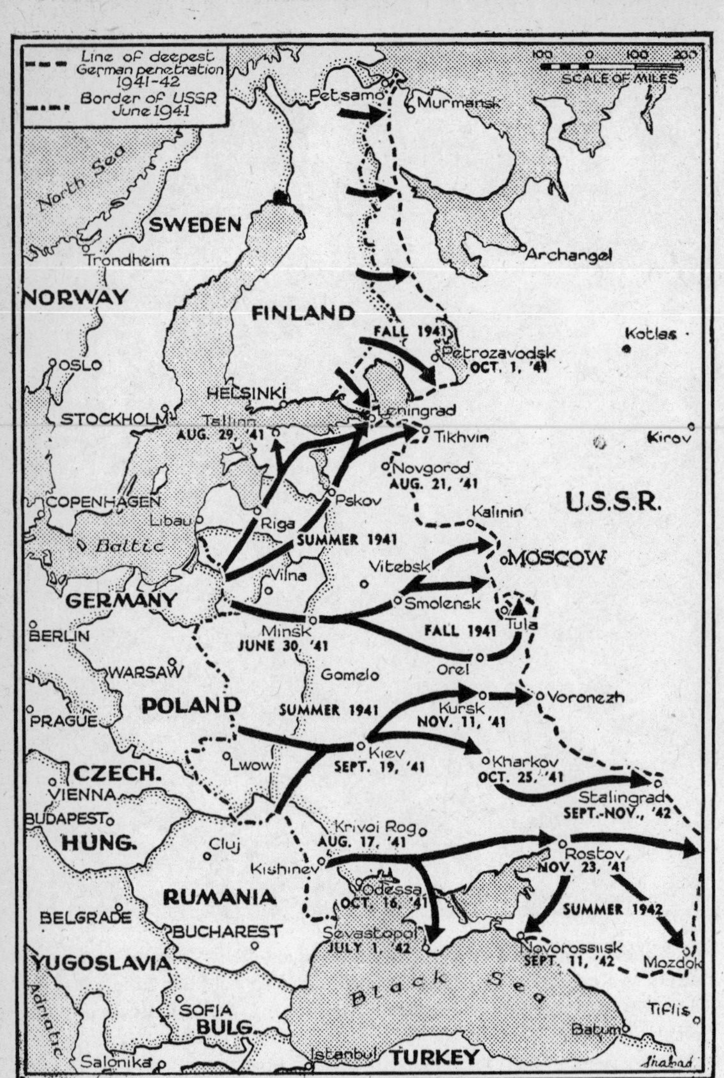

THE RED ARMY's skillful withdrawal ended when they took up their stand in the bend of the Don before Stalingrad, to defend Voronezh. That city was the scene of devastating attacks and counterattacks, but it was never in actual possession of the enemy. Nazi spearheads driving south were more successful. Voroshilovgrad, important coal center, was taken July 17, then Novocherkassk. The path to Rostov was clear at last. Its railway connections had already been cut, and after bitter fighting the Russians abandoned it. By August the Nazi steamroller was ready to roll into the Caucasus. Dive bombers, parachutists, tanks, all were hurled against the Red Army, withdrawing again, trading territory for men. Cossack cavalry, infantry, light artillery, all fought brilliantly, desperately, but they could not halt the advance. Meanwhile, to the north, Timoshenko held his ground, with the Russian line extending like a screen before Stalingrad on a line from Kletskaya through Kalach to Kotelnikov. Deliberately the Russians bided their time while the Nazis pounded their positions. Their leaders were not yet ready to draw upon the tanks, planes and guns piling up in secret storehouses, waiting for the day when the Red Army would once more startle the world with its might. In August the Nazis drove a wedge into the armies before Stalingrad. By the 17th they were driving the Russians from their position in the Don bend, clearing the path for the drive against Stalingrad and the Volga, which was to cut off the Red Armies in the north from those in the south and finish the conquest of Russia. But the Red commanders knew they had made the Nazis pay heavily. Winter would soon come to aid the defenders, and Stalingrad had been given time to complete preparations for the blow that would mark the beginning of the end for the *Wehrmacht* in Russia.

A Russian cavalry detachment crossing the Don River.

NAZI SOLDIERS SURRENDERING to Red Army men explained they had listened to Stalin's broadcast describing atrocities committed by Nazi troops and calling for extermination of all Nazi armies.

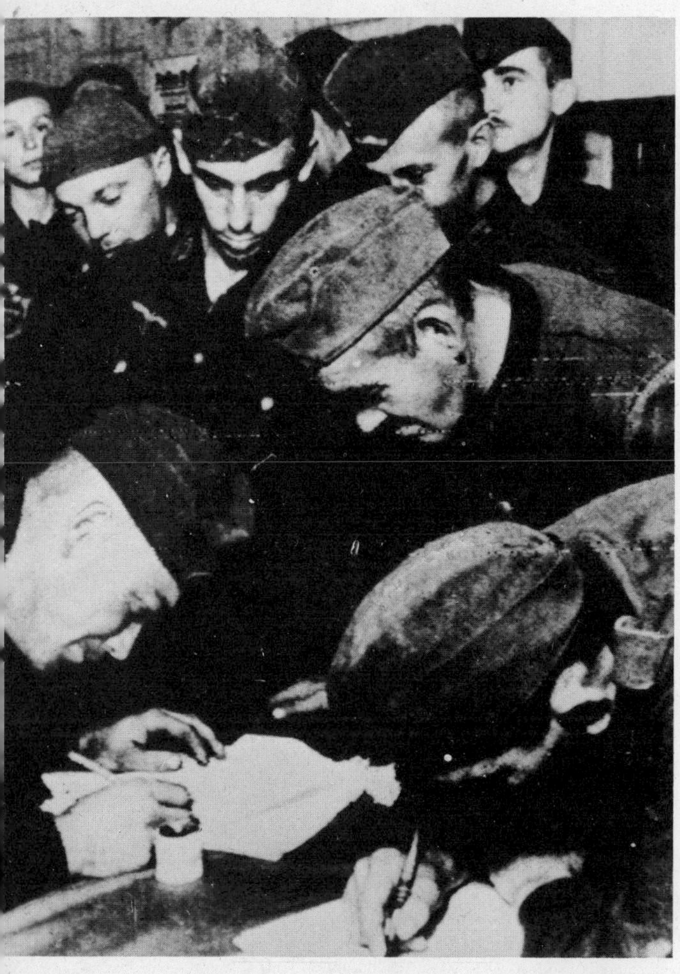

NAZI WAR PRISONERS IN RUSSIA protest against brutal treatment of Russian war prisoners in German camps. Sixty captured Nazis signed the protest, addressed to the International Red Cross at Geneva.

Nazi Hanging of Five Young Russian Guerrillas

YOUTHFUL COMMUNIST guerrillas listen to a Nazi pronounce the death sentence on them with the hope of teaching other guerrillas and recalcitrants a lesson.

BRAVELY—almost eagerly—they climb onto the crude trap that will send them to their death. Scores of partisans died this way. But guerrilla warfare went right on.

NAZIS LEFT their bodies hanging for days as an example to others. But the Nazis found their terror only deepened Russian hatred—intensified resistance.

IMMORTAL STALINGRAD

The soldiers and people of Stalingrad battled in the streets to the very end when the Nazis surrendered. While thousands of Ax
in the rubble, the Sword of Honor is presented with historic word

"THE OCCUPATION of Stalingrad, which will be concluded, will become a gigantic success. . . . And you can be of the firm conviction that no human being ever shall push us away from that spot. . . ." Thus spoke the sage of Berchtesgaden, in Sept. 1942. In the previous winter Stalin had said, "The enemy is not yet defeated . . . he will try in vain to postpone the day of defeat . . . but Hitler's war machine cannot stand up to the Red Army. . . ." Time has judged both their prophetic abilities and their generalship. Stalingrad was a symbol to Hitler of the Russian spirit that would fight until no one was left alive to fight. To the coldly practical logic of Hitler's General Staff, the city, unconquered, was a dagger at the heart of any Nazi army attempting to occupy northern or southern Russia. The first Nazi successes were misleading. Within weeks after the siege had begun in September they held a wide circle of territory about the city, footholds had been established at several points on the Volga, and Stalingrad was being jolted to pieces by tanks, artillery, low-level bombing. But fighting side by side the people and the garrison turned every block, street, falling wall, and broken doorway into a barricade and scene of hand to hand fighting. Hitler had ordered "No retreat"; Stalin, "No surrender." Lashed by Hitler, von Bock watched for every opening, hurled one suicide squad after another into the bottomless pit that was Stalingrad. All Russian communications were cut, no supplies came in to them except on barges feeling their way across the midnight Volga. It was Nov. 19 when a long-prepared offensive, launched by heavily reinforced Russian troops within and without the city, took the Nazis completely by surprise. Now the encirclers became the encircled. By Nov. 23 the Red Army was throwing a ring of steel about von Paulus and his forces inside the city, foiling all attempts at rescue. Now it was the Germans who lived—and died—in a rain of Russian artillery fire and bombs. By Jan. 26 the attackers, 330,000 strong, had been riddled to 12,000. On Jan. 31—the same day his promotion to Field Marshal was announced—von Paulus surrendered.

risoners plodded wearily out of the city, its courageous citizens returned to rebuild ruined homes, a victorious Red Army paraded The glory of the heroic warriors of Stalingrad shall never die!"

SURVIVORS FROM ONE OF 60 U-BOATS sunk by Allies in three months of 1943 are led blindfold to the gangway by British Coastal Command captors.

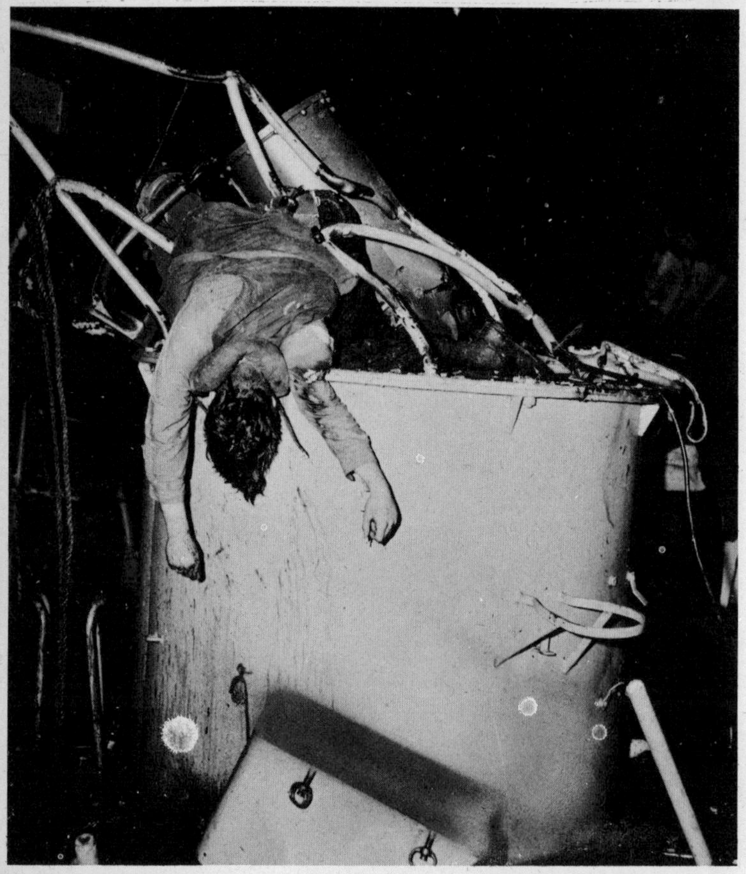

DYING AT HIS POST after his ship was torpedoed by an Axis submarine, this boy represents the blunt expression of a Coast Guardsman's duty: "You have to go out, but you don't have to come back!" Helped by observation planes and blimps, the U.S. Coast Guard's fast patrol fleet of famous PT and PC boats and small speedy sub-destroyers drove the marauders from American coastal waters – paid the price in men and ships.

BATTLE OF

UP TO the summer of 1942, when the Nazi U-boat toll of Allied shipping reached an all-time high, no really effective means of combating the menace had been found. Following President Roosevelt's inauguration of the North Atlantic patrol in 1941, which gave ships en route to Britain protection as far as Iceland, the U.S. Coast Guard tried out every possible anti-submarine device, among them the blimp. This non-rigid airship with a visibility range of five miles in all directions could cover wide areas yet pause to hover over such tiny clues on the water as oil smears, air bubbles, phosphorescent glows in darkness, the "feather" of a submarine's wake. Increased Allied bombing of U-boat bases and nests, such as the Bay of Biscay, Flensburg, Danzig, Bremen, St. Nazaire, Lorient, helped cut sinkings by destroying Nazi wolf-packs in their lairs. Allied cargo ship replacements at last exceeded sinkings. But all this was not enough. There was still a happy hunting ground for Nazi U-boats, the 600-mile gap between the limits of U.S. and British coastal patrol range. After Allied invasion of North Africa, in Nov. 1942, the Axis redoubled U-boat activities, putting submarine-specialist Admiral Doenitz in command of the German fleet, broadcasting his statement, "The entire German Navy will henceforth be put into the service of inexorable U-boat warfare." Goebbel's boasts that the U-boat would now destroy Britain were met by Churchill's stubborn insistence that ways were being found to combat them. It was summer of 1943 before it began to appear that Churchill was right. Allied shipping was increasing by geometrical progression. During two weeks in September, for the first time since war began, no Allied ship anywhere in the world was sunk by a submarine. In spite of Doenitz's frantic efforts to make his U-boats still more deadly, in 1943 submarine sinkings represented only 40% of the tonnage lost in 1942, and the 1943 curve had been steadily downward. There were reasons for this. An air umbrella was now spread over the mid-Atlantic. Coast-based planes ranged farther, and new Azores bases acquired by Britain from Portugal in Oct. 1943 placed bases closer to the scene of operation. Also, baby flat-tops had been added to the convoys. Converted merchantmen, or sturdy specially built ships, they were fitted out to carry small scouting and bombing planes. The Doenitz U-boat technique – hunting in packs, or echelons of packs, sending a "shadow" scout-sub ahead to track down the convoy and summon the rest of the pack to the kill – made the small carriers invaluable. Convoys no longer had to wait for U-boat attacks, then try to fight them off. Carrier planes went out to hunt down the hunter, finished off the shadow plane before it had a chance to report to its mates. By fall, 1942, some 570 Axis U-boats had been sunk or damaged. On the other side of the picture, Allied submarines, planes and navies had kept the continent of Europe under blockade. Meanwhile, in the South Pacific, Japan was losing shipping faster than she could possibly replace it, and shipping was the life-blood of Japanese offensive there. The Battle of the Atlantic for 1943 ended in a major defeat f . Germany.

THE ATLANTIC

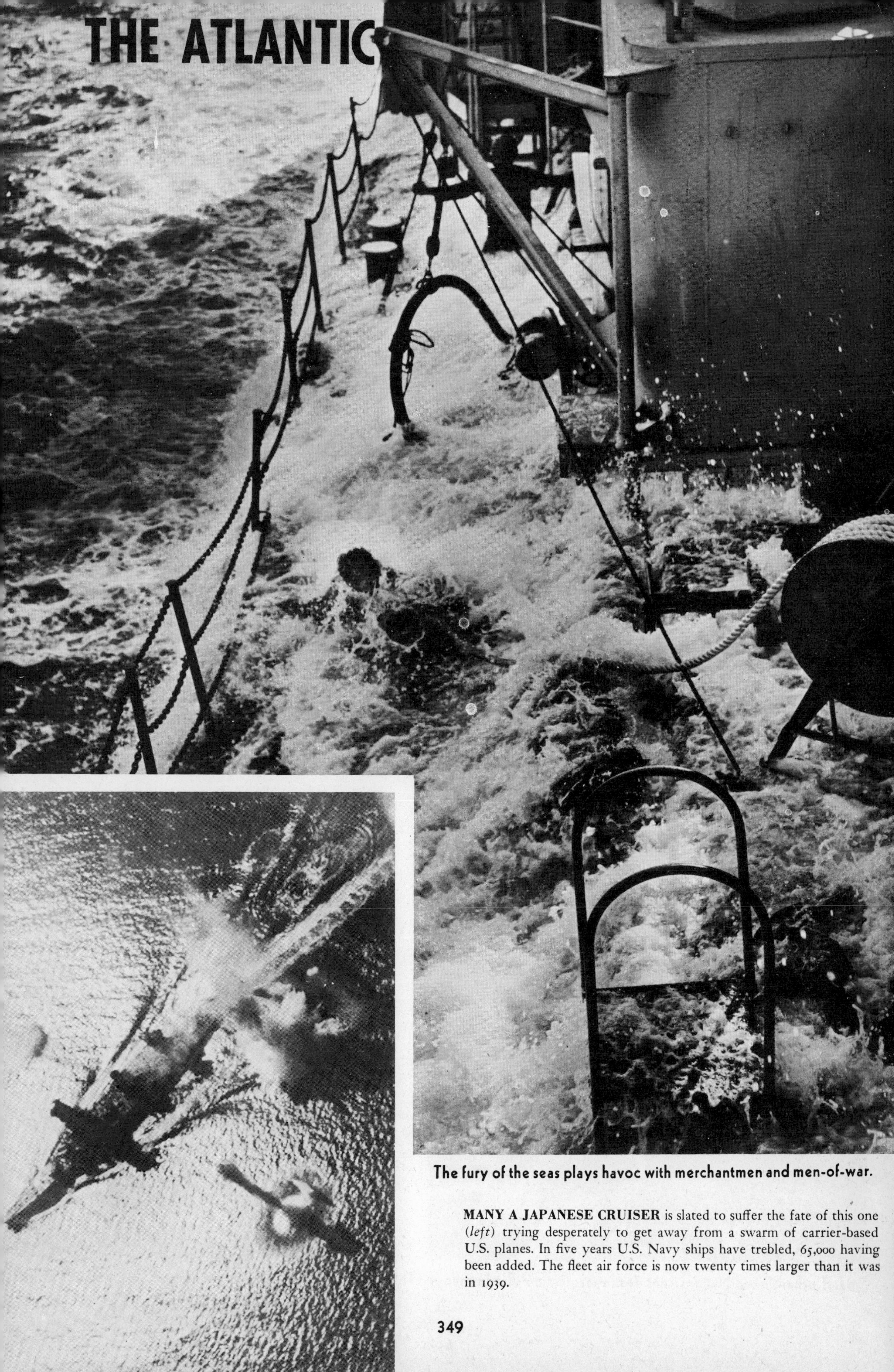

The fury of the seas plays havoc with merchantmen and men-of-war.

MANY A JAPANESE CRUISER is slated to suffer the fate of this one (*left*) trying desperately to get away from a swarm of carrier-based U.S. planes. In five years U.S. Navy ships have trebled, 65,000 having been added. The fleet air force is now twenty times larger than it was in 1939.

The "blimp," Cinderella of the air, proved her value in Coast Guard Patrol, covering 2,000 square miles of ocean every 12 hou

Poland, other United Nations, sent destroyers to aid Allied convoys.

This torpedoed U.S. tanker was saved to carry oil for fighte

THESE HUMAN TORPEDOES, used by British Navy, dive under anchored ship, attach explosive to the hull, set time fuses, escape on remainder of their strange craft.

NAVAL warfare in World War II has introduced many startling changes into the old familiar pattern of sea-borne battle. Chief naval innovation of the last war, the submarine, was forged by Germany into a major weapon of offense which came very close to winning the war for her. Today we have a hundred innovations—midget submarines, highly specialized bombing and fighting planes, rocket-type torpedoes, human torpedoes, gliders, parachutes, huge aircraft carriers, small flat-tops—the list is endless. But the one outstanding feature of this war is the extent and variety of equipment specially designed for amphibious invasion landings of a type and on a scale no one (including the men who worked them out) had ever imagined possible. Facing a global war where every battle had to be won or lost at the end of a line leading to a beach-head, American and British genius arose to the need—and the opportunity. The Japanese were taken by surprise in the Pacific, as completely as the war-wise Nazis were in Sicily, by the incredibly complex and successful Allied technique of landing armed forces, with heavily motorized equipment, on any kind of coast in any kind of weather with such speed there was no time to organize resistance.

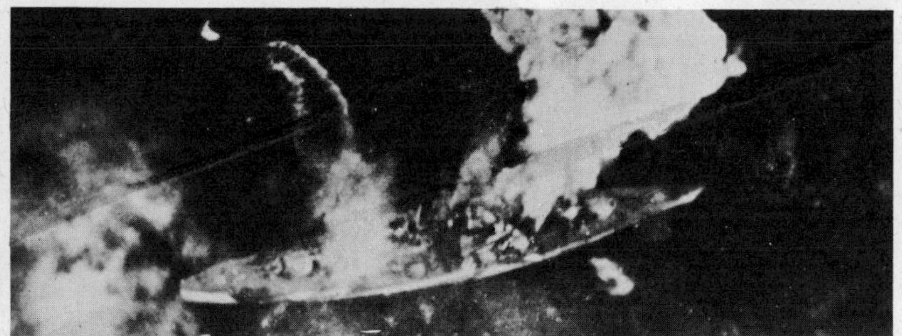

Mighty battleship, Nazi *Tirpitz*, is wrecked by British planes Apr. 3, 1944.

SS. *PRESIDENT COOLIDGE*, NAVY TRANSPORT, sank in the South Pacific Dec. 1942 after hitting a mine. Only two of her 4,000 men were lost. Mine-sweeping is one of most hazardous of Navy's tasks.

FIRE AT SEA, from time immemorial the seaman's most dreaded hazard, took its toll in many cases when a torpedo failed to sink the ship.

This unusual picture was made during a Commando raid on the Nazi base at Vaasgö island on Dec. 27, 1941.

The Commandos Take the Offensive

During the summer of 1941 when Britain was threatened with momentary invasion, Sir Roger Keyes, World War I hero of Zeebrugge, began to organize small bands of volunteers for "hazardous assignments." Christened "Commandos" by Churchill, who took the name from the Dutch "Commandos" who raided British lines during the Boer war, their first assignment was to slip across the Channel, learn the progress of Nazi invasion preparations, sabotage, and return. The Commandos included burly East End longshoremen, truck drivers, aristocrats, novelists, and play-boys. Volunteers were closely scrutinized before being accepted. Those accepted, the cream of British soldiery, were given intensive "toughening-up" training, which included much hand-to-hand fighting, naval operations, guerrilla tactics. On Nov. 16, 1941, Lord Louis Mountbatten, famous British naval commander, was put in charge of their operations. On Mar. 4, 1941, the Commandos staged their first big raid on the Lofoten islands off Norway. By the summer of 1942 Commando raids on the coast of France had become so numerous and daring that they became a major part of the effort to relieve pressure on Russia and heralded the coming full-scale invasion of the continent.

Lord Louis Mountbatten, winner of the D.S.O. at Crete was announced in August 1943 as head of a new East Asia Command organized to wage aggressive war against Japan. The Allied choice fell upon Lord Louis because of his success in his post as Chief of Combined Operations coordinating all Commando activities.

'HE VAAGSO OIL FACTORY WAS SET AFIRE by the Com-
ıandos whose surprise attack caught the Nazis napping. The British
ınded under cover of a smoke screen while British warships and
ircraft bombarded Nazi defenses. The kneeling Commandos below
re watching for snipers. Above, Commandos are shown rounding
p some of the Norwegian Quislingites on the Lofoten islands during the first big raid staged by the Commandos. Besides destroying oil stores, they captured 225 Nazis, sank all ships and destroyed a glycerine plant. Most of the local inhabitants welcomed them and some went back to England to join the Free Norwegian armed forces. The reckless daring and Indian tactics of the Commandos captured the imagination of the British and American public.

This picture, the first to show Commandos on French soil, shows raiders boarding their barges at Boulogne.

THE COMMANDOS were known to have carried out many raids on the shores of Norway, France and Holland previous to the African invasion in Nov. 1942, but only less than a dozen of these had been announced. Few lent themselves to photographic coverage, as most of them were carried out in total darkness. No pictures exist of the raid on St. Nazaire, yet of all the raids before Dieppe few were more daring or significant. Landing silently on the beaches at several points the night of Mar. 28, 1942, groups of Commandos wormed their way into the heart of the town, and the important Nazi U-boat base in the harbor. Nazi sentries fell quietly—strangled, knifed, or blackjacked. Suddenly the Commandos were discovered by a Nazi who opened fire. Dazed Nazis stumbled from their bunks, to find the British everywhere with tommy guns and hand grenades. In the turmoil that followed the Commandos fired barracks, supplies, and munition stores, while scores of Frenchmen thinking the invasion had begun pulled guns and weapons from secret hiding places and poured into the streets to help drive the hated Nazis from the coast of France. For two days bitter house-to-house fighting raged in the port before the overwhelming Nazi garrison was able to get the situation in hand. Two days later Berlin, with a bad case of jitters, ordered an immediate shake-up o the French coastal defenses. The largest and most famous-but also disastrous—of Commando raids was the reconnais sance in force against Dieppe, a strongly defended area o the Nazi-occupied French coast. The 5,000 Canadians, wh made up the bulk of the striking force were augmented b British Commandos, American Rangers, and Fighting French escorted by British destroyers and corvettes. Above them a air umbrella was put up by the RAF, assisted by Canadian New Zealand, Polish, Czech, Belgian, Fighting French, Nor wegian and American air squadrons—a truly Allied operatio Despite early Nazi discovery of their approach, before daw on Aug. 19, 1942, they made their scheduled landing, carrie out their missions, fought their way into the town, withdrew only six minutes after the time that had been set to withdraw They had tested the defenses of the coast, destroyed Naz batteries and a radio location station, captured prisoners t take home for questioning. Though they lost half their num ber, they had made the first preliminary landing on an enem coast, and pointed the way to the huge amphibious operation which were to set the pattern for war in the West as well a in the South Pacific.

These Commandos returned home after nine hours of savage fighting in the Dieppe raid, which was ridiculed by the Nazis as thwarted invasion, and described by Churchill as "an indispensable preliminary to full-scale operations."

American Rangers and British Commandos went through the same kind of training, worked together in daring sorties.

DISCIPLINE AND TIMING were the two basic rules of Commando training. In a raid, like the one above in Algeria, every man's life depended on exact and immediate obedience to any order. Each man had a specific job to do at a specific time. Men who failed to return to the barges at the appointed moment had to be left behind, lest the whole force be captured. Embarking upon a raid, they wore rubber-soled shoes, blackened their faces to make them less discernible. They were thoroughly trained in the use of a dagger and often the first men ashore were assigned the task of knifing any sentries. They were taught how to stalk and kill game so that, if left behind, they could hide in the woods and live off the land until they could either find refuge with patriots or make their way back to England. In the South Pacific, a U.S. Marine group called "Carlson's Raiders" was gaining fame in adaptation of Commando principles and technique to jungle warfare and amphibious landings. In Burma, British Brig. O. C. Wingate had trained a conglomeration of city-bred Englishmen, Gurkhas and Burmese to go anywhere, do anything, in the Burmese jungles. Wingate named them the "Chindits." Everyone else called them "Wingate's Circus." But they went into the jungle on three months' sorties —and delivered the goods. Wherever they went they blew up Japanese ammunition, wrecked their air fields, dynamited railways. One classic three-month expedition into Burma in May, 1943, carried them 200 miles into enemy-occupied country, relieved pressure on their Chinese Ally, supplied the RAF with information for raids, kept the Japanese guessing, and quite possibly prevented invasion of India. Below, right, is Brig. Wingate who was killed early in 1944. The picture lower left is typically Commando. Their jackets and hoods are reversible, white on the other side for camouflage against a snow background.

This American Ranger is scaling a wall after having made his way across the river in the darkness.

RANGERS USE TEAMWORK when they have a barbed wire barrier to cross (*below*). Commando contributions have been so great in gathering information, sabotaging barriers to attack, opening doors for regular invasion troops, that similar organizations have grown up in most of the United Nations armies. It is probable the full story of their activities will have to wait until the war is over to be told, but it is certain they have established themselves firmly as an essential part of modern warfare. A particularly valuable group is known as the Special Service Force, a Joint U.S.-Canadian Fighting Unit, trained for service anywhere at a moment's notice and in any type of operation. Whenever there is a task requiring almost superhuman endurance, versatility, courage and skill these are the men called in to do it. Very often they do not come back. They do not expect to come back. But the reports come back. Whatever they went out to do has been done.

A brave Norwegian boy shows his patriotism by leaning against an Oslo wall on which has been painted: "Long Live Haakon VII."

UNDERGROUND EUROPE

Denmark, long seething with hatred, demonstrated openly against oppressors. Here, Nazis do 'police duty' in Copenhagen.

ALL OVER Europe, in every occupied country, the end of 1941 saw the underground movement on the offensive, concentrating on obtaining arms, and increasing the flood of anti-Nazi sabotage and anti-Nazi propaganda. Desperate in the face of their victims' bitter scorn and hatred, the Nazis turned to massacre and torture on a scale undreamed of in a civilized world. Gradually the fierce individualism of early resistance efforts, hardened by the very persecution which was to stamp it out, was merged into a mighty organization, with a thousand separate units, but one unshakable purpose, one undying will-to-resist. By endless acts of sabotage, by cold refusal to accept the tyranny they must for a while endure, they cheated the conquerer of the richest fruits of his conquest, they kept immobilized for all practical purposes tens of thousands of Nazi soldiers who had to guard the occupation of hostile countries. One country after another, whose thousands had been tortured, slain, uprooted, enslaved, reached the point where its people lived for revenge. As the war in 1943 swung inexorably against the lustful tyrants who had thought to break the will of all except the "master race," the fear that walked through Europe no longer haunted the shadowy world of subjugated peoples — but turned its frightful face toward those who had first unleashed it upon the world.

NORWAY

PRESIDENT ROOSEVELT made this statement two years ago: "If there is anyone who still wonders why this war is being fought, let him look at Norway. If there is anyone who has any delusions that this war could have been averted, let him look at Norway. And if there is anyone who doubts the democratic will to win, again I say, let him look to Norway. He will find in Norway, at once conquered and unconquerable, the answer to his questioning." Since that day Norway has grown ever bolder in her stand against brutal occupation. One symbol of Norway's stubborn refusal to accept Nazi domination is the circulation of forbidden news. From underground offices like the one above more than 300 anti-Nazi newspapers carry information (obtained through short-wave radio) to readers in all parts of the country.

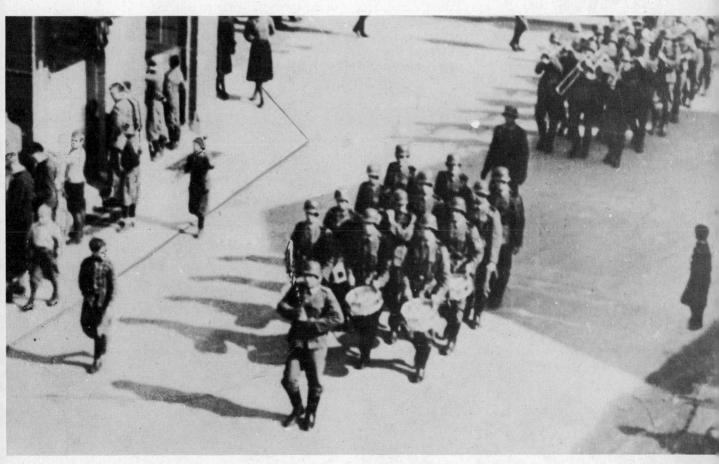

THIS PICTURE, one of the best to come out of conquered Europe, shows how the Norwegians treated the Nazis. Everyone, except two small boys, has turned his back on the parading Nazi garrison at Drobak, outside Oslo. This was an invariable rule in every country. Nazis were shunned like poison to make them feel the hatred of the people for them. Restaurants emptied if they came in. Quisling was hated more than the Nazis. When he became puppet premier in Feb. 1942, Norwegian patriots cut the wires feeding the floodlights under which he was reviewing his followers. Norway's rocky, mountainous passes made it easy for guerrillas to cut Nazi supply and communication lines by blowing up bridges and tunnels and causing landslides. When Quisling took over the schools all the teachers resigned.

A French sailor, either a hostage or trapped while engaged in underground activity, awaits the shots of the Nazi firing squad.

FRANCE

FRANCE seethed with anti-Nazi activity when it became clear that the senile Pétain intended to obey the Nazis. Frenchmen listened to BBC religiously, although it might mean death if they were caught. Underground papers sprang up everywhere, a thousand paths to sabotage were found. By D-day, in June, 1944, underground France was a thoroughly organized, highly efficient body soon accepted by General Eisenhower as the French Forces of the Interior. Ready to help the Allies drive the Nazis forever from their soil, they also took the next step leading toward establishment of peace and order under a government once more representative of that "*Liberté*, *Egalité*, *Fraternité*" which had once been France.

Protests in Paris against forced shipment of workers to Germany.

For 5 days no Nazi troops used this sabotaged railroad.

THE TWO MOST HATED MEN IN FRANCE, Marcel Deat and Pierre Laval, are shown above as they waited to inspect the Fascist brigade they had organized with Jacques Doriot to fight in Russia. A second later a 27-year-old patriot, Paul Collette, pretending he was a volunteer, stepped forth and sent a revolver shot into both of them.

THIS REMARKABLE ACTION PICTURE shows the wounded Deat being carried off by volunteers. Young Collette's aim was not good; both lived. Biggest problem of the underground was to find arms. To get them they ambushed Nazi patrols. Brave Frenchwomen, whose husbands and sweethearts were in Nazi prison camps, carried on much of the dangerous work in occupied France.

NAZIS ERECTED THIS GIGANTIC "V" on the Eiffel Tower in an effort to steal the symbol after BBC launched its "V" for Victory campaign. Within a fortnight after the BBC campaign began V's were being scratched everywhere. The Nazis claimed their "V's" symbolized the Nazi victory, but the German word for victory is *sieg*. Pétain and Laval turned French production over to the Nazis, but strikes were common and the slowdown strike almost continuous. Machinery was sabotaged, run without grease. Workers wasted precious oil. Tools were frequently lost and never could be found until the entire shop had been turned upside down. Waste was carefully but casually dropped into elevator shafts and then fired with a cigarette butt at the first opportunity.

N° 22 PRIERE DE FAIRE CIRCULER CE JOURNAL 1er NOVEMBRE 1941

LA LIBRE BELGIQUE

NOUVELLE SÉRIE DE GUERRE
FONDÉE LE 15 AOUT 1940

RÉDACTION ET ADMINISTRATION : OBERFELDKOMMANDANTUR. 1, PLACE DU TRONE. BRUXELLES
EDITEUR RESPONSABLE : PETER PAN, JARDIN D'EGMONT, BRUXELLES

J'ai foi dans nos destinées. Un pays qui se défend s'impose au respect de tous. Ce pays ne périt pas ! Dieu sera avec nous dans cette cause juste.
ALBERT, Roi des Belges.

Acceptons provisoirement les sacrifices qui nous sont imposés et attendons patiemment l'heure de la réparation.
A. MAX.

Envers les personnes qui dominent par la force militaire notre pays, ayons les égards que commande l'intérêt général. Respectons les règlements qu'elles nous imposent aussi longtemps qu'ils ne portent atteinte ni à la liberté de nos consciences chrétiennes, ni à notre dignité patriotique.
Monseigneur MERCIER.

Entre le sacrifice et le déshonneur, le Belge de 1940 n'hésite pas plus que celui de 1914. La lutte sera dure, mais nul ne peut douter du succès final. La cause de la Belgique est pure. Avec l'aide de Dieu, elle triomphera.
LEOPOLD.

Quelle que soit la durée de l'épreuve à subir, tous les Belges doivent avoir pour mot d'ordre " Fors le Roi, nul ne sera ".
F.-J. VAN DE MEULEBROEK.

Sans doute est-il nécessaire de reconnaître le pouvoir occupant [illegible]
Monseigneur VAN ROEY.

Onze Novembre

Tout le long de la rue Royale, de part et d'autre du petit square au cœur duquel à l'ombre de la Colonne l'Inconnu de 1918 dort dans sa glorieuse éternité, les sociétés patriotiques et les enfants des écoles font la haie.

Au milieu d'un peuple empoigné par l'émotion s'avancent les troupes victorieuses, d'Europe et d'Afrique. Dans le ciel nos ailes triomphantes tracent leurs V chargés de souvenir.

Et sur la tombe, encadré par ceux qui des deux côtés de la mer inviolée ont mené la lutte jusqu'à la victoire, le Roi-Prisonnier, dépose dans un silence de cathédrale, l'hommage de la Belgique à ceux qui, pour qu'elle vive, ont donné leur vie.

Ce Onze Novembre de l'an de la seconde libération, qu'il sera grand, qu'il sera beau.

Plus beau si c'est possible que le premier de tous les Onze Novembre, lorsqu'on entendit se répercuter l'écho du « Cessez-le-Feu » après cinquante-deux mois de campagne.

•

Le 11 novembre 1941, pour la deuxième fois depuis que la présence allemande souille à nouveau le sol de la Patrie, nous irons, en silence, en ordre pour ne par leur donner prétexte aux représailles criminelles qu'ils appellent « collaboration », incliner notre pensée devant la dalle de Bruxelles, devant l'humble monument de nos villages, ou plus intimement souvent devant la tombe d'hier ou d'il y a vingt-cinq ans.

Onze Novembre de guerre.

Onze Novembre d'occupation.

Jour de recueillement, de prière pour les croyants, de piété patriotique pour tous.

Nous penserons à nos morts pour penser à la Patrie vivante. Nous penserons à leur sacrifice pour ne pas perdre l'humble et persévérant courage de la résistance quotidienne. La Belgique qui a été, avec la maman, la compagne, les enfants abandonnés, leur pensée dernière doit, aujourd'hui être notre pensée unique.

Tous nos soucis, toutes nos espérances c'est de leur point de vue qu'il faut les examiner. Ils ont le droit d'exiger que nous n'abandonnions pas une ligne des raisons pour lesquelles ils acceptèrent la mort.

Onze Novembre de guerre.

Onze Novembre des souvenirs.

Onze Novembre aussi des espérances confiantes.

•

Car il suffit de se reporter à douze mois en arrière pour apprécier le chemin parcouru.

Qu'elle apparaissait enthousiaste mais peu consistante notre certitude de l'an passé !

D'alliés il ne restait que l'Angleterre, durement blessée.

Le Reich intact, écrasait de ses Panzer victorieux tout l'Occident, à la veille de voir par la force de choses s'offrir à lui des concours nouveaux. La Russie mystérieuse ravitaillait nos tortionnaires.

Un an a passé.

L'Europe écrasée est une suite ininterrompue de champs de bataille intérieurs. Dans le ciel les ailes à croix gammée fuient devant les avions anglo-américains. Le survol de nos provinces ne se fait plus de l'Est à l'Ouest mais de l'Ouest à l'Est. Et chaque nuit les bombes alliées portent la destruction au cœur du Reich. La Russie occupe, use, épuise les forces humaines et matérielles de l'orgueilleuse Wehrmacht. Les alliés forts du concours américain ne peuvent plus douter du résultat final.

L'aube de la Victoire est levée.

En Belgique les traitres, hier plastronnant, en sont reduits à réclamer la protection policière de la Gestapo. L'opinion est unanime dans la résistance.

•

A ceux qui sont morts.

A ceux qui chaque jour font pour notre Patrie le sacrifice de leur vie.

A ceux qui mènent l'obscur, le tenace, l'héroïque combat de la guerre secrète

LA LIBRE BELGIQUE, leading underground paper, listed its editor as Peter Pan, its address as that of the Nazi field commander.

THE LOWLANDS

RESISTANCE to the Nazi "New Order" in Holland and Belgium centered about the Catholic Church. The Nazis had counted on easily winning the support of the people of these countries. But they had not reckoned with Cardinal van Roey of Belgium and the Archbishop of Utrecht, J. de Jong. All Nazi threats failed to move their firm anti-Nazi stand. Cardinal van Roey forbade his priests to give communion to any pro-Nazis or to sanction masses for any who died. When the Nazis tried to take over Brussels schools, the Cardinal preferred to shut them down. He foiled attempts to divide the people by setting the Flemish against the French-speaking Walloons. His priests repeatedly warned their congregations not to join the new Nazi organizations. The Cardinal's anti-Nazi Pastoral Letter resulted in threats of violence. The Cardinal's answer was the blunt statement that the first nine months of Nazi occupation had proved worse than the three years' occupation of the last war. In Holland Archbishop de Jong and four other bishops issued a secret pastoral letter forbidding Catholics to join Nazi organizations on pain of being refused the sacrament. Dutch Catholics, Protestants and Communists linked forces, and neither heavy fines nor threats of violence could silence them.

BOTH THE DUTCH AND BELGIANS demonstrated their anti-Nazism by burying R.A.F. fliers shot down over their countries with much ceremony, keeping their graves covered with fresh flowers. This is such a grave in Belgium. The placard says these six R.A.F. fliers were killed on a reconnaissance flight "for our liberation." Dutch patriots killed many Nazis, threw them into canals. Anyone who joined a Nazi organization was shunned. Sometimes pro-Nazis were captured and their heads were shaved. To show their sympathy with Jews the Dutch wore the Star of David. Hundreds were executed for wrecking anti-invasion fortifications in June 1942. Officers and soldiers of the former Dutch army headed this phase of the underground movements activities.

GREECE

GREECE, UNDER NAZI OCCUPATION, suffered in some respects more dreadfully than any other European country. Mass executions were not so widely indulged in by the Nazi butchers, but starvation and disease reached catastrophic proportions. Still the proud spirit of Greece continued to resist. Thousands of guerrillas lurked in the hills, inflicting punishment upon hated exponents of the "New Order." These guerrillas, 25,000 strong, were kept alive only by a trickle of food brought to them by women, themselves starving, who toiled up mountain trails with pitiful bundles of supplies, and by powerful vitamin pills dropped from British planes when it was impossible to find space for anything bulkier. In the picture above, Athens University students defy Axis decrees, to observe Greek Independence Day.

"WE WILL FORCE YOU TO YOUR KNEES" – that was the challenge hurled at Nazi conquerors by the unbroken courage of crushed Greece. Inscribed on a wall by some mysterious underground hand, it spoke the innermost resolve of Europe's persecuted millions. In every occupied country were those who delighted in thus baiting the enemy.

GREEK WOMEN, like women almost everywhere in Europe, risked their lives to fight beside their men in the battle of Sabotage. They hid in the hills, crept out to steal food and arms from Axis troops, waged unrelenting warfare against the power that would extinguish an ancient race by starving its children.

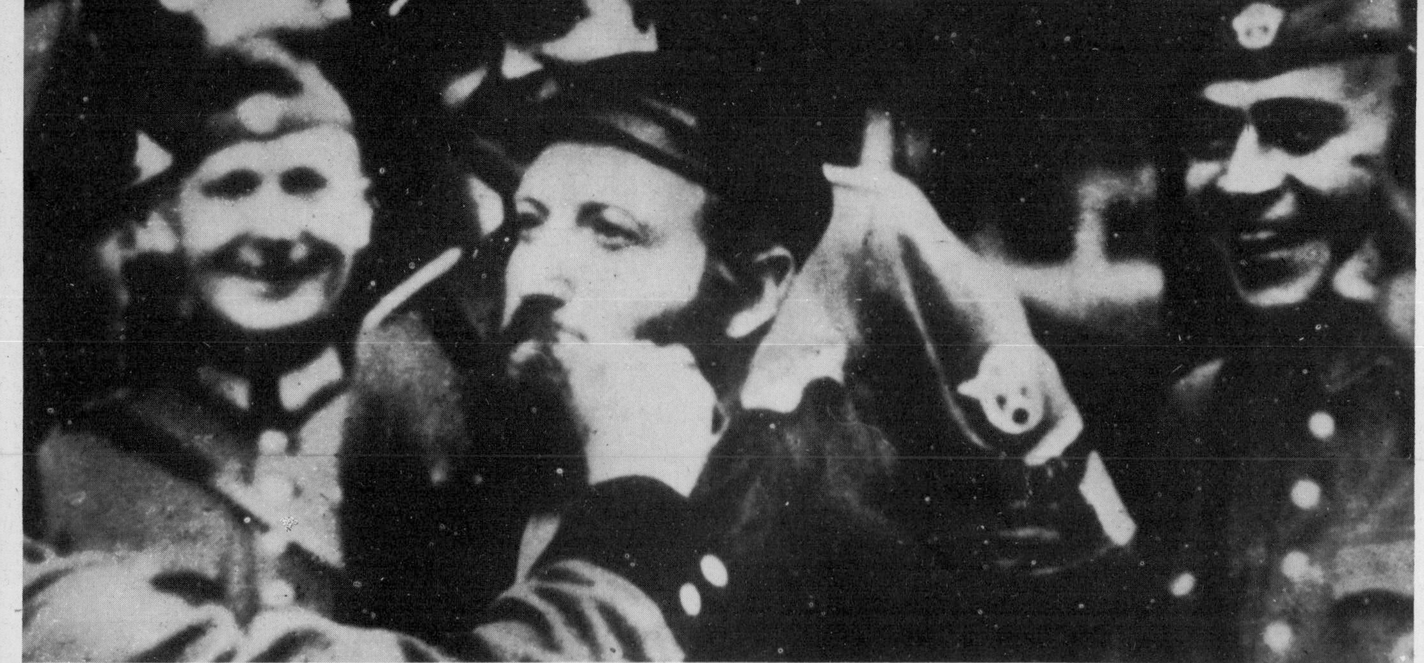

Capturing a lone Jew, some brave Nazis amuse themselves by pulling out his beard hair by hair. The dignity and courage with which the Jew looks straight into the eyes of his chief tormentor makes this one of the great pictures of World War II.

Poland

POLAND'S crematoriums, torture camps, gas chambers, will long stand as monuments to Nazi "*Kultur*." In four years Poland lost 5,000,000 people by murder and assorted tortures – disease, deportation, starvation. From a loosely knit, uncoordinated resistance movement in 1939, the Polish Underground was welded together into an efficient, deadly weapon of sabotage. Its agents became expert in outwitting the dull brutality of the typical Nazi official. They met fire with fire. Agents usually lasted six months before the Gestapo ran them to earth – then a new worker was ready to take up the fallen torch. The underground visited summary justice upon any "Quislings" or betrayers in its ranks, carried on a well-worked out sabotage program, and cleverly promoted discord and suspicion among Nazi officials. The press section printed and circulated 120 weekly newspapers, despite the death penalty for printing or reading one. SWIT, the insolent "phantom" radio station of the Polish underground, by jibing at Nazi officialdom and reporting true war news, was a powerful agent in holding together the resistance elements in Eastern Europe. This cleverly camouflaged station, operating on its own power, has been a thorn to the Gestapos for so long that they have outdone themselves in the vain effort to silence the mocking radio voice which was always on the wing, never came twice from the same place. Poland's resistance movement culminated in the stubborn stand against the oppressors led by General Bor. But it was not yet time. The superiority of Nazi numbers forced the Poles to surrender Warsaw once more after 63 days of dreadful battle.

THE BATTERED STONES of Poland's capital were yielded again to Hitler on Oct. 3, 1944, but the spirit of Warsaw waits a new day.

JUGOSLAVIA

"WE BEGAN in Belgrade," said Marshal Tito. "We will finish in Belgrade." When Hitler crushed the Balkans in his headlong plunge to conquest, fiercest resistance came from Yugoslavia. It centered then about Gen. Draga Mihailovitch, who retreated with his followers to the Serbian mountains in April, 1941, to be joined by bands of "Chetniks" (skilled Serbian guerrillas), several thousand Greeks, and a few Australians cut off by the collapse in Greece. At that time an obscure labor leader, Josip Broz, was meeting with a handful of underground leaders in a Belgrade flat to plot undying resistance to Nazi rule. Efforts were made to join the two movements, but they failed and gradually Mihailovitch's following dwindled while that of Josip Broz – now called "Tito"–grew rapidly out of the "underground" classification into a full-scale national defense military operation. The secret of Tito's success lay in his ability to promote unity among a widely divergent following, to symbolize "Unity in Equality" of all the Jugoslav peoples. "Partisans" to the world, "Jugoslavian Liberation Army" to Marshal Tito, it grew into a first-class fighting force more than 200,000 strong, equipped almost entirely with captured uniforms and arms. Tito's motto was, "If you need something, go out and get it from a German." And that is what his followers did, up to the time when the fall of Italy made closer contact possible between Jugoslavia and the Allies. Tito's army has always included both regular troops and perhaps 75,000 of the real "Partisans," peasant guerrilla fighters who made up the first resistance forces. Among these were many women, described by Tito as good soldiers "brave, enduring and able." As the day of Allied victory began to dawn, Tito emerged as a political power in negotiations between King Peter and various factions. Meantime, he had succeeded in keeping 300,000 Nazi soldiers pinned down in Jugoslavia, while he had wrested nearly half of the country from their control.

A CHETNIK SCOUT watches for the appearance of Nazi troops. Chetniks, including Mihailovitch, sometimes slipped into village taverns, mingled with Nazis, listened to their plans for smashing guerrillas.

TITO ARRIVES on the Dalmatian Island of Vis to meet Dr. Subacic, representative of King Peter's government. Tito has 3 titles: Marshal of Jugoslavia, Supreme Commander of the National Liberation Army and the Partisan Detachments of Jugoslavia, President of the National Committee of Liberation.

GERMANY

No 3.
10 Pfg
die Fahne der
Revolution
15. MÄRZ. ORGAN DER KPD SUDWEST 8. Jahrg
19. MÄRZ
Demonstration
des Todes

This 1940 leaflet called for a "demonstration of death" during a blackout.

Food is a weapon. This leaflet asks: "Is a herring and potatoes enough?"

Another Communist leaflet warns the Nazis: "The day is coming. . . ."

The day Hitler become dictator the secret anti-Nazi underground movement in Germany came into existence. Despite years of Gestapo terror it survived every attempt to root it out. Its leaders and members have been murdered, tortured and left to rot in concentration camps by the thousand. Others were forced to flee for their lives, and after Hitler's bloodless Saar conquest the strength of the underground slowly ebbed. Each new Nazi victory demoralized and decreased resistance to the Nazis except among the best organized and disciplined groups. Strongest of these were the Communists and Catholics who worked together in an anti-Nazi front. The great Catholic leaders, Cardinal von Faulhaber of Munich and Bishop von Galen of Muenster, by challenging Hitler's Neo-paganism at the risk of their lives, became living symbols of anti-Nazism. On June 22, 1941, as the Nazi armies plunged into Russia, the Communists made a desperate attempt to lead a revolt. Within an hour after Hitler announced the invasion they had mobilized their units and by early morning, with brazen recklessness, they began open agitation in numerous cities for revolt, speaking at factory gates, street corners, markets, in the Nazi army camps. They had counted on the fear of a two-front war to swing the masses of people behind them. But shortly after noon, with the Gestapo taking a heavy toll, it was clear to the Communists that they could not rally mass support and they went underground as quickly as they had emerged. The German people, growing fat with the loot of Europe and easy victories, had come to look upon war as a national pastime and, while they were uneasy, they were not ready to raise their hands against der Fuehrer. What happened to the anti-Nazi underground in Germany, after the swing toward Allied victory, has been a "black-out" almost as complete as midnight Berlin shivering in fear of Allied bombing raids. One fact emerged, however, as month after month saw every major city and industrial center in Germany pounded by thousands of tons of Allied bombs – a Germany which did not crack under the sacrifices of "total war" waged for gain and glory would not crack easily when Hitler's earlier lies about their being in danger from other countries had at last become truth. With the Nazi leaders grimly resolved to hang on at any price, with Himmler's Gestapo to stamp out any faint stirrings of revolt, with Goebbels' sinister mastery of alibi propaganda, with a population worn down by hope deferred and physical exhaustion, there seems little chance for any underground. To the outsider, it would seem that so long as the Nazi leaders hold out, the people will hold out too in the one desperate hope they have left – some kind of compromise peace.

Inside, an anti-Nazi leaflet.

AN ALLE DEUTSCHEN

VON HEINRICH MANN

Von der Befreiung Deutschlands hängt alles ab, seine eigene Zukunft und die Entscheidung, ob die gesamte gesittete Menschheit in das furchtbarste Verhängnis treiben soll.

Das erste Gedenken gilt den deutschen Helden, die im Kampf für die Freiheit gefallen sind. Die Einen haben den Kopf auf den Richtblock gelegt. Die Anderen starben in Spanien. Unsere Legionäre kämpfen für die spanische Republik und gerade damit für Deutschland. Die Freiheit der Völker ist unteilbar.

« Viele herrliche Kameraden », so sagt einer der Unseren, « sind in den letzten Kämpfen gefallen, unter anderem fast alle Politkommissare der Brigade, auch ein ehemaliger Abgeordneter des deutschen Reichstages. So schwer und ernst die Lage ist, bei den Kameraden herrscht Zuversicht und beste Kampfesstimmung. »

Ein Legionär, der Generalstabs-Offizier Ludwig Renn, rief zu Paris in eine Versammlung hinein : « Jetzt kämpf' ich für Spanien. Wenn der Fall eintritt, werde ich für Frankreich kämpfen. »

Der deutsche Freiheitskampf hat begonnen ; es führen ihn alle, die draussen ihr Leben wagen, aber ebenso alle, die im Lande der Gewalt widerstehen. Gedenken wir der deutschen Arbeiter, die auf neue Art gewerkschaftlich kämpfen gelernt haben. Gedenken wir der christlichen Gewissenskämpfer. Halten wir es nicht für unnütz, dass der schamlose Ueberfall auf Oesterreich in Deutschland

seiner Handlungen ihm von der grösseren Macht vom Kapital, erlaubt und vorgeschrieben worden ist.

Eben dies muss den Deutschen, die es nicht voll erfasst haben, wiederholt und eingeprägt werden von Allen, die an den Grenzen Deutschlands wohnen. Wessen Wort irgend Zugang findet, der spreche : Ihr sollt Landsknechte des internationalen Kapitalismus sein, dass ist der Sinn der Herrschaft Hitlers und aller seiner Unternehmungen. Der internationale Kapitalismus will euch zuletzt gegen die Sowjetunion schicken. Das ist der Endzweck. Deswegen wird Hitler geduldet, daher die Beihilfe die er findet. In allen Ländern hat er kapitalistische Verräter für sich. Gegen ihn sind die Völker.

Hier die Völker, drüben der Kapitalismus. Hier die spanische Republik, Oesterreich, die tschechoslowakische Republik, die französische Republik, die englische Demokratie, die Union der Sowjet-Republiken und die Vereinigten Staaten von Amerika, die ganz und gar antifaschistisch sind ; hier die Völker der Welt. Mit euch — wenn ihr mit diesem Regime in den Krieg ginget, wer wäre mit euch ? Eine Handvoll kapitalistischer Verräter und die Verbündeten, die der Klassenkampf dem Angreifer zuführt in jedem der Staaten ; mit ihnen kann er sie unterwühlen, solange noch nicht Krieg ist.

Im Krieg herrschen die Waffen. Die bewaffneten Völker sind gegen Hitler und wären gegen euch, der leidenschaftliche Wille der Völker wäre gegen euch, es sei denn, ihr befreit euch von dem schändlichen Regime.

TRAVEL FOLDERS WERE a favorite medium for the underground before the war. Surreptitiously stuffed into station racks, they contained anti-Nazi essays. This one was written by Heinrich Mann, noted German labor leader, brother of novelist Thomas Mann.

WOMEN BUYING POWDERED shampoo sometimes found anti-Nazi booklets inside the envelope. Almost every envelope type of package was used. Penalty for possession: death.

STAMP AND SEED PACKAGES were bulky enough to contain long booklets attacking basic Nazi theories, and giving instructions for making leaflets.

"EVERY PENNY FOR OUR PRESS IS A KICK IN THIS LIAR'S FACE," said this leaflet. The difficulties of organizing the publication and distribution of such a leaflet were enormous. Most underground meetings took place in theaters, restaurants, churches; underground units seldom consisted of more than three so that a Gestapo spy could not trap more than a few members. Until Europe was conquered much of the underground literature distributed in Germany was printed in France and Czechoslovakia, smuggled into Germany by daring anti-Nazis. Prospects of a second front in Europe resulted in an increase of anti-Nazi activity in Germany. To meet any threat of revolt Himmler increased the SS corps to 750,000.

THE AXIS BALKED

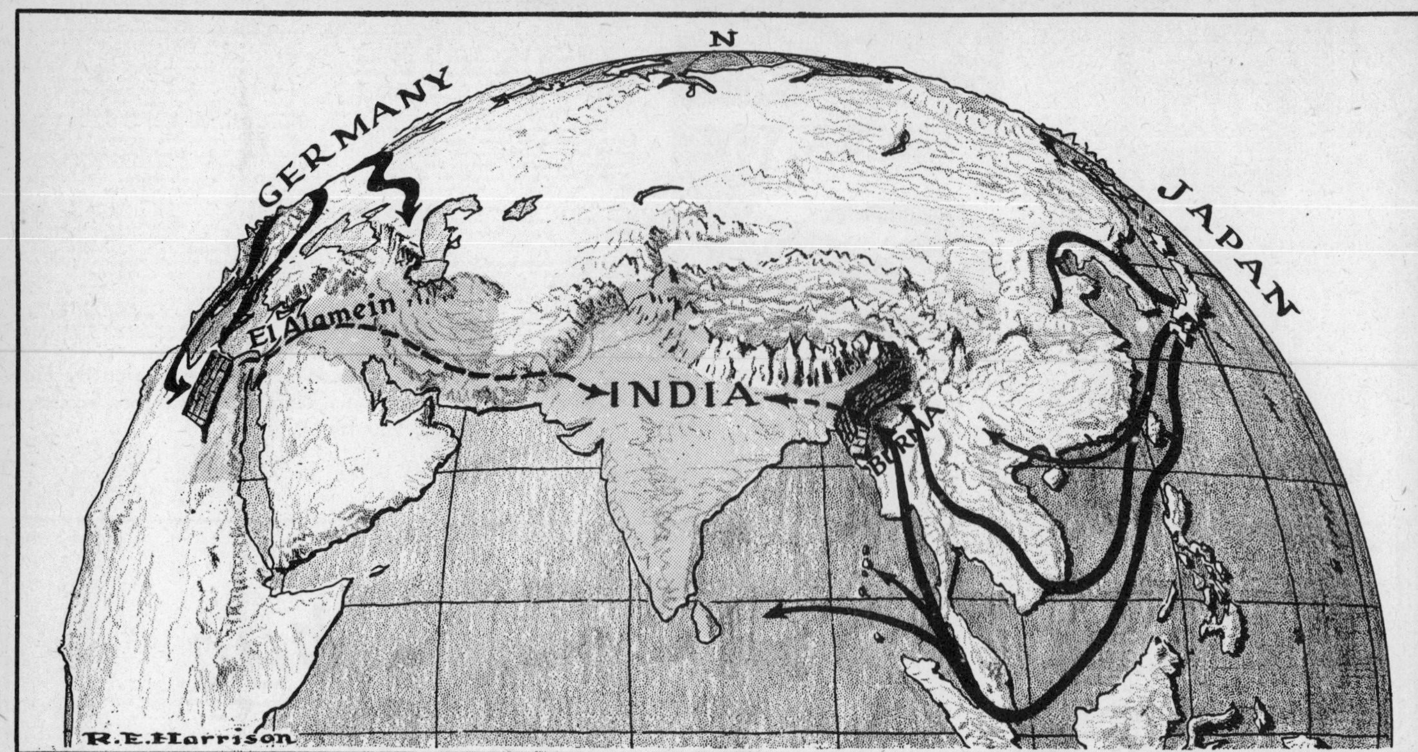

THE MAP above illustrates with startling clarity the meaning behind the phrase "global war." No "phrase" to war lords in Berlin and Tokyo, it was a simple geographical fact which seemed to make their ambitions feasible. From its island heart, the octopus that was Japan knew exactly where its long tentacles were going, where they would find soft spots to slither through on the way to their "destiny" of global power. So, from the other side of the world, the octopus that was Naziland sent forth its tentacles to seek and meet those of its unholy comrade-in-arms-and-evil. In the first sweep of conquest, when one unprepared country after another fell before them, it seemed to a dazed world that no power would be able to stop this "wave of the future." Then, alone on her little island, Britain stood fast. Against the chalk cliffs of Dover the mighty wave of aggression lashed in vain. Invasion was halted at the English Channel. The invincible *Luftwaffe* was no longer invincible in English skies. The much vaunted U-Boat failed to keep shipping out of English waters. On the land, on the sea, and in the air, Britain stood – stood alone until her Allies were ready to throw their unlimited war-potential into the desperate balance. Balked by the first link in the ring of steel which would one day be forged about her, Germany turned to the path she had planned to follow eastward – into world conquest by the back gate. But in the deserts of North Africa, at the rampart of El Alamein, the Germans were stopped, thrown back, driven out of North Africa, up the coast of Italy, back toward Berlin. Feeling for another opening to the east, the Nazis moved over Russia to the Caucasian land bridge linking Europe and Asia. Here, too, they were flung back; from Stalingrad, from the Caucasus, – and behind their retreat another link in the ring of steel was forged. Japan had moved faster and farther, over miles of vast sea lanes, through primitive unprepared countries, until her tentacles had circled a thousand islands in the South Pacific, had come to the very doors of India. But those islands they could not hold, those doors they could not open. Meanwhile air above Axis heads had been filled with Allied planes, raining death by day and by night. Allied ships and planes were blasting Axis submarines and navies out of the water. Men, supplies, munitions were flowing, in crescendo, to a hundred battle fronts. It was global war indeed. But from the fall of 1942, when the Allies invaded North Africa, held the line before Stalingrad, began throwing Japanese out of islands by capturing bases in the Solomons, it was global warfare on Allied — not on Axis — terms.

Under desert moonlight motorized death moves up to a front where artillery fire turns night into blazing day.

From Poland, first Nazi victim, come avenging fighting men.

American motor power bogs down for 24 hours in sand.

Rugged Scottish highlanders are "piped in" to a city where Mussolini left the Roman "trademark" atop the pillar.

Seen from in front of British guns the moon cannot compete with artillery fire.

THE PENDULUM SWINGS IN AFRICA

THIS AIR TRANSPORT COMMAND PLANE has brought urgent war supplies to a strategic battle zone, flying all the way across the Atlantic and the Continent of Africa. This modern "miracle bird" is passing now over the pyramids, 450 ft. high, engineering "miracles" of 3,500 years ago.

IN THE very teeth of news that Tobruk had fallen, deeply aware that Rommel, the "Desert Fox," was on deadly prowl again at El Alamein and with full knowledge that the future of Alexandria and Egypt hung in balance, Roosevelt and Churchill went grimly ahead with secret plans for a major offensive in North Africa. In June, 1942, in Washington, they worked out a gigantic pincers movement, from the east and from the west, by sea and by land, designed to sweep the whole Mediterranean clear and establish bases for breaching "*Festung Europa*," via what Churchill called "the soft underbelly" of Europe. Timed precisely to give hard-pressed Russian Armies a diversion of enemy force at the moment when they planned to take the offensive, it was a magnificent demonstration of the two leaders' faith in the will-to-victory of their people and the joint power of British and American effort. They foreshadowed in June a conviction expressed in December by a "Yank" to a "Tommy" on a bloody African battlefield – "Together we can lick the world!" During the entire summer no sign was given of momentous decisions in Washington. Churchill flew to Moscow in August, but for what good purpose was not then revealed. Stopping off in Africa where he stunned the troops by appearing suddenly in dangerous advance lines (to be greeted by admiring cries of "Blimey! It's Winnie!"), he implemented one phase of the new plans by placing Gen. Alexander in supreme command in Africa, with Gen. Montgomery in command of the 8th Army. They had been together, those two, at Dunkerque. Once again they commanded forces which could not retreat without losing all. This time they did not retreat. The race for supplies was on, between Montgomery and Rommel. And Montgomery was winning. The Battle of the Atlantic was still raging and 1 out of every 3 of Rommel's supply ships went to the bottom – but convoy after convoy got through to the Allies with planes, supplies, reinforcements – also new tanks and anti-tank guns, "tank-killers," which Roosevelt had promised to replace desperate losses at Tobruk. Allied air power was steadily increasing. All Rommel's attempts to lure the British into a trap failed. On Oct. 23, 1942, Montgomery launched a terrific moonlight assault against his wily foe, demonstrating both his brilliant strategy and the power of his new armor. The mobile guns developed by the U. S. and the battleship weight of new M-4 Gen. Sherman tanks, pitted against hitherto invincible Nazi Mark IVs, at last breached El Alamein defenses. Rommel's classic retreat left 6 Italian divisions to shift for themselves with no supplies and no water, while his badly mauled troops fled along the coast, pounded from the air, pursued by the relentless British 8th Army. Speeding across Egypt and Libya, 800 miles in 30 days, it was probably the swiftest pace set in any advance since the days of fabled Genghis Khan.

PRELUDE TO INVASION

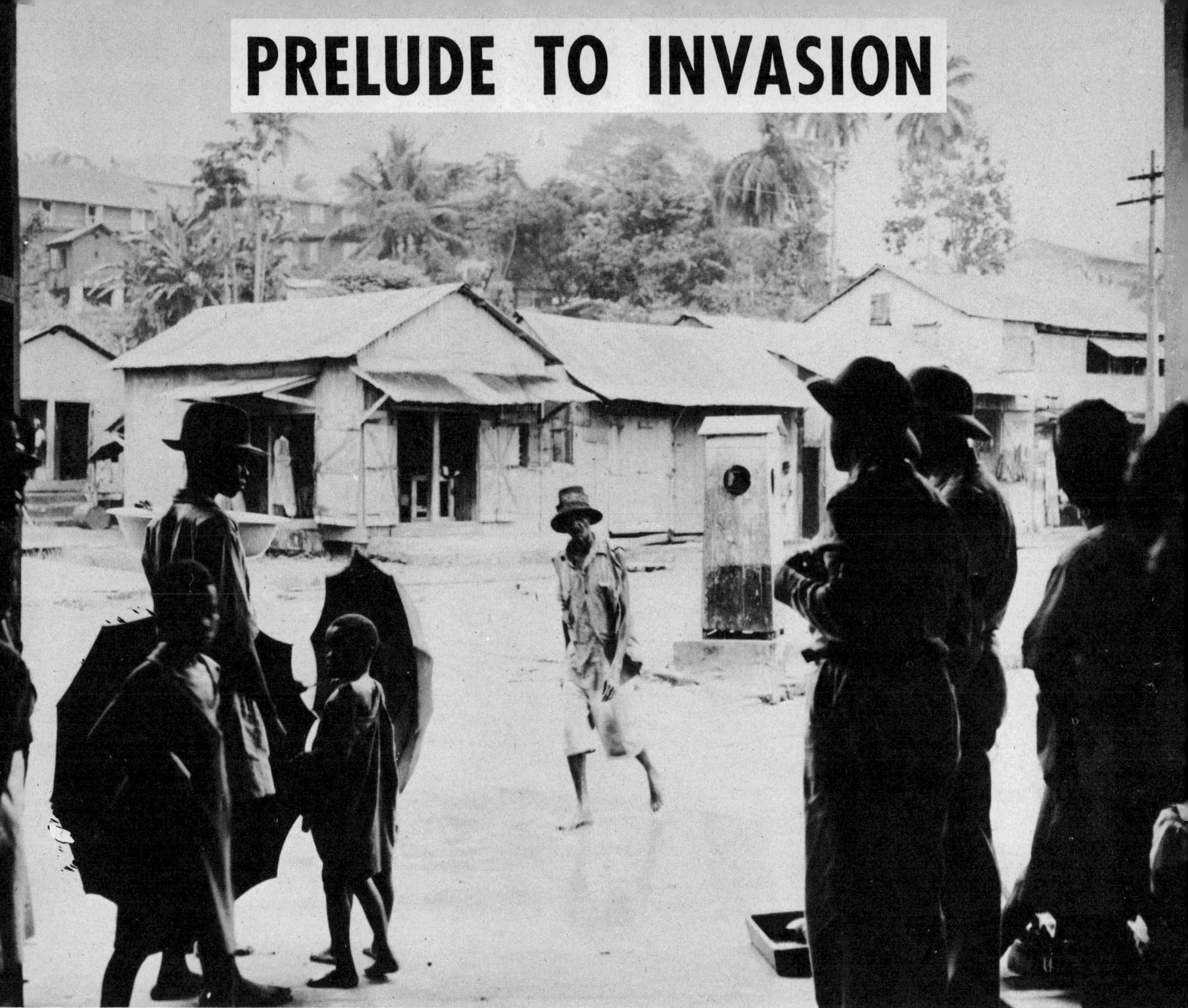

PREPARING FOR AFRICAN INVASION, American concern over keeping French colonies out of Axis hands was shown in the summer of 1942 when U.S. Army Engineer forces arrived in tropical Liberia to set up bases from which the Allies could strike at French West Africa.

WHILE from his "eagle's nest" in Berchtesgaden the Nazi vulture screamed that not even he could divine the plans of military "idiots and drunkards," the greatest armada in history was assembled by his foes, prepared for action, and despatched over a dozen sea lanes 3,000 miles long, to take the omniscient Nazis completely by surprise upon the coasts of Africa. Ever since Churchill's visit to Washington in June, 1942, preparations for invasion had been going forward on both sides of the Atlantic. To quote an official communiqué, "Never before in history have sea-borne amphibious operations been launched so far from their points of departure without secondary bases." Speaking after the historic landing Churchill said, "To transport large armies of several hundred thousand men with all their intricate, elaborate and modern apparatus secretly across seas and oceans, and to strike to the hour, and almost to the minute, simultaneously at a dozen points in spite of all U-boats and all chances of weather, was a feat of organization which will long be studied with respect. It was rendered possible only by one sovereign fact, namely the perfect comradeship and understanding prevailing between British and American staffs and troops. This majestic enterprise is under the direction and responsibility of the President of the U.S., and our 1st British Army is serving under orders of the American Commander-in-Chief, Gen. Dwight D. Eisenhower, in whose military skill and burning energy we put our faith, and whose orders to attack we shall punctually and unflinchingly obey. Behind all lies the power of the Royal Navy to which is joined the powerful American fleet, the whole under the command of Adm. Sir Andrew Cunningham, all subordinated to the Allied Commander-in-Chief." No greater tribute could be paid to the effectiveness of British-American planning than the way the North African invasion came at the most favorable possible moment, following close upon the heels of meticulous timing in Montgomery's offensive at El Alamein. The "idiots and drunkards" had done a good job preparing the political front, too, and no word revealing the actual invasion plans had sifted through to Nazi listening posts in occupied and neutral countries. In order to keep their own listening posts in operation the U.S. had patiently endured criticism of its policies in dealing with Vichy France, while the Axis was still in position to draw supplies from these same French colonies. Some of this was no doubt justified, but certainly the consular officials who distributed food were able also to gain much useful information and to find out who would be Allied supporters when the day of invasion came. They were in position to spread many subtle hints which were intended to—and did—keep Axis agents confused and uncertain. About the great blow, the Axis knew only that it must come soon, at some point and from some direction. They were pursued by twin devils of speculation and suspense. Hitler's own technique, which he had proudly labelled "war of nerves," now boomeranged.

THE HOUR C

AFTERMATH OF INVASION on the French Moroccan coast. Carefully worked out political strategy kept damage to property, also loss of life, at a minimum.

U. S. GENERALS EISENHOWER AND CLA confer with Adm. Darlan *(center)* in Algiers. C Clark, shortly before invasion date, had slipped

Early in the morning of Nov. 8, 1942, the radios of the world carried one single message. Invasion, long awaited, was under way. New courage filled the hearts of patient, countless Chinese bending under the yoke of Japanese aggression. New hope powered the mighty offensive waiting to be launched by the defenders of Stalingrad. Far away in the South Pacific, U.S. and Australian troops struggling through teeming jungles felt lift of spirit which would give them new strength. Upon every Axis minion the word sounded solemn warning that never again would the pendulum swing back, never again could the evil entente hope to "divide and conquer." At 1 A.M. on that morning of Nov. 8 an American Expeditionary Force had landed on beaches and at many points along the coasts of Morocco and Algeria. Disembarking from 500 transports by means of swarming auxiliary landing craft, while Allied Navy ships and planes stood guard, the greatest combined operation in military history had become an accomplished fact. Converging upon the shores of Africa from widely separated points of origin, convoyed by 350 naval vessels and clouds of planes, the mighty Allied fleet had reached its objective without the loss of a single ship and with a secrecy and perfection of timing that was to amaze the world. While big navy guns pounded coast defenses and carrier-based planes patrolled the skies, the waves of invasion struck at three main objectives on the coast of Algeria and Morocco—Algiers, Oran and Casablanca.

MANY COASTAL DEFENSES like the fort a had to be "neutralized" by U.S. naval batterie

IVASION STRIKES

Iorth Africa on a British sub, accompanied by nandos, risked his life to conduct negotiations French Colonial officers.

ne brief show of resistance ceased on the coast nch Morocco.

NAZI PLANES RAVAGED the Arabian quarters of this French Moroccan town after it had capitulated to Allied invasion forces.

FROM London General de Gaulle, leader of the Fighting French, called upon his countrymen in stirring words: "French commanders, soldiers, sailors, airmen, officials, colonists—rise every one of you! Help our Allies! Join them without reserve! France who fights calls on you. . . . Our Algeria, our Morocco, our Tunisia, are to be made the springboard for the liberation of France!" While leaflets dropped by plane assured the people that the Allies had no desire for territory or to interfere in any way with their own authorities, Eisenhower and others in command broadcast the same message. However, Vichy was technically in control and some resistance had to be expected. Allied land and naval forces and parachute troops cut road and rail communications, took over port installations, occupied air fields and landing grounds. French warships which offered resistance at Casablanca harbor brought the Allied fleet into action, leaving a flotilla of French destroyers and several cruisers at the bottom of the harbor and the new 35,000-ton battleship *Jean Bart* a flaming wreck. Algiers fell on the 9th, Oran on the 10th. On the 11th a conference at Algiers between Lieut. Gen. Mark Clark and Adm. Jean Darlan resulted in a proclamation by Darlan calling upon all French armed forces in North Africa to cease resistance to the Americans and their Allies. This capitulation meant the Axis could use no part of North or West Africa as a base for operations.

EXTRACTING A NAZI DUD BOMB from its crater after it has been disfused. Thousands of land mines (*insert*) and "booby traps" were used by retreating Nazis in North Africa in an effort to slow up pursuit.

NOT SOME QUEER AFRICAN BIRD, but a Douglas C53 which "buckled under" upon hitting soft ground over a muddy field while taxi-ing to the runway with a full cargo.

AFTER THE CAPITULATION OF ALGERIA AND MOROCCO, the plan worked out in Washington began to emerge—the invaders would strike at the western flank of the Axis while Montgomery applied pressure from the east. The Nazis recognized the plan too. They occupied Bizerta and Tunis, and began pouring reinforcements into Tunisia from Sicily. British-American-French troops drove into Tunisia to meet them. British paratroopers dropped at key points seized airfields and prisoners. Planes from Malta and Algerian bases bombed Axis airfields and transports, while Allied planes and submarines made a determined effort to cut Axis supply lines. In late Nov., 1942, the British 1st Army occupied several towns within a few miles of Tunis and cut the rail lines between Tunis and Bizerta.

SOMETIMES CALLED "EISENHOWER'S SECRET WEAPON," WACS were first of women's divisions to see foreign service. Eisenhower called them "fine soldiers." WAC above looks over Cairo.

***YANK* AND *THE STARS AND STRIPES*,** the two newspapers of, by and for service men, are "hits" wherever they go. Eagerly awaited, worn out by reading, they are rated No. 1 as morale builders.

Home is where you hang your helmet.

High Allied officials surround the coffin of Adm. Darlan assassinated Dec. 24, 1942.

ADMIRAL DARLAN achieved a brief and tragic prominence when the Allies found he was the only one who might be able to swing thoroughly Vichyized French colonies into Allied ranks, preventing much invasion bloodshed. General Giraud, smuggled out of France by British submarine on the eve of invasion to represent French patriots, at first proved unacceptable to colonials. Darlan's record was not too clear as to Vichy, but he was in Algiers self-appointed High Commissioner in French North and West Africa, and he was able to deliver co-operation from the army and several colonial governors—also possession of the port of Dakar long a danger spot to Allied shipping. Strangely, only the fleet ignored its admiral's call, and remained in Toulon harbor instead of escaping to North Africa.

THE FRENCH FLEET AT TOULON had been a picture to trouble sleep for Axis and Allied leaders alike, ever since the Armistice had immobilized the 75 warships and lesser craft while shipping and sea-power became dominant factors in a global war. During months of humiliation and despair "The Fleet" had been one symbol left to Frenchmen of the power and pride that had once been France. Inert and useless, still it was there, ready for that "day of glory" when Frar should arise from the deadly lassitude that had gripped her in 194(arise, and throw off the hated yoke. Yet on Nov. 27, 1942, when N forces drove into the harbor to revenge invasion of Africa by seizi the French ships, Admiral de Laborde issued ruthless orders to "scut the fleet!" and the great ships became a mass of tangled wreckage.

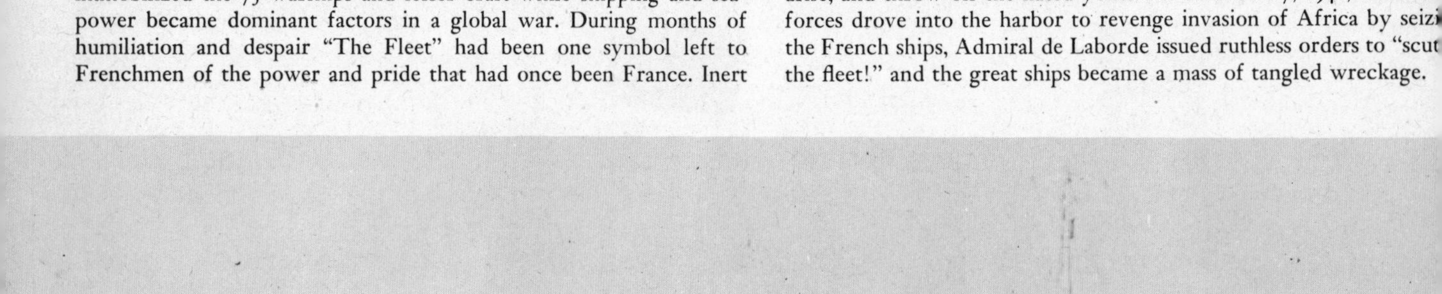

FRENCH WARSHIPS AT ALEXANDRIA were eventually saved for the Allies. They were not to be compared to the main fleet which had committed suicide at Toulon by sending 230,000 tons of shipping to the bottom, but they were valuable at a time when the Battle of the Atlantic was still raging and America had not yet swung into full production. Under Egyptian "protection" since 1940, when they had demobilized themselves at Alexandria, they now became pawns in the political game the Allies had to play in North Africa. Here Nazi-La interests had spent both money and skill in a campaign to turn Fre colonials against the Allied cause, and by placing their henchmen all key positions had gone far toward making the Colonies pro-Fasc However, the Allies won the diplomatic battle and all remaining u of the once great French fleet joined with them in the war agai Fascism.

NCH MAQUIS, originally guerrillas from the e Savoie, set a pattern of resistance to occu-n; later organized as French Forces of the In-:, or as one of the other patriotic groups.

Gestapo men could not prevent patriotic demonstrations, like this one at Lyons, on Bastille Day.

OLITICAL CRISIS faced Gen. Eisenhower in th Africa after Darlan was shot to death by a ber of a French patriotic youth organization Christmas Eve, 1942. Caught in a tangle of con-ng interests and ideas, the Allies supported the ointment of Gen. Giraud, then head of the army, to succeed Darlan. This appointment ushered in a period of political turmoil which threatened to disrupt all that had been accomplished, with supporters of Gen. de Gaulle (still in London) bitterly denouncing any other authority than his. Meanwhile fighting was slowed down by heavy rains. In Dec., with some 20,000 men and air superiority in Tunisia, Axis troops forced the British back, leaving Nazis in control of a 30-mile circle about Tunis and Bizerta – with a coastal door open toward Libya and Rommel.

Shadowed by Pyramids, a flimsy tent city accommodated military police, signal and other personnel at Allied conferenc

"UNCONDITIONAL surrender" – that was the verdict of Casablanca, announced by President Roosevelt and Prime Minister Churchill following their conference in Africa, Jan. 14-24, 1943. Meeting with diplomatic agents, military leaders and technicians, just behind actual battle lines, they were able to see the war picture from both political and military angles. Concentrating upon immediate problems of North Africa and European invasion, they were in touch with the two other Allies, pledging all possible help to Russia and all strength to be thrown against Japan once Nazi power was broken. Progress was made toward an accord between de Gaulle and Giraud factions, changes in war plans were mapped, new commands announced. The Middle East was separated from the Mediterranean, with U. S. Gen. Eisenhower in full control over the Mediterranean theater, British Gen. Alexander as Deputy Commander-in-Chief, British Air Marshal Tedder in charge of Allied air operation, British Adm. Cunningham directing Allied naval activity. De Gaulle and Giraud were persuaded to attend the conference, and a gradual easing in their relations followed. Agreeing on French liberation and Nazi defeat, they were far apart on all other issues. Giraud's faction found excuses for many Vichy appointees in North Africa, while de Gaulle and the Fighting French demanded vigorous action against any tainted with collaborationism. By April, 1942, the Council which Giraud headed had made provision to restore laws of

President Roosevelt drops in upon President Barclay of Liberia, welcomes him to an American Jeep.

UNCONDITIONAL SURRENDER

in Cairo, 1943.

the Republic and had repudiated all decrees passed under the Vichy régime. On the military front, plans were laid at Casablanca for new vigor in the conduct of the war in Africa. The 8th Army's epic pursuit of the *Afrika Korps*, 1,400 miles in four months, had brought Tobruk, Tripoli, Benghazi, and the entire coastline of Libya back into Allied hands. By the middle of Feb. Rommel had entrenched his forces just inside Tunisia.

New French Army gets U.S. equipment.

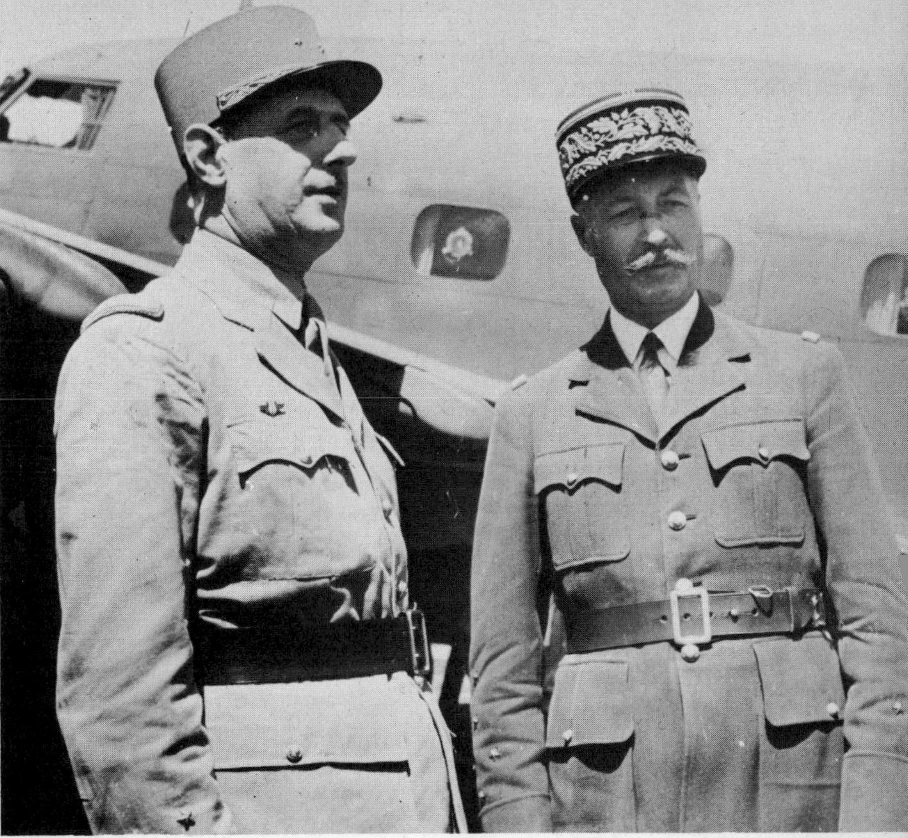

VICTORIES WERE MAPPED OUT at meetings of combined Chiefs-of-Staff in North Africa in 1943. At the one above, on the U. S. side of the table, *(L to R)* are: Gen. Arnold, Gen. Marshall, Capt. Royal, Adm. Leahy, Adm. King, Col. McFarland. On the other side, British, are: Comdr. Coleridge, Sir Hastings Ismay, Sir Andrew Cunningham, Sir Alan Brooke, Sir Charles Portal, Sir John Dill, and Brig. Ridman. In lower picture Giraud and de Gaulle meet in Algeria.

A German soldier, killed trying to escape in his half-track.

TUNISIA CLEARS PATH TO ITALY

MARCH 1943 in Tunisia found the *Afrika Korps* entrenched behind the Mareth Line, strongly fortified from the sea through the Matmata Hills, to the dune belt of the Sahara which had been considered impassable when the line was built. Montgomery's discovery that, with ingenuity and persistence, modern motorized equipment could negotiate those dunes, opened the door to final conquest in Tunisia. In the north, from Bizerta and Tunis down to Sfax, von Arnim's 100,000 Axis forces had been getting in supplies and reinforcements from near-by Sicilian bases, though probably a third were lost in transit, from Allied bombs or submarines. Along an interior line, 150 miles or so running through the Gafsa area, French, Americans, and British extended thinly northward toward the Allied main body where the British 1st Army, U. S. 2nd Corps, and the newly organized French Colonials were holding von Arnim and seeking a break-through to Tunis. Offensives and counteroffensives all along this line had served to keep Allied assistance from being sent to the 8th Army, but it had meant heavy fighting and much loss inflicted upon the Axis. They had taken bloody Kasserine Pass from the Americans in Feb., lost it again before they could push their way through and fan out over the Algerian plains. Just as new Gen. Sherman tanks had saved the day for Montgomery before El Alamein, so now the huge new Churchill tanks which had been the British answer to the Nazis' latest bigger and heavier Mark IVs, went into action in the Kasserine fighting and turned the tide for the Americans. On Mar. 6, 1943, Montgomery issued a characteristic order of the day to his troops, notifying them that the enemy was about to attack: ". . . because he is caught like a rat in a trap and is hitting out in every direction, trying to gain time to stave off the day of final defeat in North Africa. This is the very opportunity we want . . . This attack really helps us . . . and we must show our gratitude in no uncertain terms." In abortive attempts, such as this one, to dislodge Montgomery from his position facing the Mareth Line, Rommel lost much precious armor and helped to hasten his own defeat.

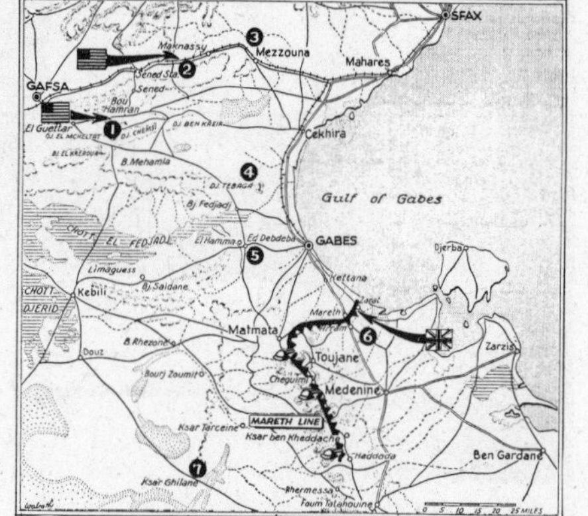

THIS HALF-TRACK will never again roll across the sands of Tunisia. Below an American Army doctor comes to the aid of an Arab mother whose baby has been severely burned. "Babies are babies the world around" to Allied doctors and soldiers. Everywhere they go they find a place in children's hearts, share everything they can with them.

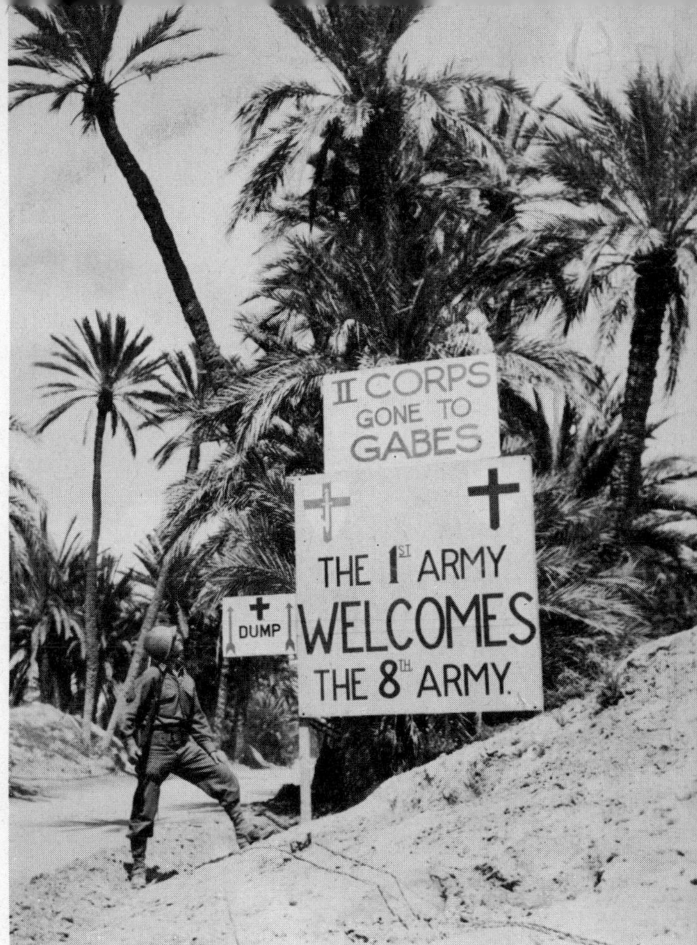

TRAFFIC IN TUNISIA points the way to victory. While Montgomery flanked the Mareth Line, other Allied troops fought through Gafsa down toward the coast. When they made contact with the 8th Army in April, 1943, the fate of the *Afrika Korps* was settled. Below, right, Allied fighters storm an entrenchment in Tunisian hills.

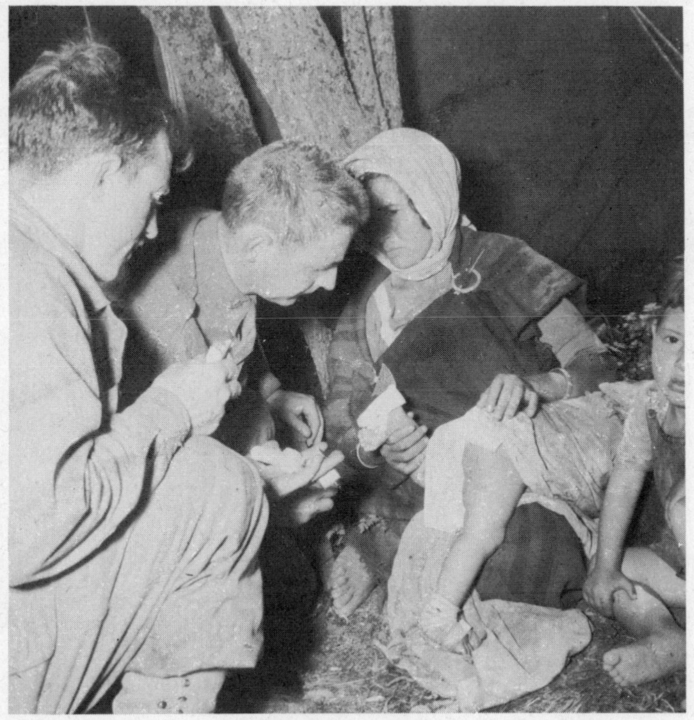

COLLAPSE OF THE MARETH LINE came with the capture of Mareth, Toujane and Matmata on Mar. 28, 1943. It began on the 20th when Montgomery sent New Zealand, Greek, and Fighting French troops, under Gen. Freyberg, around the Matmata hills to flank the line via the "impassable" dunes and take El Hamma in the rear. By Mar. 30 the *Afrika Korps* had been driven back to above Gabes. On April 6 Gherkas, Highlanders, and British "Tommies," under cover of a terrific night artillery barrage, stormed and captured Akarit. This finishing blow sent the *Afrika Korps* reeling back along the coast, leaving Italian troops behind as usual to cover the retreat. Thousands of prisoners were taken and the road to Sfax was littered with wrecked tanks and equipment left behind in flight.

In one day alone 9,000 disillusioned Axis fighters were taken into this prisoner-of-war camp near Mateur.

END OF ROMMEL'S *AFRIKA KORPS* came about when it was incorporated into von Arnim's forces, herded back into the "coffin-corner" of Tunisia behind an inland front running from coast to coast. The port of Sfax was captured by the 8th Army April 10, 1943, Sousse on the 12th, and along the coast Montgomery pressed forward. By May, armies in the north were ready to move. Americans had taken Mateur on May 3. On the 6th the British 1st Army launched a final offensive on Tunis, with the heaviest artillery barrage and the greatest concentration of air power used, up to then, on any single field o battle. On the same day U.S. and French troops drove towar Bizerta. By afternoon, May 7th, both objectives were in Allied hand Above, left, Nazi prisoners go in for landscaping. At right a captur Axis paratrooper seems to be enjoying his cigarette – an Americ one.

LCI invasion barges concentrate in Tunisia for the next move—Sicily.

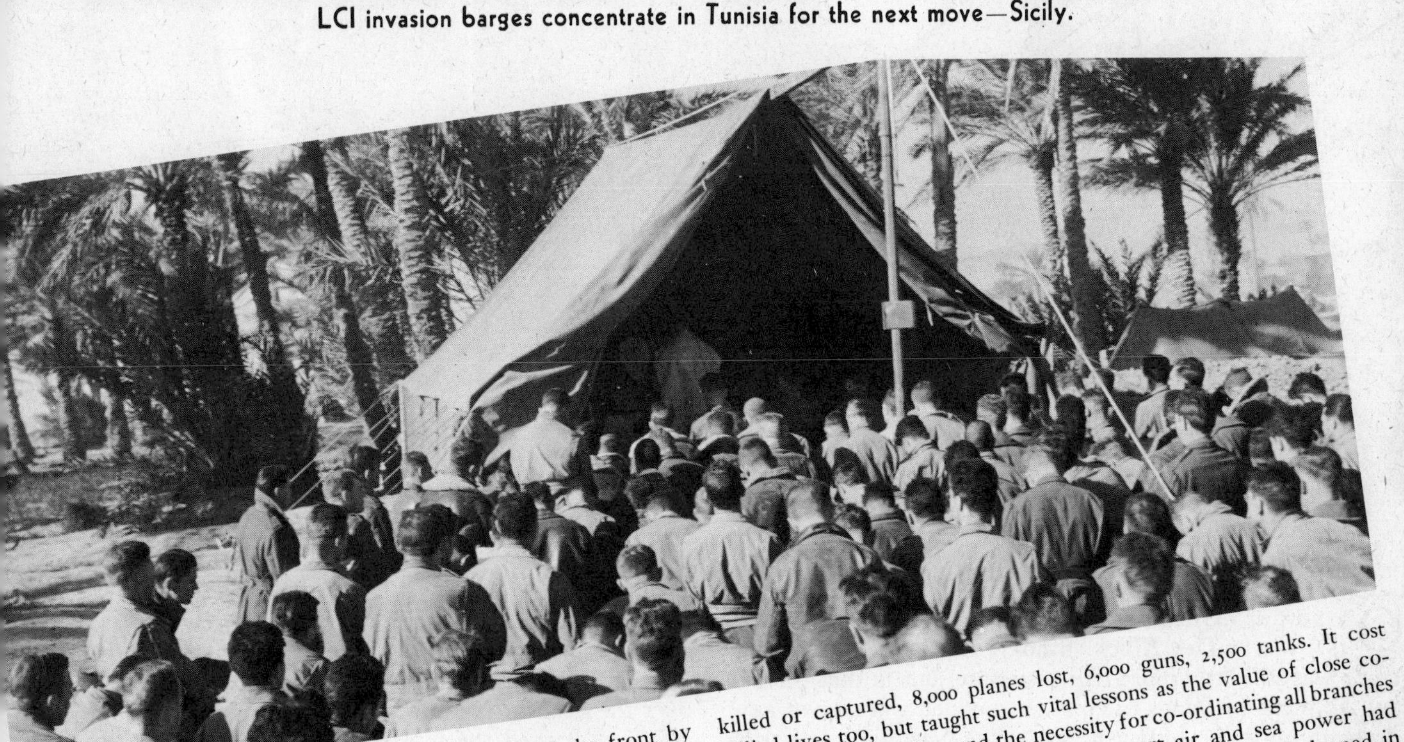

CHURCH SERVICES (*above*) were held just behind the front by U.S. chaplains, who go wherever their men go in this war. In Tunisia, Cape Bon was the last refuge of the harried Axis. By May 12 practically all enemy forces were rounded up, including von Arnim who was captured by proud Gherkas, and 24 other generals. Churchill summed up Axis losses in three years of African warfare as almost 1,000,000 men killed or captured, 8,000 planes lost, 6,000 guns, 2,500 tanks. It cost Allied lives too, but taught such vital lessons as the value of close co-operation among Allies, and the necessity for co-ordinating all branches of service. There was no mistaking the part air and sea power had played in the land victories of 1943—while those pincers, planned in Washington, were closing in Tunisia to doom Axis dreams of empire.

ON NOV. 8, 1942, one word electrified the waiting world. INVASION! The Allies invading Africa! The second front was still little more than a gesture, but in that gesture lay the shape of things to come. It sounded warning of new demands upon the *Luftwaffe*, upon the Nazi hordes swarming almost unchecked over Europe. From Leningrad to Nalchik the Russians felt a stirring of new life. This was the moment they had waited for. To the amazement of the Axis (of the Allies, hardly less) great armies of fresh troops, trained and magnificently armored troops, began to march. Fleets of tanks and motorized equipment began to roll from hundreds of camouflaged factories and warehouses of new industrial centers safe beyond the Urals. New Russian planes rose into skies which for so long had seemed almost the native element of the *Luftwaffe*. The Red offensive which broke over the head of Nazi General von Paulus in Stalingrad on Nov. 19 marked the first revelation of this new power so carefully built for the critical moment when an exhausted enemy, with dangerously extended lines, must face the dreaded Russian winter, a fresh new powerful army, and a western second front—all at the same time. From the surrender of von Paulus (*insert*) at Stalingrad in Feb. 1943, tens of thousands of Nazi supermen gave themselves up or fell into the hands of the forward-pushing Red Army.

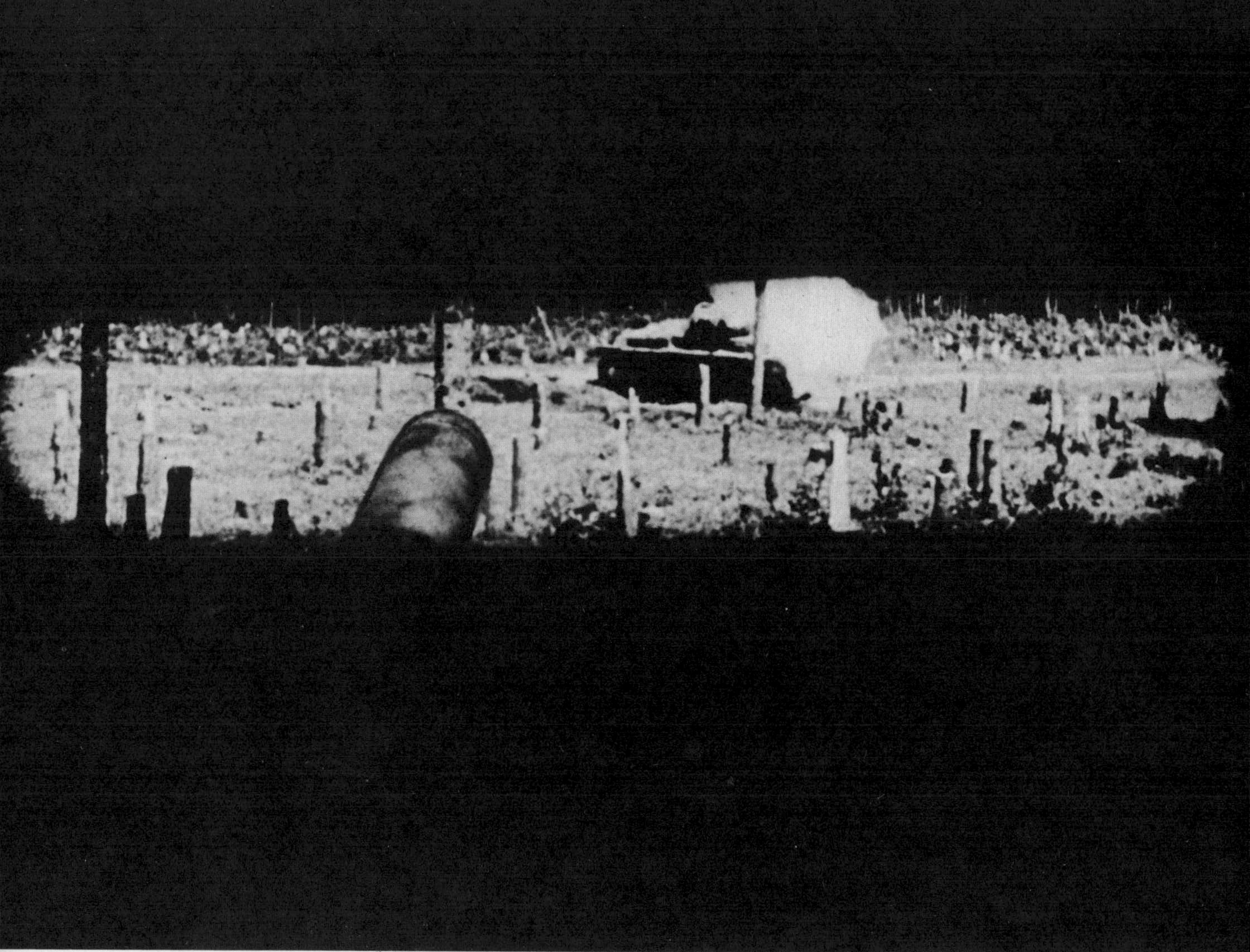

Through a slit in his Red Army tank, driver gets a good view of Nazi tank he has just demolished.

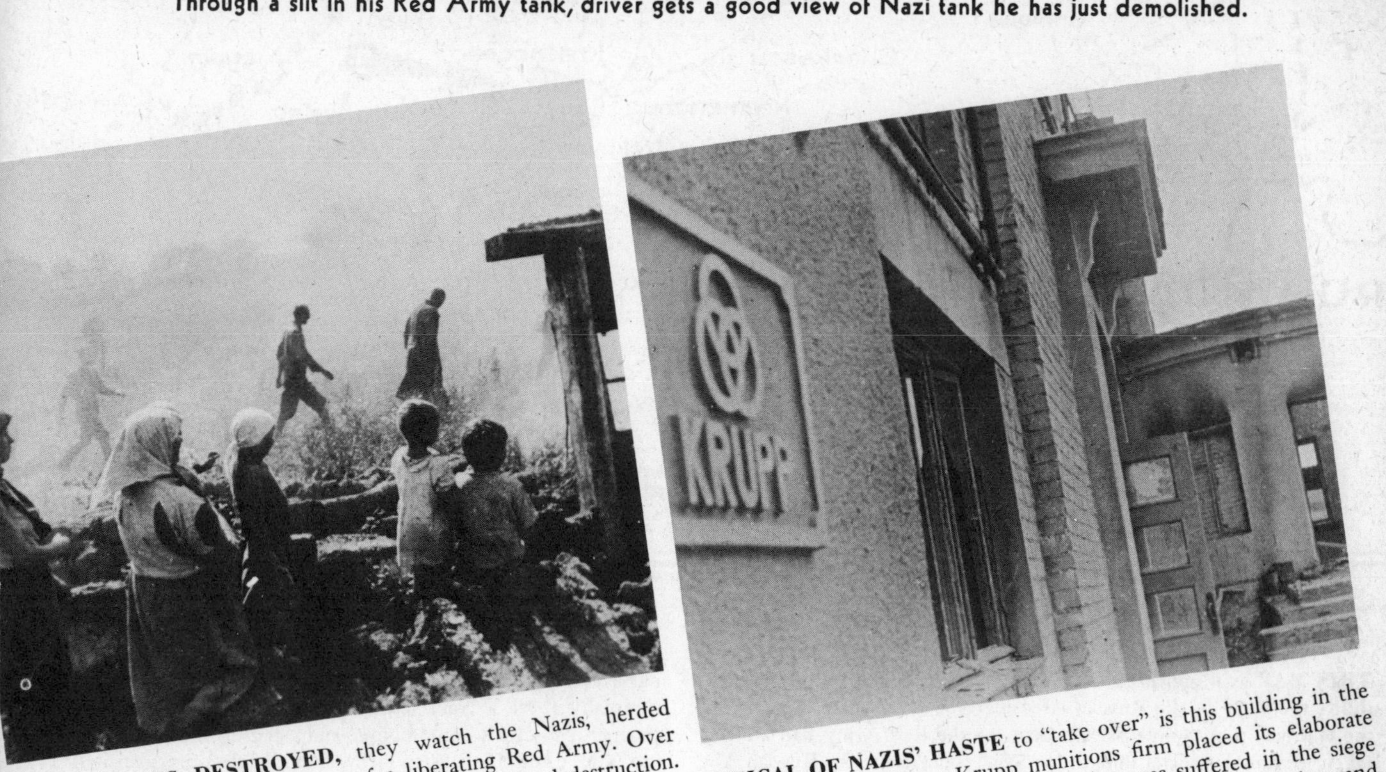

THEIR HOMES DESTROYED, they watch the Nazis, herded through the village, war prisoners of a liberating Red Army. Over mile after mile of Russian earth, these Nazis had spread destruction. Thousands of villagers were carried away to slave-labor (or death) in Germany. Others were tortured, robbed, left to starve or freeze.

TYPICAL OF NAZIS' HASTE to "take over" is this building in the Ukraine. Here the great Krupp munitions firm placed its elaborate nameplate before attempting to repair damages suffered in the siege of the town. By the time the Red Army had retaken Kharkov and Kiev, largest cities of the Ukraine, they were blackened shells of cities, not a power plant left—only Nazi time-bombs in their ruins.

GAINS ALL ALONG RUSSIAN FRONT PILED UP BY RED ARMY

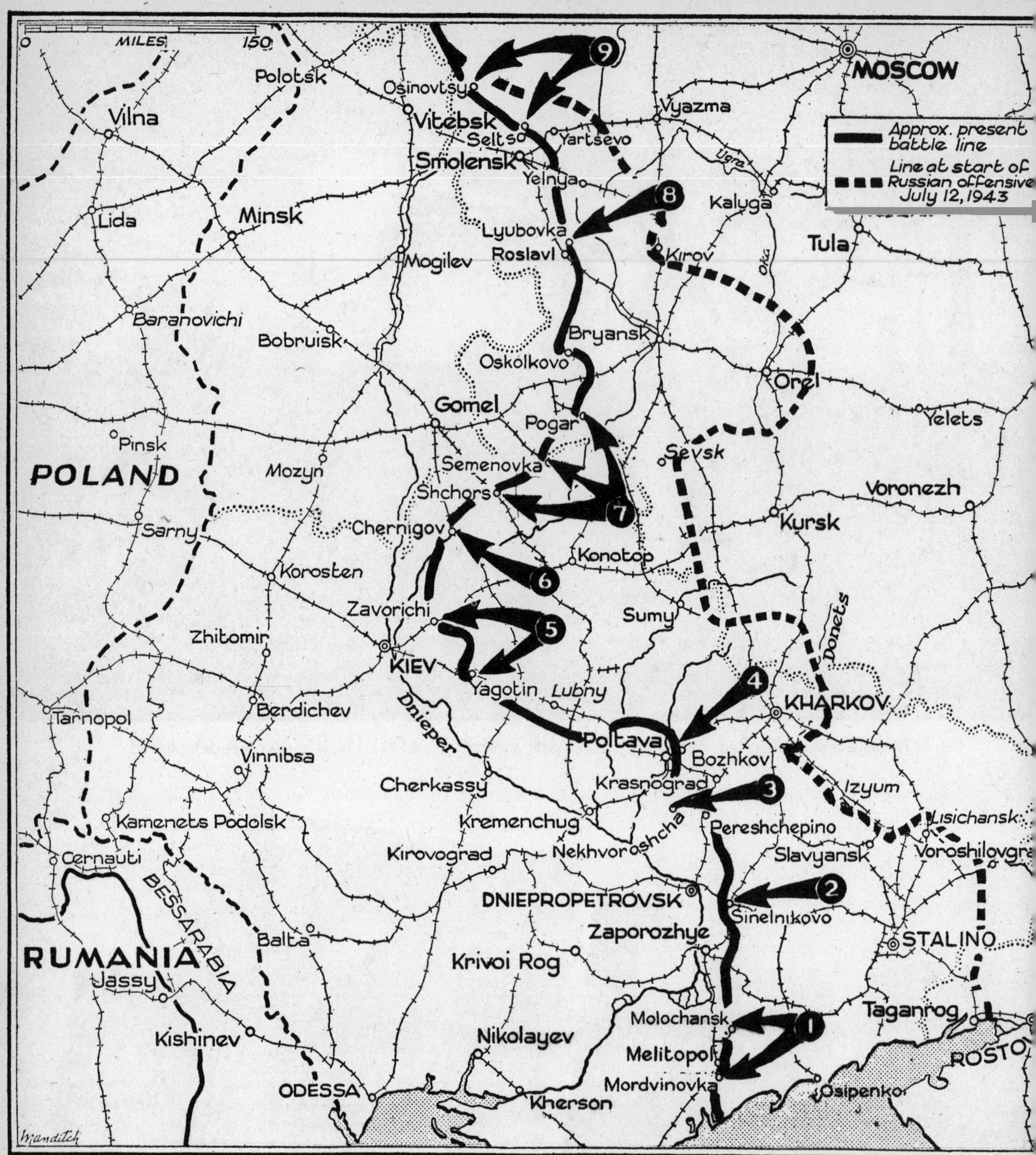

THIS MAP as it appeared on the date of publication, Sept. 22, 1943, shows the story of the Russian offensive as it stood three days before the Russians took Smolensk. On Sept. 17 the Red Army had already taken Bryansk, central hinge for Nazi operations in Russia. The Red tide then rolled along the roads to Gomel and Kiev, taking Kiev Nov. 6. By capturing Zhitomar a few days later – an important railway junction near the old Polish border – they split the Nazi front by driving a wedge between the northern and southern forces. The capture of Gomel, pivotal point in the Nazi defense system, and a powerful drive from Velikye Luki to the outskirts of Vitebsk, marked the beginning of the gigantic Russian offensive which would eventually force a Nazi retreat all the way from Leningrad to the Dnieper. Moscow's communiqué summarizing the fighting from July 5 to Nov. 5 said the Russian Army had liberated approximately 133,000 sq. miles, killed 900,000 officers and men, captured 90,000 prisoners, destroyed or captured 10,000 airplanes, 17,700 tanks, 18,000 guns. By mid-November the Nazis had been driven back almost half the distance from Stalingrad to Berlin. And with the exception of a few attempted counterattacks, the *Wehrmacht* was still in retreat on the road back to Berlin.

RED ARMY, pushing defeated Nazis steadily westward, vowed undying vengeance the despoilers of their country.

S PARADED behind the bier of King Boris Sept. 5, 1943, in vain attempt to impress n countries with Nazi-Bulgarian friendship.

NG RUSSIAN GIRLS work long hours in munitions plants, then put on dances like : night to entertain Red soldiers and sailors.

WITH the launching of the second Red winter offensive at Stalingrad in Nov. 1942, the Russian campaign swung into action in a series of blows, following a pattern worked out during days of siege at Stalingrad. While Hitler's "intuition" drove him into one mad gamble after another, Stalin and his advisors were evolving a new strategy for the offensive. Their objective was to combine close integration of action on all sectors of the front with fluidity of movement, so enabling them to capitalize quickly and effectively upon any favorable situation which might develop. The three main fronts—northern, central, and southern—must be reorganized to make twelve, each under independent command but all under General Headquarters. The approach of winter found the Nazi front highly vulnerable. While the Nazis still held at Stalingrad, new Red offensives launched in the middle Don region garnered in small towns, and by Dec. 31 had regained most of the area within the Don bend. While this drive headed toward Rostov, Russian troops far to the south seized the offensive in the Caucasus, sending large bodies of ski-troops swooping down upon the Nazis and wresting several key towns from them. When Russians recaptured Mozdok, on Jan. 3, 1943, the Grozny oil fields were snatched from Nazi reach. At this same time the "*Herrenvolk*" were having their troubles in the north. On Jan. 18 a powerful Russian assault broke the siege of Leningrad and liberated the city, while other smashing drives freed hundreds of villages, took Kursk, Rostov, Voroshilovgrad, all between Feb. 8 and 14. Kharkov fell on the 16th, to be retaken a month later. Rzhev fell on Mar. 3. When the spring thaws brought the usual spring stalemate to the Russian front, both armies rallied their forces for victory in the next blows. The Nazis struck first, on July 5, 1943, in the Orel-Kursk-Belgorod sector, with a concentration of fire power so terrific it seemed as if nothing could stand against it. But the Russian technique of "blitz-grinding"—wearing the enemy down by prolonged defense, then attacking when he had reached the point of exhaustion—was paying dividends. The Nazi attack was held. And on July 12 Red forces plunged into action. Along a 500-mile front, from Orel to Taganrog, they launched their drive to regain the rich Donetz basin, directing their main assault against the Orel salient anchored on the west by Bryansk and Smolensk. Orel and Belgorod fell Aug. 5, with the Red Army fanning out from Belgorod to drive the Nazis back in tumultuous disorder—which did not look at all "according to plan." Kharkov was taken—once more—on Aug. 23, Sievsk on the 27th; to the south the Donbas area was retaken, Taganrog on Aug. 30. Early in September Lisichansk, Stalino, and Mariupol on the Sea of Azov fell. In the Kuban valley, Nazis were losing Novorossisk, which deprived them of any foothold east of the Kerch straits and forced them to fall back from Caucasian bridgeheads into the Crimea. The main Russian drive was now turned toward Smolensk, one of the Nazis' greatest eastern front bastions, where for two years they had been busy building a hedge-hog system of defenses with strong points covering the major avenues of advance. The Red Army took Smolensk on Sept. 25. Within a week the Nazis were cleared from a 400-mile stretch on the east Dnieper and Russians were thrusting across it.

NAZIS TAKE the "road back to the fatherland," leaving useful war material, fuel, and even Tiger tanks behind.

RED ARMY EXECUTES Nazi War criminals—justice as decreed at the Moscow Allied Foreign Minister's conference in the fall of 1943.

FRESH FROM THEIR MEETING at Cairo with Chiang Kai-shek, President Roosevelt and Winston Churchill met Marshal Stalin at Teheran, Iran's capital, on Nov. 28, 1943, for a four-day conference. Their report, "We leave here friends in fact, in spirit, and in purpose."

MOSCOW...TEHERAN ...CONFERENCES

"ADVERSITY makes strange bedfellows"—but no stranger than World War II. The amazing spectacle of an "Axis" partnership between the nation which had made a fetish of "race purity," and the one Oriental people farthest from kinship with all Occidental concepts, had been accepted by a puzzled world as part of the general madness of war-crazed leaders. Many Europeans and Americans found it even harder to believe that essential unity was possible between "capitalistic America," and "imperialistic Britain," and "communistic Russia." But the struggle for survival is rooted in instincts more deeply seated than theoretical ideas, no matter how fervently adopted. When it became increasingly clear that the Axis actually meant to destroy whole segments of the human race, to conquer and absorb the rest, to implement the paranoia of an individual with the will and resources of a whole people through creation of the most powerful war machine known to history—prejudices all over the world began to vanish. Since prejudice precludes understanding—or even knowledge of the truth about anything—many people on both sides of the Atlantic were agreeably surprised to find that Russia did not seem to be the least interested in "Red" plots to overthrow all existing governments, but was very busily engaged in trying to make up for all the time she had lost in the fields of popular education, economic recovery, industrialization of industry, and development of cultural institutions. Also, fortunately for the world, she had been interested in building an army for a war which, it seemed, she alone in Europe had seen on the horizon. With this background in mind, the results of the Moscow conferences fall into their proper perspective. When it became clear that military necessity required closer co-operation in conduct of war, and removal of all unnecessary causes of friction in working out a program to keep the peace, the conferences between British and American leaders were expanded to include first Chiang Kai-shek at Cairo in Nov. 1943, then Stalin at Teheran immediately afterward. The separation of the two councils was not the most desirable arrangement, but was made necessary by the fact that Russia was not a partner in the war against Japan. Preliminary to the meeting of the leaders at Teheran, a conference of the three Foreign Ministers—Molotov, Eden and Hull—was held in Moscow from Oct. 19 to Oct. 30. Military reasons made it impossible for the results of the conference to be reported in detail, but a general feeling of good will was apparent, and the countries involved were assured that there were "frank and exhaustive discussions of the measures to be taken to shorten the war." Politically, the principles of the Four Freedoms were upheld, and continued co-operation pledged for war and peace. The dramatic meeting of Roosevelt, Churchill, and Stalin in Teheran in Dec. brought forth the statement that complete unity had been reached in concerted military plans, pledged the nations to decisions already made at Cairo with regard to "unconditional surrender" and other fundamental policies.

STALIN

STALIN WAS BORN JOSEF DJUGUSHVILI on Dec. 21, 1879, in Gori, near Tiflis. His peasant father had become a cobbler and earned little. Fellow revolutionaries gave him the name "Stalin," meaning "steel" in Russian, during his underground days before the revolution.

STALIN'S MOTHER, Ekatrina Djugushvili, was determined he should not be a cobbler. When he was nine she sent him to the Gori ecclesiastical school to become a priest. Interviewed years later by H. R. Knickerbocker, she said Stalin had always been "a good boy."

PATIENTLY easy-going yet determined, a theoretician and an intuitive politician, coldly analytical and frank, pipe-smoking Joseph Stalin has had the most remarkable career of all the world's leaders. His story is that of the Russian revolution. For years the most controversial figure in world politics, charged by his political enemies with every crime imaginable, Stalin won the respect and confidence of free peoples everywhere by the skillful way in which he organized and led Russia's fight against Nazism. His name will go down in history as the man who developed socialist Russia in twenty short years from a backward, illiterate, undeveloped agricultural country to one of the most highly educated, powerful, modern industrial countries of the world. Stalin's energetic political career began when he was expelled from a seminary in his native Georgia in southern Russia for studying Marx. He got himself a job reading scientific instruments in the Tiflis Observatory, spent his nights organizing oil workers, studying more Marx and Lenin. Unions and strikes were illegal under the Czar and it was there that Stalin, much harried by the police, first developed the determination, the patience, the political sense, organizing ability, and "long view" of events for which he is now famous. These elements in his character were forged in the unsuccessful 1905 revolution and the decade that followed when Stalin stuck out the police terror, built the Communist party into a formidable, well-knit revolutionary organization. When Lenin died in 1924 the job of building socialism had only begun. Yet through Stalin's three Five-Year Plans, Russia was industrialized, her farms mechanized and collectivized, her living standards raised, her people educated. Those were grim, hard, struggling years for Russia, years of toil and sacrifice. There were blunders and mistakes. Stalin himself had to reprimand the overzealousness of the Communists in collectivizing the farms. There was sabotage and suffering. At times, it would seem today, only the determination of Stalin bridged the gap between chaos and socialism. But the plans did succeed, and when the war broke out Russia was well on the way to becoming one of the most powerful industrial nations of the world. The Five-Year Plans were the backbone of Russia's preparedness. Without them the Red Army would have been powerless. As head of Russia's Communists, Stalin has been the bold, resolute leader of the "dictatorship of the proletariat." He has struck with full vigor at anything within Russia which threatened its life. Yet in 1936 Stalin voluntarily insisted that education and socialism had advanced far enough to relax the "dictatorship." Correspondents have noted his warmth, personal magnetism, that he laughs easily and often. He refuses credit for Russia's advances, gives it to "the people." When he is applauded by an audience, he applauds too—but he is applauding "the people." When H. G. Wells asked him what he was doing to change the world, he said: "Not so very much."

THIS RARE PICTURE of Stalin (XX) was probably taken about 1894 when he was graduated to the Tiflis Theological Seminary. He began his political career at 15.

AT THE SEMINARY Stalin became acquainted with Marx's work, quarreled with the corrupt Russian priests, was expelled as a "radical" for organizing trade unions.

BY 1900 STALIN was the leader of the revolutionary movement in the Caucasus. He is shown here urging the oil workers to strike. His fame spread through Russia.

THE CZARIST POLICE hunted Stalin daily. This record was taken from their files after the revolution. He was arrested 8 times.

THIS IS THE SIBERIAN log cabin to which Stalin was exiled from 1913 to 1917. Exiled eight times, he escaped seven times.

MOLOTOV, STALIN, AND LENIN are shown in the editorial offices of *Pravda,* of which Stalin was editor. Stalin corresponded with Lenin for years before he met him. In 1910, when Lenin formed the Communist party, Stalin joined it immediately.

STALIN WAS A LEADER OF THE RED ARMY, then ragged, starving, poorly armed. His superior ability as a strategician defeated the counter-revolutionary armies in three major battles—Leningrad, Smolensk, and Tsaritsyn.

STALIN, LENIN, the founder of the Soviet Union and father of the revolution, and M. I. Kalinin, now president of the Supreme Council of the U.S.S.R., posed for this picture in 1919 when Stalin was People's Commissar for Nationalities. The Czarist regime had attempted to Russianize the 160-odd nationalities within its borders, suppressed their languages, maintained its own rule by keeping the various national groups fighting one another, refused them schools and economic development. To win full support of these national groups for the Soviet Stalin encouraged these national cultures and tongues, insisted on the fullest political equality for every nationality and race, and the economic and educational development of every region. This was his greatest contribution to Marxist theory.

LEON TROTSKY, who had not been a Bolshevik before the revolution, fought Lenin's "N.E.P." policy of 1921 which temporarily delayed collectivization. Lenin and Stalin argued socialism could not be built without the fullest support of the people, that they were not ready for socialism. Trotsky was voted down. On Lenin's motion in 1922 Stalin was elected general secretary of the party. With a handful of followers Trotsky continued to oppose Lenin and Stalin, who had become Lenin's right-hand man.

BUT STALIN, shown here crossing the Kremlin yard to a party conference, decisively defeated Trotsky in every debate and denounced him as traitorous. Trotsky was exiled in 1929. Years later, in 1937, Trotsky was found to be working with the Nazis for the overthrow of the Soviets. Trotsky's agents included eight Red Army generals and numerous top Soviet officials. At a public trial they confessed their guilt and were executed. Trotsky was assassinated by one of his own followers in 1940.

STALIN'S CHIEF ADVISERS on foreign policy were Molotov and Maxim Litvinov. In the 1930's, certain war was coming, Stalin sent Litvinov to the League of Nations in the hope of making it a stronghold of collective security. Though Litvinov was the ablest diplomat at Geneva, he was unable to prevent the continual appeasement of the Fascist powers, wrecking the League.

MEANWHILE, WITH ORJONIKIDZE Stalin was pushing the development of heavy industry, particularly at Magnitogorsk, deep in the Urals, where they built one of the largest steel centers. By a series of Five-Year Plans which were fulfilled by the Soviet people with much suffering and sacrifice the Soviet Union was made practically independent of the world and more fully prepared for war.

IN 1935 STALIN decided the U.S.S.R. had progressed far enough in education and industry to permit the extension of democratic rights to all citizens. At his suggestion a new constitution was drafted to replace that of 1924 which, while permitting non-Communists to hold office, barred rich kulaks and others from voting. The new constitution, adopted in 1936, introduced universal, equal, and direct suffrage with secret ballots. Stalin warned the party it must reduce inefficiency, bureaucracy, and produce results if it was to maintain its leadership under the new system. Above: Stalin voting.

JOSEPH STALIN RECEIVES THE ORDER OF VICTORY from his friend and associate of 40 years, President Kalinin. Stalin lives and works in the massive Kremlin. From the beginning he has taken an active interest in all matters concerning Russia's defense. He has emerged as one of the great military strategists of the greatest war in history, has become Marshal of the Soviet Union. In domestic affairs he has shown increasingly liberal trends, encouraged the teaching of Russia's historic past, and religious tolerance. In May 1943 he helped to formally dissolve the Comintern (Third International) which had long been inactive but continued to furnish fuel for anti-Red propaganda. Already Stalin is planning two new "Five-Year Plans" to assure post-war prosperity. Firmly entrenched, he is called by many Soviet millions "Father Russia."

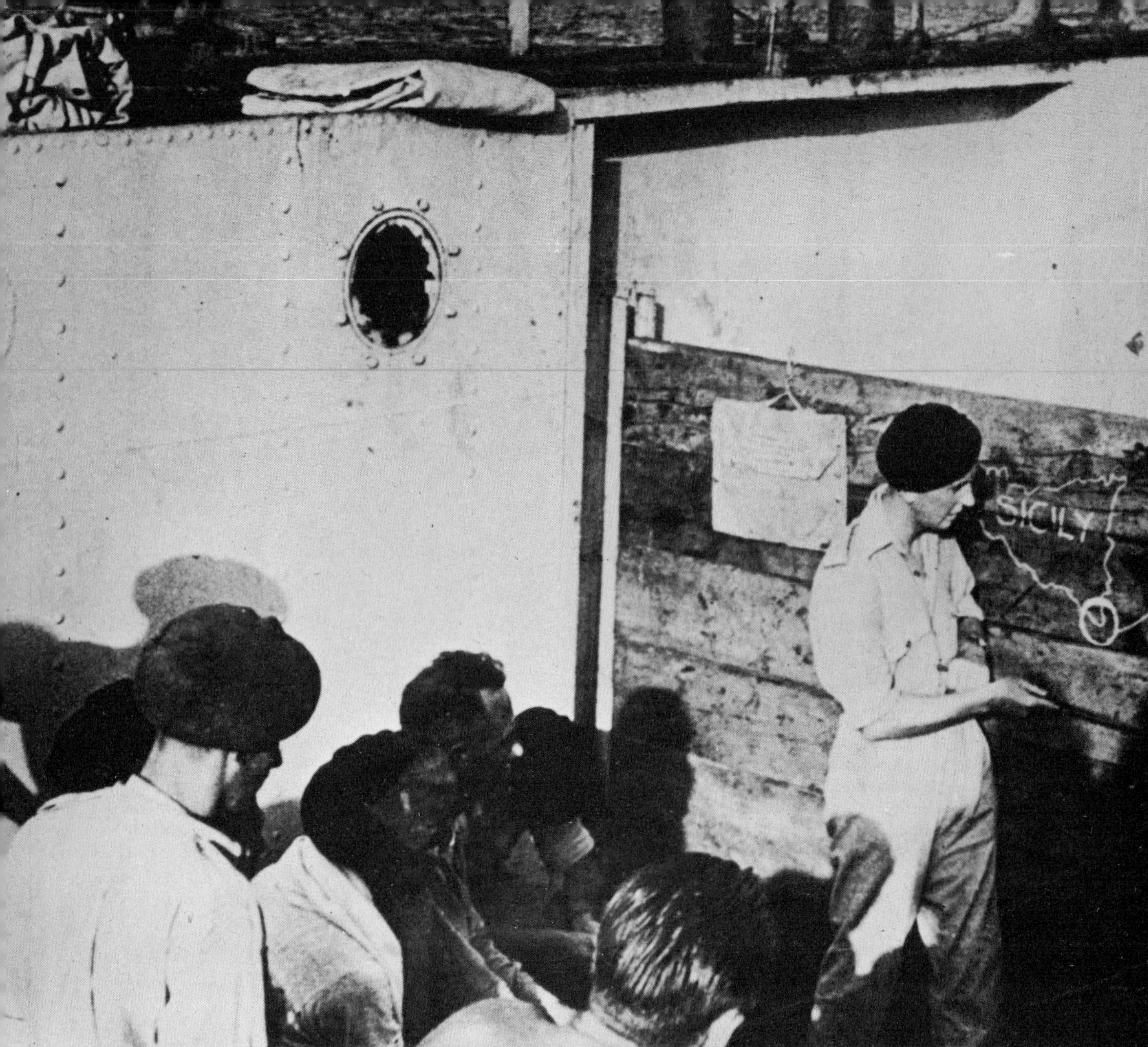

LCI invasion barges concentrate in Tunisia for the next move—Sicily.

SICILY—STEPPING-STONE TO EUROPE

Over the dark, sullen waters of the Mediterranean a vast armada of Allied ships, 2,500 of them, bore toward Sicily, remnant of an ancient land bridge between Europe and Africa, which for centuries has lain in the path of wars. It was the night of July 9-10, 1943; and the Allies were ready to breach the first outwork of Fortress Europe.

The co-operation of air and sea power was the deciding factor in the success of the Sicilian campaign. Ever since the loss of the *Prince of Wales* and the *Repulse* in 1941, it had been axiomatic that warships could not be risked within striking distance of shore-based aircraft without complete cover by fighter planes. But now the tide had changed, and it was the Italian Navy which skulked in harbor while the Allied landing force approached the coast with impunity, so great was their supremacy in the air. For a month the ports of Sicily had been mercilessly bombed by the North African Air Force in a preparatory softening-up process.

Warships not only covered the landing of the ground forces, but supported the invasion by shelling coast cities ahead of the Army's advance, bombarding the road from Catania to Messina, and covering the flanking sea-borne landings which marked the final stage of the campaign.

The Sicilian invasion was not entirely unexpected by the enemy, but they seem to have expected it to come on the western side of the island, nearest to Tunisia. Instead, the Allies landed in two forces, the American 7th Army, under General Patton, along the stretch from west of Licata to Cape Scalambri below Scoglitti, with Gela in the center; the British 8th Army, under General Montgomery, which included the 1st Canadian Division, on the east coast south of Syracuse. The two forces together numbered about 13 divisions, of which 2 were armored; while the Axis had 12 divisions, but only 3½ of them German. The first three days showed that the island would fall to the Allies; and it took until Aug. 17 to capture Messina and complete the conquest of the island.

ON THE EASTWARD DRIVE FROM PALERMO TO MESSINA, water bugs ferried American troops and equipment around road blocks and blown-up bridges, saving hours upon hours of priceless time. Tanks, half-tracks, trucks, jeeps were unloaded at Patti in one such amphibious operation, and then rolled up to the town of Falcone. The Germans employed routine defenses against sea landings—mines off shore, hit-and-run air raids, concealed gun emplacements on shore; but all their efforts proved inadequate in face of Allied naval and air supremacy.

DURING THE FIRST TWO DAYS OF THE INVASION, the Allies put ashore 80,000 men and 300 tanks. Both sides used tanks freely, but the Sicilian terrain precluded their being the decisive factor they had proved to be in Tunisia. The use of tanks was confined to supporting local attacks in small parties. In the picture civilians of Sciacca cheer the entry of a full-track.

DESTINATION SICILY – The men shown above had been at sea for three hours before they learned that their goal was this first outpost of Italy.

Right: In a Sicilian dooryard a U.S. private administered life-giving blood plasma to an American soldier wounded by shrapnel. The remarkable portrait studies of the women looking on show a mingling of awe, curiosity, and compassion.

CATANIA, key to the German east coast defenses, was liberally bombed during the pre-invasion softening-up. The coastal advance of the British 8th Army was checked for three weeks on the plain below Catania. Fierce German resistance from mountain strongholds forced General Montgomery to throw his weight onto the left flank, where the Canadians were advancing inland. Capture of Regalbuto, Catenanuova, and Centuripe forced the Germans to withdraw along the whole eastern flank; and at last on August 5 the British entered Catania.

THE ALLIED MILITARY GOVERNMENT follows on the heels of invading Allied armies. Here a civil-affairs officer and a member of AMG supervises the posting in Catania of proclamations giving details of the orders to be carried out by the civil population. Sicily has been the proving ground for the British and American version of military government for occupied territories. On the basis of their experience there, AMG has revised and corrected the Allied pattern of military government for use in all countries to be occupied.

DURING THE FIRST DAYS after the Germans had been driven from Sicily, the people were obliged to live in such makeshift homes as this ancient Roman amphitheater. But with the help of the AMG they pitched in to bring their country back to normal. From the beginning the AMG found that it could rely upon co-operation from the Sicilians, most of their minor officials could be retained, and the civil police could be trusted to maintain order. As a result, officers of the AMG could confine themselves to purely supervisory functions. For administrative purposes the AMG is organized into six sections—financial, civilians' supply, legal, public health, public safety, and Allied and enemy property—all under the command of a chief civil-affairs officer and his deputy. The AMG also carries with it advisers on education and the preservation of fine arts and monuments. Members of the AMG are selected for special administrative qualifications and trained in the AMG school. The organization was established on May 1, 1943; and hundreds of officers were trained between then and July 10.

THE FALL OF A "SAWDUST CAESAR" is graphically illustrated by this mutilated portrait of *Il Duce* hanging on a tree in Messina. After 21 years of oppression, Italians greeted their release with vigorous expressions of joy. The bankruptcy of Fascism was evident early in 1943. Frantically Mussolini swept away civil and military officials, expelled party members for defeatism, and established a new Direc torate to strengthen his failing hand. Implacably the schism in th party widened, until, when the Duce brought back the news th Hitler had abandoned Italy at the Verona meeting, a demand for h resignation was carried 19 to 7 by the Fascist Grand Council.

THE ARMISTICE WITH ITALY was signed on Sept. 3, 1943, in an army tent in Sicily. General Castellano, the civilian in the center, signed on behalf of Italy after weeks of see-saw negotiations between the Allies and the Badoglio government. The picture was taken while General Smith, American Chief of Staff, was in the act of signing the historic document with his own pen.

THE CARABINIERI IN NICASTRO, typical south Italian town, were not disbanded by the AMG. They kept at the police work in which they are experienc but now they wear special armbands to show that Allied military authorities are behind them.

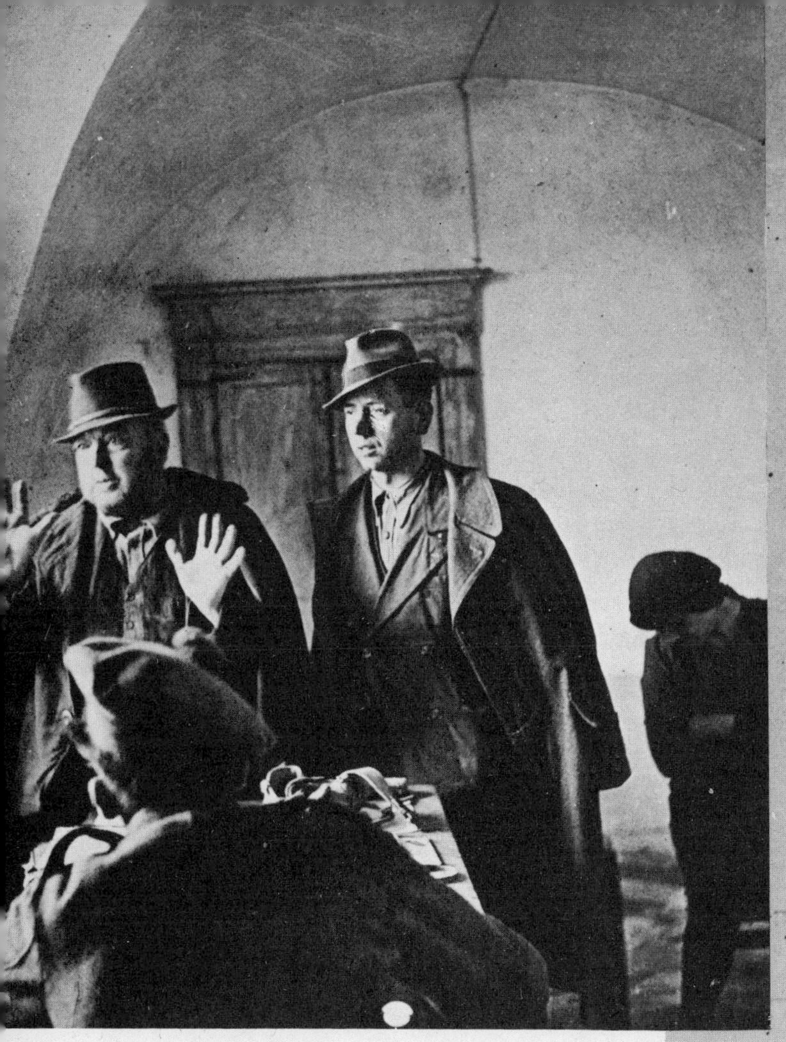

ONE OF THE AMG'S first tasks in administering occupied Italian territory was the weeding out of rabid Fascist officials. Every effort was made to continue civil officials in office, but a die-hard party member was anathema to his fellow citizens. Here one, accused before the AMG, obviously denies everything.

"AN ELEVATED POSITION – The Duce has again assumed his state office in close contact with the Nazi armed forces." So read the caption to the above Russian cartoon, commenting on Mussolini's rescue from prison by Nazi paratroops on Sept. 12. On the 23rd, Germany announced that he had been made president of Fascist Italy; he later denounced the King.

IN OBEDIENCE TO THE TERMS OF THE ARMISTICE, the Italian fleet put out to sea before the Nazis could interfere effectively. The *Roma* was sunk by air attack, but all other capital ships except the unfinished *Impero* steamed safely into harbor at Malta. Most of the remaining cruisers and destroyers also reached Allied ports between the 8th and 10th of September. The picture shows the seaplane carrier *Guiseppe Miraglia* in St. Paul's Bay.

THE BRITISH and Canadian 8th Army, "deservedly first," as General Montgomery put it, to set foot on Europe as an army of vengeance, crossed the Straits of Messina in the early hours of September 3, 1943. The two-mile stretch of water was lit by searchlights from the Sicilian coast and tracer bullets. So thoroughly had the ground been prepared by bombing and barrage that, for the first time in history, masses of troops landed on enemy soil without the loss of a single soldier through enemy action. The sea was as safe as a mill-pond that night. Of the 300 ducks, several hundred landing craft, and scores of warships which did the invasion job, not one was lost by enemy action. The landing was on the beach between Reggio and San Giovanni. The Germans had some 16 divisions in Italy, among them veteran troops—the and 16th Armored, parts of the Hermann Goering Panzer, Parachute, and 29th Armored divisions. But it was soon parent that they were making no effort to defend Calal and southern Apulia. Instead, they concentrated their fo in the Salerno area where British and American forces lan on September 9. After the invasion of western Europe, I became the forgotten front; but a tour of European bat fields by the House Military Affairs Committee in 1944 minded the country that the Italian battlefield is one the toughest in the world and that fighting all the up the Appenines has never before been tried in the hist of wars.

INVASION OF ITALY

Above: Day and night, without letup, equipment was loaded on waiting landing craft for the big invasion of Italy.

Right: General Dwight D. Eisenhower snatches noon mess by the roadside. The menu is hot C ration—hot because it was packed next to the manifold of the General's car.

BLOODY SALERNO

"THERE are no certainties in war," said Churchill. "There is a precipice on both sides—a precipice of precaution and a precipice of daring." On Salerno's beaches the balance was rather on the daring side. There was no possibility of actual surprise. Its shelving beaches, its location within striking distance from Naples and fighter range from Allied bases in Sicily, made it the one logical spot for the first full-scale attack on the mainland. So sure were the Nazis that it would be the spot, they had spent two weeks fortifying heights overlooking the beaches and had five divisions ready to drive back the invaders. Under U.S. General Clark, American and British units landed at dawn on Sept. 9, 1943, at points between Salerno and Agropoli, landed to find themselves almost at once under fire both from artillery and dive bombers. Unexpected mine fields delayed the big landing boats which carried heavy equipment. Those men on the beaches had to dig themselves in, try to keep themselves alive with small arms against heavy artillery on fortified heights. Naval gunfire and Allied fighters held off Nazi bombers, pounded Nazi fortifications. For four days the outcome was in balance, while the bloody struggle on open beaches went on. It was a week more before the issue was finally settled—a week of attack and counterattack, of bloody nights and bloody days—before Churchill could speak of Salerno as "an important and pregnant victory." The picture to the left shows British soldiers, first to land at Salerno.

THE WHITE ENSIGN flew over Reggio Harbor after the Allies had landed along the toe of Italy the first week in Sept., 1943. Italy's "unconditional surrender" to the Allies was announced on Sept. 8, and declaration of war against Germany Oct. 13. Above, Gen. Eisenhower receives Marshal Badoglio on board the battleship *Nelson*.

LST BOATS, those huge naval freight cars, are part of the fleet of water bugs without which amphibious warfare would be impossible. Many of the Landing Ship Tanks, Landing Craft Tanks, Landing Craft Infantry, to give them their full titles, have traveled down the Mississippi River, across the Gulf of Mexico, and across the Atlantic in order to transport men and equipment for the armies. These are being loaded at the docks of Palermo, protected by barrage balloons.

SELDOM HAS AN INVADER been welcomed the way the Italians did the Allies. The picture below, a typical street scene in a liberated city, shows how the civilians greet the military. In Reggio even the soldiers of the Italian Army ran down to the harbor to greet their "çonquerors" with smiles. Before the Nazis left they backed trucks up to the doors of shops, fastened grapples to the fronts of the buildings, and pulled the whole fronts away, the better to do their looting.

Top: British army engineers crossed the Volturno River in Oct. 1943 in a "shore-landing-deck-craft" which they built themselves. They used it to move reenforcements, ammunition, and food across the stream.

Bottom: The town of Ortona, key port on the Adriatic, lay in the path of the 8th Army's northward drive in December 1943. The picture shows the square after Canadian tanks have broken in. **Insert:** Field Marshal Sir Harold R. L. G. Alexander, now in command of the Mediterranean theater.

"GALLOPING GHOST OF THE SICILIAN COAST" was what her crew called the U.S.S. *Philadelphia* because she ran along the shore between Cefalu and Messina and shot away German positions which the land army could not reach. In the picture she is weaving a veil of artificial fog off Anzio, to hide ships anchored in the beachhead harbor from marksmen in the Nazi artillery. Purpose of establishing of the Anzio beachhead on Jan. 22 was diversion of German strength.

RAIN, SNOW, AND MUD; mountain passes blocked with snow; German machine guns raking slopes up which Allied soldiers must grind their way—that was the nightmare picture of the "third front" in Italy during the winter of 1943-44. When winter and the strong German defense positions on the Gustav line blocked progress up the peninsula, a flanking movement from the sea was tried to divert part of the German strength at Cassino.

HUGE CAVES in the Nettuno area of the Anzio bridgehead afforded a natural bomb shelter. The donkey and cart are a familiar part of the Italian landscape, whether above ground or under it. In various sections of the country, as the liberating armies moved in, the people were found living in caves, stables or whatever refuge they could find.

AT THE END OF MAY Allied forces at Anzio finally launched their successful attack. The picture shows a British infantryman cleaning up a captured German position. The Germans have a habit of hiding in a slit trench until a company has passed, then sniping from the rear. The soldier in the foreground was killed in this manner.

GUSTAV LINE

CASSINO, guarded by this six-mile belt of strong mountain positions and other fortifications, was the chief obstacle in the Allies' road to Rome.

British vehicles move along near San Angelo.

Gun positions like this raked the open areas.

Men, vehicles and armor cross the Gari.

ALTHOUGH LONG SINCE REDUCED to existence at subsistence level, these Italian villagers did their poverty-stricken best to accord the last rites to a civilian killed in the fighting when the Allied soldiers drove the Germans out of Alife. This affecting scene is duplicated every day in hundreds and hundreds of towns all over the world.

THE NEW ORDER in German-occupied Italy is graphically illustrated in this scene of mourning at Rionero. Shortly before the British 8th Army reached the town, the Germans had massacred 16 Italians in reprisal because one desperate Italian peasant had killed a German chicken thief. The bereaved families are gathered at the graves of the victims.

MONTE CASSINO, ancient monastery founded by St. Benedict, was spared by the Allies until there was no doubt it was used by Nazis as a fortress from which to command Allied lines, take heavy toll of Allied lives. Reduced by bombing, it held out until it was taken by assault May 18, 1944.

ALLIED TROOPS marched through the ancient wall of Rome in June, 1944, nine months after Nazis seized the city upon Mussolini's fall. The bombing raid on San Lorenzo marshalling yards in Rome was United Nations' declaration that not even the veneration accorded Rome by all Christendom could make them lose sight of military necessities. Vatican City, however, was carefully "briefed" for protection from bombing, and the Pope's influence was helpful in the Italian situation.

PIETRO CARUSO was a symbol of Italy's troubled heritage from Fascism and war. First to be tried before the Tribunal for the Punishment of Fascist Crimes, this former police chief was accused, among other things, of furnishing hostages for Nazi execution purposes. On the opening day of his trial, mob violence swept into the Palace of Justice, seized another defendant in the belief it was Caruso, beat him, drowned him, strung his body up in a prison window. But the mistake in identity did not help Caruso. He was convicted in Sept. 1944, and executed the next day at Fort Bravetta. His summary trial high-lights the Badoglio government's determination to "purge" all Fascist collaborators, with the death sentence for ones like Caruso. All Fascist legislation and decrees were abolished by the Badoglio Government, and by occupation authorities—everything now points toward the democratic way.

A corporal watches for enemy snipers while his comrades set off mines, heavily sowed along the street. The black smoke is a mine.

THIS SCENE OF RUIN is Rosignano, but it might be any of countless talian towns which testify to the stubbornness with which the Germans esisted. Rosignano was taken in July 1944 by the 5th Army. Two American infantrymen of the 34th Division were snapped as they trolled through the streets with an Italian partisan to look over the ituation.

FRESCOES IN THE CAMPO SANTO, in Pisa, Italy, were badly shattered during the fighting. Here one of the specialists in the preservation of fine arts and monuments attached to the Allied Military Government is carefully searching through the fragments of a Tuscan fresco in preparation for its complete restoration under supervision of the AMG.

AS SOON AS ALLIED ARMIES moved into a liberated Italian town, the people crept back to salvage anything left of their possessions. Above, old and young, they pick a precarious way across the River Arno, balancing on a rail of the Ponte Allegrozie, one of six famous ancient bridges which spanned the river in Florence until retreating Nazis blew up five of them in August, 1944. Florence, "Cradle of the Renaissance," storehouse of its treasures, escaped complete destruction, but the exquisite bridges were gone, some of the loveliest among the city's storied palaces, and the Santo Stephano Church—all irreparable losses to the world of beauty as well as to Italy. In towns completely ruined by bombardment, as Reggio was, returning citizens felt their way through shell-torn streets, turning over heaps of rubble, searching for what remnants of bedding and cooking utensils they could find. With these poor possessions they took up life in cellars or stables, or crowded with peasants into surrounding villages. The people were hungry, diseased, frightened, ashamed; and above all sick of war. Some had not been fed regularly for three months, and they hated the Nazis who had abandoned them, as well as the Fascist hierarchy which had bled them for 20 years. Frank Gervasi, a commentator who talked with Italian soldier-prisoners when Montgomery first invaded Italy, describes them as "tired men, exhausted spiritually as they were broken physically." Few of them had any interest in peace terms and seemed not to care whether Italy retained her identity as a nation. They wanted only *lavor e pane*—bread and work.

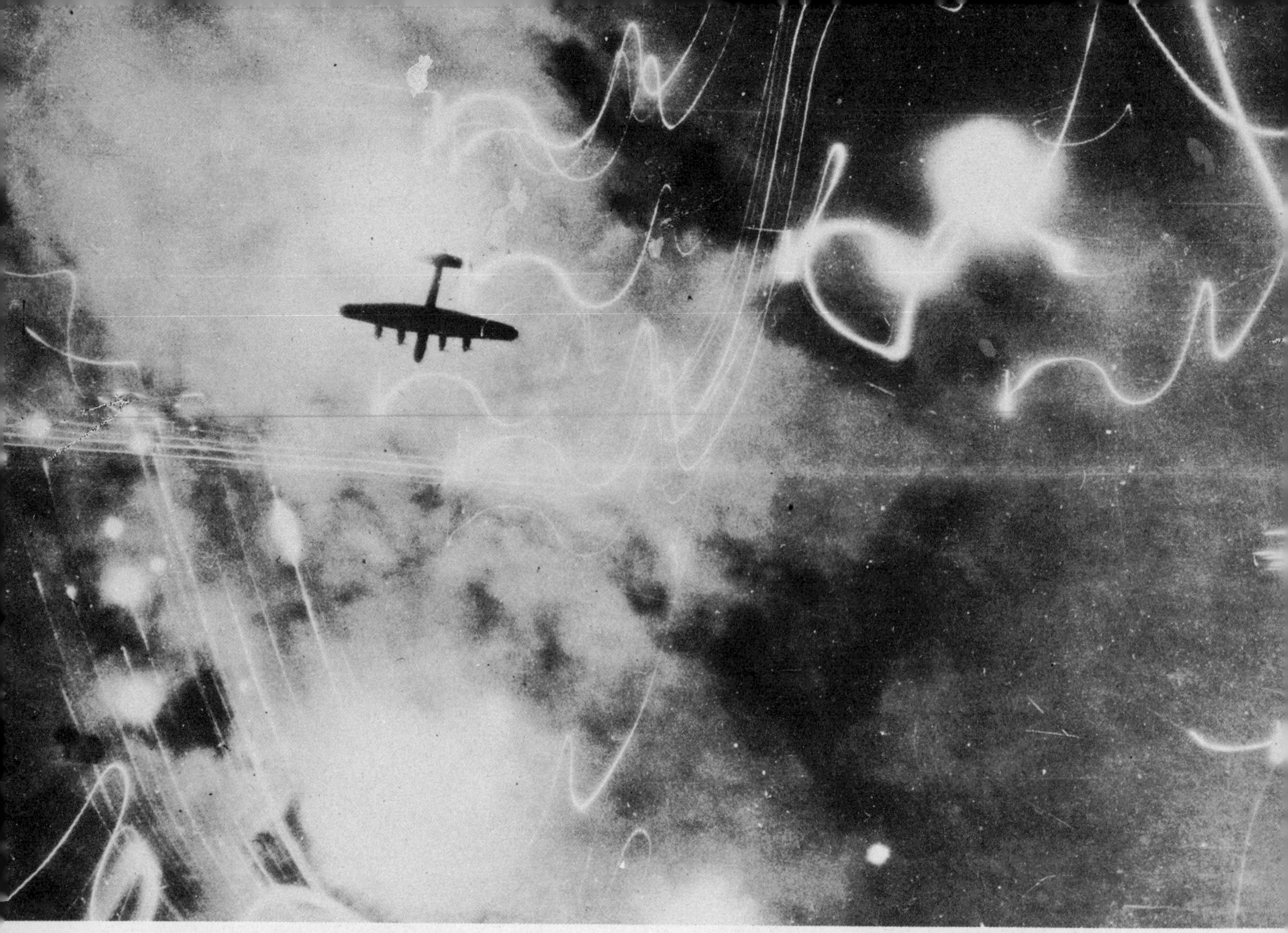

Silhouetted against fire and flak, on a night raid over Hamburg, this Lancaster leads the way for others.

BOMBING 'ROUND THE CLOCK

WITH the Luftwaffe tied up in Russia giant R.A.F. night bombers struck heavier and heavier blows at Nazi Germany in an attempt to force Goering to withdraw planes from the Russian front and to smash the Nazi industrial might. The night raids of the winter were followed by daring, low-level daylight raids on Nazi harbors, plants, and rail junctions in occupied countries. Late in March 1942 the R.A.F., which had grown steadily stronger, began the devastation of the Nazi war-production machinery at

THIS UNUSUAL PICTURE, taken when the R.A.F. raided Nazi-held Vaasgö island, shows bombs exploding on runways of Herdla airport. On May 3, R.A.F. bombers severely damaged Nazi battleships *Gneisenau* and *Scharnhorst* and cruiser *Prince Eugen*. It was Dec. 1943 before the *Scharnhorst* was sunk, in battle with a British fleet unit guarding the Murmansk convoy route.

Boys of the Eagle Squadron relax in the Pilot's Dispersal Hut while waiting for orders to "scramble."

its key points. A series of heavy raids reduced Lubeck and Rostock to ashes: Lubeck was a major Baltic outlet for Nazi supplies going to Finland, while Rostock was both a vital Baltic port and site of the Nazi Heinkel aircraft plants. Devastated streets, like the Lubeck street pictured below, helped bring home to Nazi Germany the meaning of "total war" in the air. In this raid on March 28, 1942, heavy damage was done to vital port installations and great quantities of matériel intended for use against Russia were destroyed by fires raging after the attack. In April, 1942, the R.A.F. began its now famous 1,000-plane raids on German industrial cities. Monster Wellington, Halifax, Stirling bombers roared eastward to converge over one industrial center after another. Thousands of incendiary bombs from the first planes lighted the target for those with the heavy demolition bombs. The glare could be seen for 150 miles. The populace of the Ruhr valley fled. Frantically the Nazis set about moving their factories eastward out of bombing range.

THE COAL-HANDLING PLANT of the Cologne power plant goes up in smoke. Though not as destructive as mass night raids, the daring daylight raids did much to build up morale of conquered peoples. The three-day continuous raiding of Rostock completely destroyed the Heinkel airplane factory there. Mannheim, Stuttgart, Copenhagen, Hamburg, Kiel, Trondheim, Pilsen, Essen were raide repeatedly, as was the entire coast of France and Paris. The pictur below shows devastation of Cologne after it had been hit on consecu tive nights by thousand-plane raids. The cross-shaped building in th left foreground is Cologne's famous Cathedral.

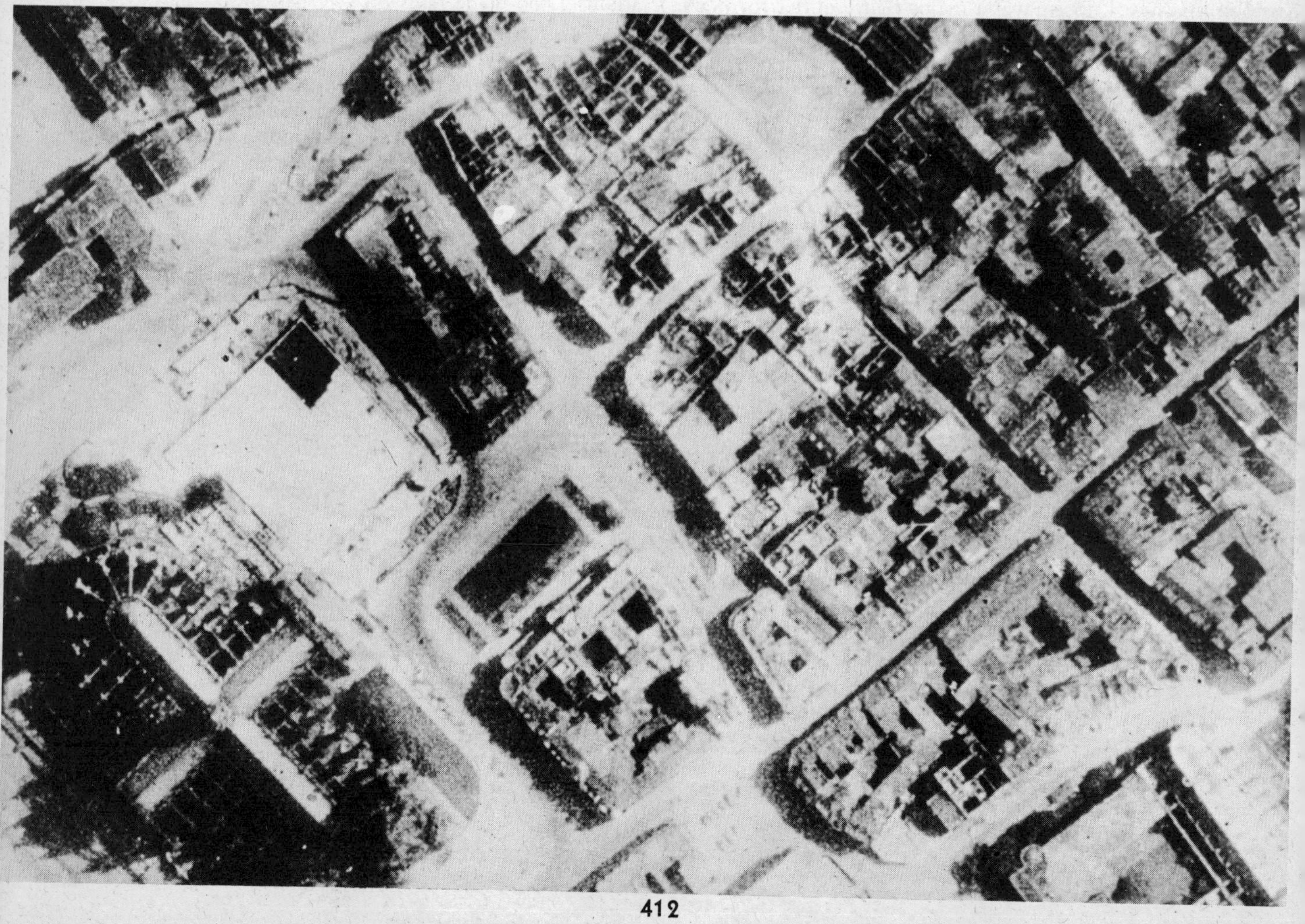

ESE PICTURES SHOW the Renault Works in Paris after they been gutted by R.A.F. raids in March, 1942. Pétain and Laval turned French factories over to Nazi use, and the Renault plant producing tanks for Hitler's spring offensive in Russia. The re-kable picture above shows some of the destruction. The circular object at the top of the photograph is a gas tank. By looking closely one can see some of the unfinished tanks in the extreme lower right corner. The picture below is a close-up of another section of the Renault plant. It shows the smoking ruins and the skeleton sheds that were left after the R.A.F. raid.

Heroic Malta, the most bombed spot on earth, received the "George Cross" award from Britain's King, late summer, 1942.

Allied bombs knocked out Nazi tank obstructio

By the autumn of 1943 mighty streams of U.S. bombers were arriving in Britain. On Mar. 26, 1944, Churchill announced that the U.S. Air Forces actually outnumbered the R.A.F. But it was not numbers alone which counted in this historic partnership of two great air powers; it was the unique circumstance that each air force had developed a special technique which fitted into and complemented the special technique of the other to create a round-the-clock bombing machine such as Goering had never dreamed of when he launched his *Luftwaffe* against England. The R.A.F. excelled in night flying, with "area" or saturation bombing. The U.S. Air Command, having the advantage of the t miraculous Norden bombsight, had prepared its long-r Fortresses and Liberators especially for day flying, with the-spot" or precision bombing. This fortunate combin released over Europe the rain of destruction which w contribute so heavily to Allied victory. The R.A.F. c now go out at night over an industrial or military ta spreading in loose formation to devastate the whole area hour-long avalanches of block-busters, so called because was capable of knocking down a block of buildings. At d the American 8th Air Force could follow the same co

ɪtreets of Sousse in the North African campaign.

Pantelleria's surrender to Allies June 11, 1943, marked first bastion to fall under siege almost entirely from air.

ɪng over in small close formation to drop its bombs from ɔoo feet upon those precise spots in the target which had ɪped liquidation the night before. It was precision bomb- which made it possible to devastate railway yards at ne, in the spring of 1944, without other damage to the ', as is shown in the picture below at the left. At the right, remnants of Cassino, blasted to clear the road to Rome, r shattered witness to "area destruction" wrought by sat- tion bombing. Round-the-clock bombing, aided by the uisition of bases in Italy in the fall of 1943, placed the ch under an aerial siege from which there was to be no respite before the day of "unconditional surrender." The Allied bombing program followed the Nazi production line from points of manufacture to distribution of finished products. Preliminary to invasion, the *Luftwaffe* was as far as possible to be paralyzed at its source. Feb. 13, 1944, marked the opening of a major Allied bombing offensive against aircraft factories, ball-bearing plants and airplane parts centers, now widely dispersed and carefully hidden in the interior. As D-day approached the "bottleneck" air strategy, developed to cripple the Nazi war potential, was applied on an ever widening scale.

THE BATTLE OF BERLIN was opened in Nov. 1943 by heavy, long range night bombers, in an intensive air campaign designed to eliminate this vital nerve center as a functioning part of the Nazi war machine. The picture above shows what air power had done in the following months toward taking Berlin out of the war.

BREACHING OF THE EDER DAM on the night of May 16-17, 1943, revealed new possibilities in aerial warfare. The RAF's daring raid released raging flood waters down the Eder Valley to damage and destroy power plants, factories and industrial installations. In the picture water is still pouring through the gap, racing downstream toward Kassel. In this raid mines were employed instead of bombs.

"You must win the air battle before you can fight : land or sea battle." Those words were spoken by Gen Montgomery, in farewell to the 8th Army before leaving t take up his new command of ground forces preparatory t invasion of the continent in June 1944. "I have never fough a land battle until the air battle was won. I believe that to b the first principle of war." That was also the belief of th Allied High Command around the world. Wherever inva sion was planned, battles were not fought until bombers ha softened up enemy defenses. The air arm had come into it own, over land and sea. The 3-year battering of German wa industry, followed by special concentration against aircraf production, turned to the next step in the process of "soften ing up" for invasion. Key rail points and transportation sys tems, strategic roads and bridges, coast defenses, munitio dumps, tank and truck depots, all were added to the No. list of bombing objectives. The bottleneck strategy, so ef fective against production sources of Nazi war potential, wa applied to communications. With spring, 1944, Allied a activity increased to a concentrated crescendo. The invasio coasts of Europe, Nazi air fields in France, Holland an Belgium, all were blasted by heavier and more destructiv block busters. Allied air force over Europe was now so tre mendous that a number of large-scale air expeditions coul be sent out at the same time, over widely scattered target In desperate efforts to protect war plants, the *Luftwaffe* sac rificed many planes it could not afford to lose, with invasio looming darkly upon the horizon.

NEWEST NAZI "Revenge Weapon"—Vergeltunswaffen—plunges toward some quiet English home, death and destruction in its wake.

V-WEAPONS

The insert above shows an air reconnaissance picture snapped by the R.A.F. on Nov. 8, 1943. When it was checked by a WAAF, she discovered a queer-looking ridge (arrowed), a launching ramp with a "fly-bomb" already in position. The site of the picture was a Nazi experimental station at Peenemunde on the Baltic. Despite repeated R.A.F. bombing of this and other stations, the experiments went on —but the launching had been delayed past D-day, too late to turn the tide of the war. Rather, it had the opposite effect. Amazing new weapons had become almost a commonplace in World War II, but it had remained for the Nazis to outdo even their own record in wanton destructiveness. When their long-threatened "secret weapon" smashed into England on June 12, 1944, from some mysterious launching point, the last faint hope of "soft peace" for Germany flew into as many fragments as the robot itself. The ever tolerant British had let themselves almost forget the horrors of the *Blitz* of 1940. Sure of ultimate victory, the British could discuss comparative merits of mild or bitter peace terms—but not after that June day when once again the Nazi revealed his evil hand. Serving no military purpose, these "Revenge Weapons," V-1 and V-2, destroyed homes, hospitals, schools, killed thousands, before the advancing Yanks and Tommies could root out launching sites across the channel. Still they came, from more distant sites, while the Nazis boasted of a forthcoming "V-3" which would speed across the Atlantic to blow up New York.

"SHUTTLE BOMBING" gave Allied planes new striking power. With the great Italian airbase at Foggia in Allied hands, Sept. 17, 1943, planes could make the long hop to Rumanian oilfields, drop their bombs, then go on to new nearby bases in Russia to reload and refuel for another raid on the way back. In June, 1944, a new shuttle technique carried a fleet of planes from England to attack Berlin, fly on to Russia, raid oil targets in Poland, stop over in Italy, fly home again to Britain. Above is the finale of an air battle on the road to Ploesti's oil fields. In the picture below King Michael inspects the ruins of the once-great refineries which had supplied a vital part of the special gasoline which kept the *Luftwaffe* in the air. Hammered by incessant Allied raids, the destruction of the fields helped force Rumania out of the war, Aug. 23.

MEN OF A FLYING FORTRESS CREW battle to save their blazing ship. The "snow" in the picture is fire-smothering foam which blankets the men as they spray it over the bomber. It took 20 minutes and 12,000 gallons of foam to save their plane. The picture below shows the flight deck of a carrier shepherding a convoy through dangerous waters. Dramatic rise of the carrier to a dominant position in the fleet parallels rising importance of air power in modern warfare. Close co-operation between land, sea, air forces requires use of carriers to an extent foreseen by few military experts before World War II. Wherever convoys travel, wherever invasion impends, the carriers are there—from majestic "flat-tops" of the battlefleet, swarming with planes, to "baby flat-tops" with improvised flight decks and only a few small planes.

AIR WAR PLAYED A MAJOR ROLE in the South Pacific where vast distances stretched between island bases. At the time of Pearl Harbor, in Dec. 1941, the U.S. had one carrier in the South Pacific—in 1943 there were a hundred of them, their planes ever on the alert. In the picture above an A-20 is shown "skip-bombing" a Japanese freighter headed for New Guinea. In this technique a plane flying perilously close to the surface "skips" a bomb along the water until it strikes the ship's side. Below, in one of our finest examples of aerial photography, is an island in the Tarawa group after a terrific cannonade and aerial bombardment by U.S. ships and planes. Despite the havoc from explosives, the entrenched Japanese rose from pill boxes and fought almost to the last man in one of the most bloody battles in the Pacific.

"COOLIE" MEANS "BITTER STRENGTH." It has taken bitter strength—and bitter toil—to build the roads that bring in supplies to China's armies and the airfields their Allies' planes must use. Inch by inch, foot by foot, acre by acre, a field grows under the magic of thousands of willing hands. With only hand-made tools and a few pony carts, Chinese men, women and children have moved tons of boulders, crushed them, paved the runways, turned out the fields from which B-29 Superfortresses could take off to bomb Japanese industry. The plane in the picture below is over *Yawata*, the "Pittsburgh of Japan"; the target of this daylight attack is the "Japan Iron Manufacturing Co.," largest steel plant in the nation. Bombing results of this third attack on Yawata by Superfortresses were officially described as "good."

FOOD FOR STARVING WAR-TORN MILLIONS is a major preoccupation of the United Nations. At their conference on food and agriculture held in Hot Springs, Va., in the spring of 1943, an Interim Food Commission was appointed to function until plans for a permanent body could be worked out and approved. Meanwhile United Nations' Relief and Rehabilitation Administration (UNRRA) continues to arrange for distribution of all goods.

ONE WORLD

THE DEATH of Wendell L. Willkie on Oct. 8, 1944, came with a shock of personal loss to people of many nations who had come to think of him both as a friend and as a crusader in the cause of international understanding and co-operation. Returned from his globe-girdling tour in 1942, he formulated through his writings and speeches a creed for Americans. He had seen for himself that from the advent of the radio and the airplane distance had vanished from the face of the earth. Physically, Chungking was closer to New York than Chicago had once been, and after the war, new jet-propulsion planes would bring Paris almost within commuting range. For better or for worse, in war or in peace, the globe had become "*One World*" and nothing henceforth could alter that fundamental fact. With so little distinction between "near" and "far," Willkie visualized for his country a great responsibility which was at the same time a great opportunity. In his own words: "We are not living in several worlds. Our small American farms, our huge American factories, have close bonds with what is produced in the Andes and the hills of Szechuan, with the complex trade mechanism of London, with the cargoes that sail from Bombay and Oslo and Melbourne. Whatever we do at home constitutes foreign policy. Whatever we do abroad constitutes domestic policy. This is the great new political fact. . . . All the world is looking to us to set the pattern of the future."

WENDELL L. WILLKIE, liberal, political "amateur," entered the 1940 Presidential race without "professional" party backing, yet polled the largest popular vote ever given a Republican candidate. On his world trip in 1942 he became unofficial Ambassador of Good Will from America to every country he visited. Everywhere he went he made friends. Above he is shown with President Lin Sen of China.

THE MONETARY CONFERENCE AT BRETTON WOODS, N. H. in Sept. 1944, was an expression of United Nations' determination not to have repetitions in the post-war world of scenes like this one, when unemployment riots in U.S. cities had to be broken up with tear gas. The conference planned world economic stabilization through an International Monetary Fund and an International Bank.

DUMBARTON OAKS MARKED the first step in a United Nations' program to make sure that history should not repeat itself in a third world war growing out of World War II. Meeting in Sept., 1944, in Virginia, the conference agreed on fundamentals of plans for lasting peace. Above, U.S. troops in the Army of Occupation march out of Coblenz after World War I, when America refused to join her former Allies recognizing the League of Nations, thus helping to sow the seeds of another war.

LENINGRAD DOUBTLESS FOUND good use for the metal in these piles of Nazi helmets. Never before had such mountains of matériel fallen to the victors as in the Nazis' 1944 spring retreat.

THE PENDULUM SWINGS IN RUSSIA

RUSSIA'S winter campaign in 1943-44 was even more spectacular than those which had already amazed her Allies, – and the Axis. The mounting strength of the Red Armies kept pace with the ebbing of the *Wehrmacht*. It was clear that defense psychology no longer played any part in Russian planning, but was becoming the sole property of Nazis, who had arrogantly refused to include the strategy of retreat in their military manuals. With bold decisiveness the Red Army ignored lengthening supply lines, ignored autumn rivers of mud that had been roads in summer, pressed on after retreating Nazis, giving them no time to rest, no time to consolidate positions, pushing them back to the Dnieper. Behind the Dnieper lay the Leningrad Railway, linking Nazi forces north and south, and the great base of Minsk, heart and nerve center of Nazi supply lines. The front extended from Leningrad down to Kiev, then followed the Dnieper, around its deep bend to the Black Sea. That deep bend was an invitation to encirclement, as the bend of the Don, before Stalingrad, had been a year before. From the direction of Poltava the Red Army smashed toward Uman. Overwhelmed in the Cherkassy area, surrounded, cut off, floundering in February's snow and ice, the Nazi 8th Army fought desperately but in vain. Supported by *Stormovik* planes, by Cossack cavalry, the Red Army rode the retreating Nazis down without mercy. Nazi planes from von Mannstein's armies farther south dropped leaflets to encircled troops promising "Help near"—but *Stormoviks* dropped leaflets too, saying "Position hopeless." As usual the Russians were the truer prophets. Not even Viking SS troops could stand up under the Russian punishment. They fought until there were only a few thousand to surrender, leaving miles of Ukrainian steppes littered with dead men and abandoned equipment. Farther north a second phase of the Red offensive was pounding at Vitebsk and Pskov, while at the lower rim of the huge steel circle flung about von Mannstein, between Uman and Odessa, the Russians took Nikopol (Feb. 8), source of half Germany's supply of manganese, and on Feb. 22 Krivoi Rog, in the copper-coal-iron ore region. By this time spring had brought the usual deep thaws—but not the usual expected stalemate. Again the Russians gave the Nazis no breathing space. They put broad special treads on all motorized equipment for navigation through mud, used cavalry and horse-drawn transport—and kept right on encircling bogged-down Nazis, smashing ahead toward Rumania. The Nazi 6th Army was wiped out. By mid-March, 24 Nazi divisions had suffered fatal decimation. The Nazis had to face the fact that the Ukraine was lost. By Mar. 25, 1944, the Red Army had raced across Bessarabia, blocking Nazi escape routes from the Ukraine, to stand for the first time on a boundary they had held when the Nazi invasion began.

ONE OF THE SITES SELECTED BY NAZIS for a cemetery was in front of Alexandrovsky Palace, a favorite home of the tzars at Tzarskoe Selo (now called Pushkin), not far from Leningrad which was then St. Petersburg. The town, turned into a miniature fortress by Nazis, was freed when the corridor surrounding Leningrad was at last cleared of the enemy on Jan. 27, 1944, after Novgorod had fallen to the Red Army on Jan. 20, and Staraya Russa on Feb. 18. The picture below illustrates the wanton vandalism of exponents of Nazi "*Kultur*." The statues they have left in fragments had been parts of the monument erected at Novgorod to commemorate the 1,000th anniversary of the Russian State. Wherever the Nazi blight passed in Russia, libraries and museums were burned, treasures of art and science destroyed or stolen, in addition to the countless millions of defenseless civilians ground under the conqueror's ruthless heel.

APRIL SAW DESPERATE NAZIS in Odessa trying frantically to evacuate their garrison and equipment. Besieged from without, harassed from within by guerrillas hidden away in the city's catacombs, the last of the defenders fled on April 10, 1944, while victorious Russians moved in to find the port a scene of utter destruction (*below*). On April 8 a Crimean offensive was launche[d] With a thunderous artillery barrage an[d] waves of dive bombers, it took only thre[e] days' fighting to carry Red forces to th[e]

se line at the base of the Crimea, while
he forces (*above*) from the Kerch pen-
tip closed in on Kerch, taking it April
44.

ODESSA LEARNS ABOUT THE "NEW ORDER"

THIS YOUNG WOMAN OF ODESSA is obviously happy as she rips off the board bearing the world's most hated name, secure in her faith that the Red Army will never again allow Hitler's name to deface her street or Hitler's idolaters to pollute her city.

THE GESTAPO ALWAYS RUNS TRUE TO FORM. This dreadful scene shows bodies of Odessa citizens burned alive in the compound of the Nazi Gestapo and their Rumanian confederates, the Siguranza. Scars like this take more than one generation to heal.

A SUPER JUNK-YARD FOR SUPERMEN. Odessa's streets were almost impassable because of the battle-field wreckage brought in by her Nazi masters from the surrounding countryside and dumped without rhyme or reason into the streets of the city.

Nazis came into Russia, riding proudly in fleets of mighty tanks—got out any way they could!

BLITZKRIEG IN REVERSE

FRESH from victories at Odessa and Kerch in April, 1944, the Red Army poured into the Crimea. Nazi and Rumanian defenders fell back to Sevastopol, were driven out on May 9. Mighty Russia had at last hurled the invaders back to borders they had treacherously violated almost three years before, had battled her way through to her much-needed sea ports, and her speed showed no sign of slackening. Russian engineers performed miracles restoring transport lines as fast as territory was retaken. Supplies from the U.S. and Britain increased steadily as the Murmansk sea-route became safer. Large bodies of Nazi troops were tied to the Italian front, the air-blitz against Germany was daily reaching a more furious pace, while over uneasy Nazi heads hung the shadow of major invasion in the west. On June 6, 1944, that shadow became grim reality. The Allies invaded Normandy, in force. On June 9 the Russians launched a drive against Finland's Mannerheim Line, prelude to a Russian summer offensive that was to out-*blitzkrieg* anything Nazis had ever accomplished in the days of their most colossal success. In a series of swift co-ordinated blows, aimed at the chief bastions of the Nazis' stolen empire, four powerful Soviet armies estimated at 1,000,000 men were speeding across White Russia toward Poland. In one week the Red Army had stormed throug Nazi barriers, killing or capturing 183,000 enemy tr Their losses were 30,000 a day, as Red forces pushe toward Minsk, at a pace of 20 to 24 miles a day. Fro Baltic to the Carpathians—the longest active land front world—the Red Army was driving the Nazis before it first time anything like this had ever befallen the m *Wehrmacht*. By the end of July Soviet vanguards we miles from Warsaw, 385 miles from Berlin. Many citie been taken, including Brest Litovsk in the Kovel secto Lwow in Galicia, one of the largest rail centers in Eu The Bug River had been crossed, one spearhead had re the Vistula, another had driven to the suburbs of Wa The month of July, 1944, had proved to be the grimme experienced by the Nazis in the whole of World War I August 15 Nazis brave enough to look eastward saw an darker picture. In the north, trapped by a corridor d through Latvia to the sea, west of Riga, Nazi forces being ground to annihilation by Red Armies. Below Pskov they were driven back into Estonia. In the center great battle lines stretching down through Poland fighting was in progress around Warsaw, while Polish u

"MOST IMPREGNABLE LINE IN THE WORLD," the Finnish Mannerheim Line was called. But the Red Army breached it in June, 1944, taking Viipuri on the 20th. The Russians had also recaptured a 150-mile enemy-held section of the Leningrad-Murmansk railroad which enabled them to ship supplies landed at the port of Murmansk directly to Leningrad. On the Karelian side of the front Russians had gained the whip hand. Finland would not be able to stand up much longer against Russian and Allied pressure.

THE GIANT UPPER PAW OF THE RUSSIAN BEAR crushed down upon Nazi-occupied Minsk on July 3, 1944, then hacked and slashed on to cut the railway line at Vilna. 150,000 Nazis were trapped at Minsk. Scores of Red bombers were blasting the roads to Vilna and Köenigsberg, to Bialystock and Brest Litovsk. Above, residents of liberated Minsk watch their homes burning, fired by Nazis as they left. Below, Red Army machine gunners help clear Vitebsk of the enemy before Russian troops move in, June 26, 1944.

ad joined the struggle. In the , Russian troops had reached ow, ancient capital of Poland, other Reds captured Sambor, r of communications lines open- ve possible routes to Czechoslo- n oil fields. In a Nazi order e day Field Marshal von Model "Fear of tanks, fear of encircle- incessant retreating and such like otions of those weak in spirit and estations of cowardice that must nd room in the heart of a German r." At almost the same time a n communique read, "There is ubt that fear of tanks and fear of clement are at present organic es of the Germans . . . and the er of wavering soldiers and offi- n the German Army will grow every day despite the appeals and s of Field Marshal Model."

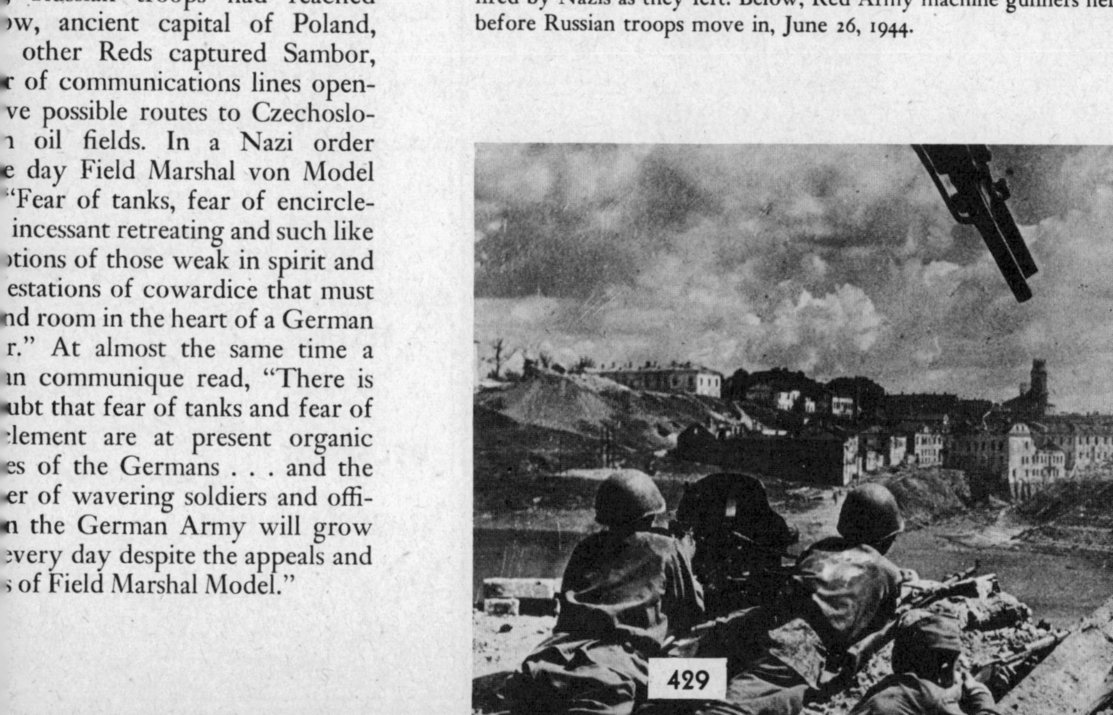

RUSSIA RESURGENT

In the continuing offensives of 1944 the Red Army had proved its staying power as well as its superior leadership. Its magnificent strategy had been improved, perfected—constant use of surprise and mobility developed to an unparalleled degree. The Stalingrad tactical pattern—the swift outflanking thrust of encirclement to cut rear communications, combined with massed frontal assault from infantry, tanks, artillery—was repeated on an ever larger scale, always with flashing speed, with deadly brilliance in execution and timing. Military results had been spectacular. Along "roads back," from 2,000 miles of front, wreckage of costly Nazi equipment littered the countryside. Columns of Nazi prisoners—ragged, unwashed, hungry, tired—testified to the headlong Russian pace overtaking fleeing Nazis, brushing them griml from the map of Russia. Now in August of 1944 Soviet Ru sia was to try her skill in the political as well as the militar arena, with one objective—a protective ring of friendly stat between her and the country whose armies had twice in generation invaded Russian territory. On Aug. 21, 1944, th Red Army struck with great power on the Rumanian fron On the 23rd young King Michael dramatically announce Rumania's decision to join the Allies. Within a week Russia advance through the Balkans had changed the entire polit cal and military picture there, and the Red Army was racin for the Ploesti oil fields, pushing into Transylvania, thrustin toward Yugoslavia. Russia's declaration of war against Bu

THE MUTUAL ASSISTANCE PACT between the U.S.S.R. and the Czechoslovak Republic, signed on Dec. 12, 1943, marked full emergence of Soviet Russia as a political power in Europe. Above, Gen. Svoboda, commander of Czechoslovak troops in Russia, signs a message to the oppressed Slavs of Europe.

THIS VETERAN OF AN EARLIER BULGARIAN WAR (1877) talks to a young Soviet officer in Sofia about those days when a Russian Army liberated Bulgaria from foreign domination and helped her become a state. In 1944 Russia again helped Bulgaria —this time by forcing her to throw off the yoke of Nazi slavery.

garia brought that country in a hurry to the anti-Axis side. By Sept. 10, 1944, Red troops had joined Tito's Yugoslav Partisans and Allied forces in a drive to trap Nazi armies in Greece and Bulgaria. Now, Finland became the third Axis satellite to come into the fold, signing peace terms with Russia on Sept. 19, while a new Red offensive in the north was driving the Nazis out of Estonia, sealing escape routes, taking Tallinn, capital and chief port of Estonia. All the way along the line Red Armies advanced, converging on Budapest, crossing the Vistula to establish contact with the Polish Gen. Bor still defying Nazi might in beleaguered Warsaw. October brought high lights and drama. On the 13th Riga, Latvian capital, fell while Red sea-and-land forces drove the Nazis out of Petsamo, Finnish naval base they had still held. Now for the Red Army all roads led to East Prussia. Drives were aimed at Mazurian Lake regions, at Memel, at Tilsit where Czar Alexander had once met Napoleon on a raft in the Niemen River to sign a treaty with terms most humiliating to Russia. On Oct. 15 Nazis seized the Hungarian capital, while Red Armies were taking Szeged and the Transylvanian capital Cluj. By mid-November activity had flattened out into a period of suspense on both eastern and western fronts. The Soviets had settled down to the job of clearing Nazis out of East Hungary to broaden a base for attack on Budapest while waiting for the strategic moment to drive into East Prussia. World attention was focused now on the dramatic return of U.S. Gen. MacArthur to the Philippines on Oct. 19, and the opening of phase three in the offensive on the widening western front, where the Allies prepared to hurl from 3 to 4 million troops against Hitler's Fortress Germania.

THE FREE GERMANY COMMITTEE was made up of Soviet prisoners-of-war who under Soviet sponsorship broadcast appeals to their countrymen to rise against the baleful cult of Hitlerism. Third from the left is Lt. Count Heinrich von Einsiedel, great-grandson of the famous Bismarck.

SCRAPING BOTTOM OF THE MAN-POWER BARREL, to meet the threat to East Prussia from fast-driving Red Armies, Nazis drafted everybody from "Hitler Jugend" to the lame, halt and blind. Here they are waiting for a train to take them to the job of digging defense trenches somewhere in East Prussia.

GERMANS LEAVE MESSAGES on city walls. Communication lines cut, postal service overstrained by years of war and disregard of the individual's needs by the dictators, civilians have to tell their friends that they are still alive by means of notes chalked on the ruins of homes.

INSIDE GERMANY

"INSIDE Germany" – two words connoting a riddle to which nobody really knows the answer. Neutral travelers cheerfully give interviews in Stockholm or Ankara. But what do they say? Nothing that we can really depend upon. Bombed-out squares are walled off or repaired with tremendous speed, to give the impression that nothing has happened. Those in whom the Germans are interested are offered the best, in order to show that the people are not suffering. Whoever has seen behind the veil, even though a neutral, is warned that if he talks he cannot hope to escape the Gestapo dragnet. One fact has become clear, however– the German people have grown weary of a *krieg* which is not a *blitzkrieg* any more. It is not only the frightening Gestapo which keeps them from revolting. Each of them knows that he shares the guilt of cruelty toward those in the overrun countries or toward foreign workers enslaved inside Germany. Conquered countries, counted upon as granaries, do not produce any more, and the German diet, too, although much better fare than that of any enslaved people, consists mostly of vegetables and potatoes. At the front, "supermen" started to surrender, but soon the fear of being shot in the back on the spot made this a poor alternative. Today we know that the Hitler gang will destroy not only the spirit, but all life inside Germany as well, wherever and whenever the Allies approach their soil.

MARKET DAY IN BERLIN. Against the background of a bombed-out building – one of Germany's most fashionable department stores – the empty benches of the vendors show that Hitler's promises of a well-fed people are gone with the wind.

THE BRANDENBURGER SQUARE – symbol of Prussian pride is now a mass of waste. German women set up a mobile canteen.

Behind the barbed wire of the ill-reputed concentration camp in Dachau, near Munich.

Concentration camps were originally an English institution, established to unite at one location a mass of foreigners from the country with which a nation was at war. They were foes, but non-combatants, forced to live together to prevent their giving aid and comfort to the enemy. They were maintained like human beings. Today there is no word—no institution—in all Europe more dreaded than the concentration camp. Hardly had Hitler come to power on January 30, 1933, when concentration camps were established, large and small, dotting the country. Prisoners were herded in, crowded together. At first it was only the opponents of the régime, labeled "Communists," from the lowliest to a member of the Diet, who were sent to these camps. But soon it changed. Any Nazi, feeling a grievance against even the most honorable citizen, found it easy to wreak vengeance by having him sent to a camp. There the sadistic guards revived Egyptian slavery practices to get the last ounce of work from the prisoners—work which lacked that usefulness to the community which was so highly lauded by Hitler. Mansions were built by this slave labor for Nazi leaders, play courts erected for their children—day after day, twelve hours a day. Each of the camps contained its torture chambers, where prisoners had their nails torn out—where they were burned—beaten—where they became wrecks. But the information the Gestapo was seeking almost never was given. In their blind rage they tortured the innocent, who accepted their fate rather than betray their compatriots. Here were found the gas chambers where millions of Jewish people were exterminated. Here many thousands of silent and innocent heroes of the conquered countries found their end. Many of their relatives have never been informed of their fate, while others received sarcastic requests from Hitler's men for contributions in order that they might get the ashes in a little wooden box.

"OUR WALLS ARE BROKEN BUT NOT OUR HEARTS," is the translation of the sign on the wall of this shattered building. With slogans like this the Nazi soldiers desperately try to prevent the collapse of their followers' morale.

ALLIED BOMBERS CARRY THE FIGHT to a people who were promised that they never would see enemy planes. But city after city is being bombed and Nazi war production crippled, thus giving the Nazis a dose of their own early medicine. Note that under a dictatorship the injured and homeless are attended by the police – not by Red Cross or other social workers.

ROBBERY AND LOOTING became the creed of Nazi Germany. Here Hitler and Himmler enjoy a painting filched from an occupied country. Goering is reported to have turned Karin Hall on his country estate into an art gallery.

DOES HIMMLER TAKE OVER?

IN JULY, 1944, the world received definite proof that all was not well between Hitler and his Army, through an abortive attempt on his life, engineered by high-ranking Junker officers. It had been known there was a rift between the SS troops and the regular Army, which had been subordinated to the common cause until things began to go badly on the military fronts. Meantime, the German officers had never forgotten their classical tradition that lives must never be sacrificed unnecessarily or without military advantage. The enormously costly Russian campaign, combined with the fact that Hitler personally dictated the entire battle strategy in an unmilitary, wasteful, and mystical manner, drove the old-line Army generals into open revolt. They felt that Hitler was leading Germany to catastrophe. Stimulated by the broadcast of the Free German Committee in Russia, they attempted to assassinate Hitler as the first step toward taking over the country. A badly shaken *Fuehrer* immediately ordered a *putsch* which killed, disgraced, or shuffled around many of the outstanding Army leaders—thus mastering the threatening revolution. Himmler was appointed Chief of the *Wehrmacht* inside the Reich, assuring Nazi Party domination of the Army and at the same time checking Hitler's interference in purely military affairs.

HIMMLER VISITS FRANCO to bring the little puppet back into the German orbit. Aware the Germans thought he owed a large debt, Franco knew the sympathies of his countrymen were with the Allies. He gradually changed his non-belligerent status on the Axis side to so-called strict neutrality. Nevertheless, the Allies had to employ economic pressure to curb his sending of vital materials to Hitler's factories.

SHORTLY BEFORE HIS FALL, Mussolini appealed to Hitler for aid. Assisted by his son-in-law, Ciano, he tried to persuade the Germans to send divisions of men to help defend Italy against Allied invasion; also to send food for his countrymen starving to death since he sold them out to the Nazis, who were careful to feed themselves but not the Italians.

GENERAL HOEPPNER tried and found guilty of "the most cowardly and indecent crime in German history"—the attempted liberation of the world from Hitler and all the things for which Hitler and Fascism stood.

British Tommies land June 6, 1944, on the Normandy beaches from which William the Conqueror sailed away to invade Englan

"THE BATTLE will be bloody, for the English will never yield; and though driven back and thrown into confusion they will always return to fight as long as they have a breath of life." So wrote a Venetian Ambassador, in France, to his Doge in Venice in 1588. It might easily have been one, Erwin Rommel, writing from France to his Fuehrer in Berlin, in 1944. That same Montgomery who had staged the longest "fox hunt" on record when he chased the "Desert Fox" for 1,400 miles along the coast of North Africa, was landing now on the shores of France with vastly greater resources in men, equipment, armor. The American Gen. Eisenhower, once more in supreme command of Allied armies, had with him gifted leaders who had learned the lesson of teamwork on lesser fronts. At the right, these leaders are pictured as follows: seated, left to right, Air Chief Marshal Tedder, Deputy Commander; Gen. Eisenhower, Supreme Commander; Gen. Montgomery, Commander-in-Chief British Group of Armies; standing, Lt. Gen. Bradley, Senior Commander U. S. Ground Force; Adm. Ramsay, Allied Naval Commander; Air Chief Marshal Leigh-Mallory, Air Commander-in-Chief; Lt. Gen. Walter B. Smith, Chief of Staff Supreme Headquarters. Under their leadership began the long awaited Allied invasion of the Continent—the real Second Front.

The "brain trust" of the invasion.

D-DAY

Four years after Dunkerque, another kind of D-day saw the world's mightiest armada draw near the coasts of France.

AMERICA'S "SECRET WEAPONS" go into action. Massive jaws of a Coast Guard LST (Landing Ship, Tanks) spew out British motorized equipment onto the flat deck of a low-riding "Rhino," portable dock, while Coast Guard gun crews on the LST watch for N bombers. The tanks and loaded trucks emerging from the hold roll to posts at the fighting front in Normandy.

-FABRICATED harbors (*right*) insured
of supplies to Allied armies. Picture
vs pier leading to a wharf with concrete
kwater beyond.

Roadways appear as if by magic, as long lines of men and materiel stream ashore at a beach in Normandy.

THE BATTLE OF THE BEACHES

"THE HISTORY of war does not show any such undertaking so broad in conception, so grandiose in scale, and so masterly in execution." This was the tribute of Josef Stalin to the greatest invasion of all. Stalin knew well what all fighting men know, that no other military hazard is so great as sea-borne invasion against a fortified and defended coast. He knew, too, as did invasion leaders, that for months the Nazis had used their best skill to make the coasts of France impregnable. There had been no secret about these preparations. Herr Goebbels had loaded the news channels of the world with propaganda designed to chill the ardor of "decadent" democracies for the perils of invasion. The beaches, shouted (through both words and pictures) would be a long chain of death to any foe rash enough to attempt a la ing. Invaders would be hurled back with hardly a man to tell the tale. In the face of this, U. S. Gen. Bradley, shor before D-day, spoke to his troops in Britain, waiting word to go. "This talk about 90% casualties," he said, tommyrot . . . I'll see you on the beaches." And he did. G Bradley knew what even the shrewdest Nazi generals did —the extent and completeness of Allied planning for D-d probably the most detailed and far-reaching that had e preceded any kind of military operation. The little island Britain was weighted with men and their complex mod equipment. Gen. Eisenhower and his advisors had taken heart every lesson learned in "blood, tears, and sweat" in Pacific, in North Africa, and in Italy. They were ready w "something new under the sun" in the way of amphibi landings—something which would amaze the world and st

Men of French 2nd Armored Division join in liberating France.

zi prophets of Allied doom. In the early morning light of t forever memorable day of June 6, 1944, France awoke, er 4 years of bitter rebellion against all-powerful Nazi sters, to find the tide which had ebbed so tragically at Dunque sweeping back upon the coast of Normandy. It was a ghty tide of Allied power, released against Hitler's "imgnable" fortress of Europe, to beat against its bastions, to each its defenses, to sweep onward across France, freeing from her long nightmare of "collaboration" and shame der the edicts of the Pétain-Laval clique at Vichy, to reach outer barriers of that magic fortification-circle which the ny Nazi self-made god-of-battles had flung about the sacred of his 3rd Reich. All through the night the armada of ps, 4,000 strong, converging from every direction, moved toward the beaches. Battleships and transports carried the edition safely through mine fields cleared out of the rough ter by daring minesweepers. First ground assault waves nt in at 6.30 A.M. in full daylight, while the big naval guns pounded away at enemy shore batteries and hissing rockets hurtled overhead. Together with amphibious tanks, the rocket craft appeared for the first time in this invasion, and the vital role played by naval bombardment was as great a surprise to the world as was the extraordinary display of new amphibious landing craft. Some landings were immediately successful. Others met with heavy fighting and bitter losses in men, assault boats and equipment, blown up by mines or mowed down by mortars and machine guns on the bluffs. Nazi guns poured their hate upon landing ships as they let down their ramps. Vicious crossfire pinned down troops trying to find shelter in foxholes, making their position precarious in the extreme, as in the case of those Americans who landed east of the Vire estuary. Soon beaches were strewn with mine-wrecked bull-dozers, with landing craft piled up along heavy wire entanglements and concrete barriers—still, more men, more vehicles, more guns, more tanks moved steadily toward battered shores.

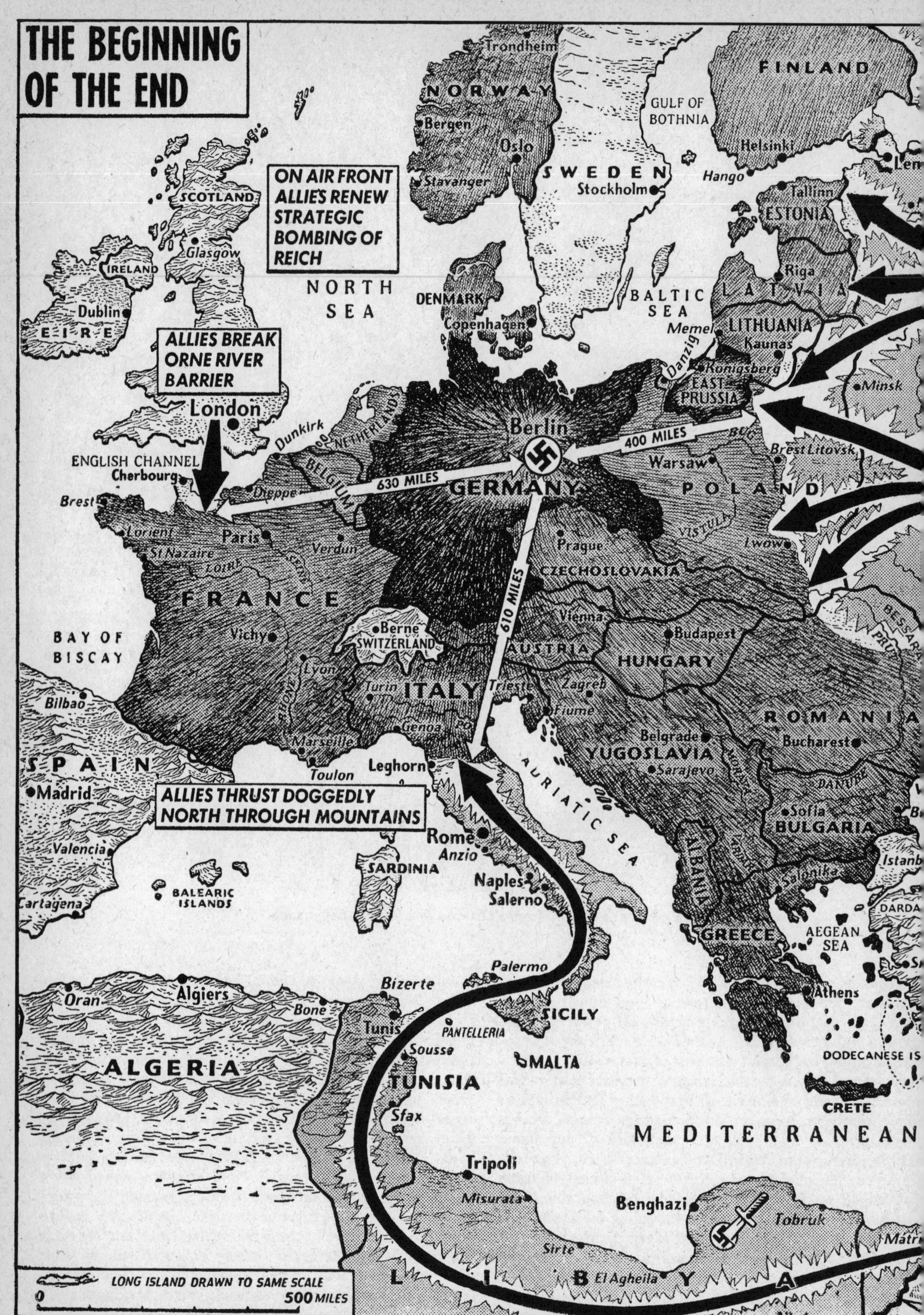
THE BEGINNING OF THE END
ON AIR FRONT ALLIES RENEW STRATEGIC BOMBING OF REICH
ALLIES BREAK ORNE RIVER BARRIER
ALLIES THRUST DOGGEDLY NORTH THROUGH MOUNTAINS
630 MILES
400 MILES
610 MILES
NORWAY
SWEDEN
FINLAND
SCOTLAND
IRELAND
EIRE
NORTH SEA
DENMARK
BALTIC SEA
GULF OF BOTHNIA
ESTONIA
LATVIA
LITHUANIA
EAST PRUSSIA
GERMANY
POLAND
CZECHOSLOVAKIA
FRANCE
SWITZERLAND
AUSTRIA
HUNGARY
ROMANIA
YUGOSLAVIA
BULGARIA
ALBANIA
GREECE
ITALY
SPAIN
ENGLISH CHANNEL
BAY OF BISCAY
ADRIATIC SEA
AEGEAN SEA
MEDITERRANEAN
SARDINIA
BALEARIC ISLANDS
SICILY
MALTA
PANTELLERIA
CRETE
DODECANESE IS
ALGERIA
TUNISIA
LIBYA
Trondheim
Bergen
Oslo
Stavanger
Stockholm
Helsinki
Hango
Tallinn
Riga
Memel
Kaunas
Danzig
Konigsberg
Minsk
Glasgow
Dublin
London
Dunkirk
Cherbourg
Brest
Dieppe
Lorient
St Nazaire
Paris
Verdun
Vichy
Lyon
Marseille
Toulon
Copenhagen
Berlin
Warsaw
Brest Litovsk
Lwow
Prague
Vienna
Budapest
Berne
Turin
Genoa
Trieste
Zagreb
Fiume
Belgrade
Sarajevo
Bucharest
Sofia
Salonika
Athens
Leghorn
Rome
Anzio
Naples
Salerno
Palermo
Bilbao
Madrid
Valencia
Cartagena
Oran
Algiers
Bone
Bizerte
Tunis
Sousse
Sfax
Tripoli
Misurata
Sirte
El Agheila
Benghazi
Tobruk
LONG ISLAND DRAWN TO SAME SCALE
0
500 MILES

On the beaches of Normandy, under the impact of magnificently co-ordinated attack by land, sea, and air—including the new techniques for airborne troops, and sea landings without benefit of conventional harbor facilities – the over-extended *Wehrmacht* felt itself reeling again, this time in the west. Thrown back already a continent's length in the east and south, those French beaches were the arrogant Nazis' last hope of holding, against flood-tides of power sweeping in upon them from every direction. Once more the Seer of Berchtesgaden had been betrayed by his intuition. Surprise attack was possible, because he had failed, in his frantic guessing game, to uncover the mystery of where the Allies would strike first, clinging to the old belief that armies must have harbors to land in force. Allied leaders were open to conviction because they were plunged into war which made sea-borne landings imperative for them, docks or no. After experiments in Africa, Sicily, the Pacific, they settled down to turning out the huge, incredible fleet—every type and size of invasion craft—seagoing, but capable of putting men and heavy equipment ashore on any coast with never before dreamed-of speed. That was the thing which made huge-scale surprise invasions possible, just as the new Nazi *Panzers* had made their revolutionary type of *blitzkrieg* possible in 1939. Without plenty of these ungainly amphibious craft which no one had even thought of until after Hitler had plunged a whole world into war, the western Allies could never have taken the offensive, would have had little chance of victory either in the Atlantic or Pacific. A thousand technical problems were solved by joint Allied ingenuity; tremendous mass production was achieved in America by prefabricating sections in inland cities; and before the all-wise Axis knew what was going on, a vast fleet was ready for use on every invasion front. Even then the Normandy landings, on such a terrific scale, might have failed except for another thing that "couldn't be done." Prefabricated synthetic harbors, each the size of Dover, with concrete caissons, floating breakwaters and piers, were built in Britain by Allied engineers and towed to their new home—one of the most remarkable engineering feats of all time. Adding to this the versatile "steel-box" technique of adjustable, expandable, portable pontoon bridge and dock construction dreamed up by our Navy engineers, it was possible for Allied armies to land their amphibious craft practically anywhere, without notice, while it was practically impossible for defenders to make any coast line unbreachable. While the Nazis hung back in Normandy, expecting a thrust in the Pas de Calais area and therefore hesitating to concentrate their limited strength in Normandy, Montgomery's 2nd British Army, with the 3rd Canadian division and the U. S. 1st Army, were striking along the coast, past Cherbourg, all the way to Brest. With Nazi troops held on other fronts by continuing Russian and Italian drives, von Runstedt and Rommel had been afraid to take the initiative while there was still time, and the Allied foothold was still insecure.

CAEN HELD OUT until July 9, 1944, when it fell to British and Canadians. Heavily mined, much destruction was engineered by retreating Nazis. Above, a "Tommy" carries a little girl past a Nazi defense post.

CHEERING CROWDS greeted Allied forces entering Bayeux, June 8, 1944, and officers addressed the townsfolk. The two little girls on the platform are children of local residents deported to Germany. Beyond this town Nazis continued to resist stubbornly, while Montgomery fought just as stubbornly for elbow room along the Allied beachhead. British troops pushed forward slowly.

THE BATTLE OF FRANCE

BEYOND Caen were the plains, and beyond the plains—straight ahead 120 miles away—lay Paris. Sloshing through mud and water, soaked by cold drizzling rains, British and Canadians hurled tanks, guns, infantry against Nazi *Panzer* formations. Gradually the whole Nazi left flank was pushed back to a line running from Periers to St. Lo. Rommel's tank strength was now estimated at half what it had once been, while Allied power was growing steadily stronger. A regrouping of forces created for the first time an independent Canadian Army, augmented by British troops and a Polish division, while the American 3rd Army appeared on the right flank. Montgomery as usual had harried Rommel by shifting tactics which kept the "Fox" in uneasy lack of equilibrium, preventing transfer of troops from one point to another, leaving him with inadequate strength for defense at any given point. Rommel had been kept so busy he had had to leave the Nazi garrison at Cherbourg to shift for itself, while 3 U. S. spearheads were reaching out toward the port. By June 21, 1944, Bradley's 1st U. S. Army had surrounded Cherbourg. While Allied warships pounded from the sea, and air and artillery bombardment gave the defenders no respite, the infantry stormed the garrison, forcing it to surrender on June 26th. By July the whole peninsula was in the hands of the Allies, with 35,000 prisoners. On July 18, the day St. Lo fell to U. S. Forces, Montgomery staged a dramatic breakthrough, cracking open Nazi defense lines east and southeast of Caen, spreading out on the plains to breach the Orne River. When Gen. Bradley added the weight of his armor in the sector between Coutances and the coast, the stage was set for the final drive against the main Nazi forces in France.

THIS U.S. TANK DESTROYER and its driver never got beyond entrance to St. Lo, center of real Nazi resistance until finally surrounded and taken by U.S. troops July 18, 1944. Fighting every step of the way, in wet swampy country, Rommel's forces were being slowly but surely worn down—and no reserves appeared to reinforce him. By July 24 almost 600 of his tanks had been knocked out.

AS LIBERATION PROCEEDED in France, Maquis, Free French, other resistance groups came into their own. Their sabotage-ingenuity and desperate heroism known to all the world, were a decisive factor in Allied strategy and in the outcome of the Battle of France. *Maquis* went into action beside the Allies in the northwest and southeast, operated daringly on their own along Swiss and Italian borders. In the central sector Maquis, now recognized as French Forces of the Interior (F.F.I.), moved grimly in upon Vichy. Gen. Eisenhower credited French "resistance" with having kept so many Nazi troops busy they could not be sent into Normandy as reinforcements for Rommel. Eagerly thousands of young men like these above – and women, too – waited their chance to serve France.

With Cherbourg in Allied hands, in July, 1944, preparations went forward for assault upon major Nazi positions in France. The battle opened on July 25, 1944, with the greatest single air blow ever recorded up to that hour. But from that time on everything that happened had a strangely reminiscent quality, as if a motion picture film, already seen, should suddenly reverse itself and start unwinding backward. Step by step, the story of France in 1940 was told again—but in reverse. Allied drives now split the Nazis, flanked them, cut them off in flashing surprise encirclements, seized their supplies, their equipment, their troops, broke up their "orderly withdrawals," disorganized them to a point where more than once bodies of Nazi troops taken prisoner discovered they had headed straight into Allied lines under the impression they were running away. The pursuers moved so fast that one bewildered young American officer in the northern sector asked his superior what country they were in that morning. American armored divisions, British and Canadian tank forces, roared over open roads with infantry perched on the outside ready to jump off and go into action. Then they would come back for the rest of the ride. Nazi lines broke. More than 1,000 prisoners a day were taken. Strafed from the air, they fled in broad daylight, while east and west of Coutances terrific tank battles still raged. Montgomery's arr and tanks rolled ahead over the countryside, different colu roaring toward different objectives, all part of the caref planned master strategy of a mammoth invasion. Bradl columns roared across Brittany, through Rennes, on to Nazaire. Nantes fell Aug. 9, Le Mans the same day, and umns pressed on toward Brest, toward Paris. The Allies now overrun an area containing a sixth of all France—alr half of the quadrangle bounded by the Seine and Loire Riv the English Channel and the Bay of Biscay. Still the "b krieg in reverse" roared on—the Allied *blitzkrieg* which flicted heavy losses instead of taking them, and pushed battle lines back toward the Reich. It was Nazi cities wh shuddered this time under bombing raids, Nazis who c out of Paris, Allies whose racing columns converged upo When on Aug. 22 the British captured Lisieux, scene of t last battle before Dunkerque, when on Aug. 25 the A entered Paris, when on Sept. 1 the Canadian 1st A marched in triumph into Dieppe where in Aug. 1942 they lost more than half their force engaged in their fan Dieppe raid—there remained only invasion of German to make the symbolism complete.

ROADWAYS IN FRANCE became Nazi race-tracks. They disposed of everything which might impede their flight, leaving the countryside strewn with hand grenades, blankets, mess kits, personal belongings, while the roads were cluttered with tanks, half-tracks, all kinds of vehicles. In the picture above, U. S. soldiers are checking a discarded tank for booby traps, time-bombs, etc., while one of them stands guard against enemy sniping.

NO LIFE WAS LEFT IN ST. LO, after its capture July 18, 1944, except Allied trucks which kept even the farthest-thrusting Allied spearhead supplied with necessities of war. In an amazing demonstration of efficiency behind the front, every road was made part of a vast shuttle system in which filled trucks moved up, empties moved back, to be reloaded at once and routed out again. Result—quick repairs to equipment, soldiers fed, advance maintained.

ENEVER MARS chanced to spare a ch village, retreating Nazis took care of oversight. They carefully planted land s at strategic points, hid time bombs in lings where people were likely to be ered—churches, schools, anything they not have time to destroy before they left. cy, above, with piles of burned-out Nazi matériel mingled in rubble, is such a . By Aug. 1944, Allied pursuit of re-ing Nazis was moving at a pace of from 50 miles a day. The bridge at the right only one of many blown up in vain ts to delay the headlong pace of Allied s racing at the heels of fleeing "super-" in France.

"FOUR STARS" IN FRANCE

An American General, Dwight D. Eisenhower, leader of the biggest army in the world, was appointed Supreme Commander of the Allied Expeditionary Forces in the most crucial theater and critical period of war in the west. He directs operations of 4 U. S. Armies in northwestern Europe, British and Canadian Armies, divisions from other Allied nations, and the Allied Air-Borne-Army. In addition to this he co-ordinates all ground armies with naval and air activities of the U. S. and Britain. All responsibility for political phases of any campaign is also his, at a time when European politics have never been more complex or difficult. This makes Gen. Eisenhower a strategist in a larger sense of the word than its purely military interpretation — he must be both fighting man and statesman. He is shown below with U. S. Chief of Staff Gen. George C. Marshall, who gave him the tools for his tremendous job and raised his fighting arm from 400,000 men in 1940 to 10,000,000 in 1944. Below (*left*) is Lt. Gen. George S. ("Blood-and-Guts") Patton, leader of the 3rd Army in its historic conquering sweep in August and September over terrain familiar to all World War I veterans — Rheims, St. Mihiel, Verdun. Working in complete harmony with the British, Canadian, Fighting French, and other Allied units, these Americans helped carry through in France, in the summer of 1944, one of the brilliant campaigns of this or any other war.

GEN. EISENHOWER, on July 21, 1944, pins the Oak Leaf Cluster to the Distinguished Service Medal on Lt. Gen. Omar N. Bradley, Commander of the U.S. 1st Army in the great Allied July offensive of that year in France.

Somewhere between Nice and Marseilles, the sky is filled with parachutes bringing men and supplies to new beachheads.

D-DAY in the South of France, Aug. 15, 1944, was a strange contrast to previous Allied amphibious landings in the South Pacific, or Normandy. The Nazis had been forewarned, but offered so little opposition that in the first few days the Allies lost only 500 men and took 10,000 prisoners. Maj. Gen. Patch, who had cleaned up Guadalcanal, scrambled ashore with the first wave of the American 7th Army. In the next few hours American and French troops poured onto the beaches between Toulon and Cannes, to fan out in every direction. The securing of the beachhead was so easy that the armies were able to get it organized and begin their drive inland almost at once, whereas it had taken weeks to accomplish the same thing in Normandy. While the French 1st Army closed in around Toulon, which was taken Aug. 27, and the Americans were capturing Marseille Aug. 23, Patch was preparing to drive straight through to the north to link up with the Allied armies located in the central part of France.

THE TOWN OF LAVAL, FRANCE, does not model its feelings after its name. Gen. Charles de Gaulle was wildly cheered when he visited Laval on Aug. 22, 1944, soon after its deliverance from Nazi occupation. After his return to French soil, Gen. de Gaulle made steady progress toward uniting various French political factions into a working organization with two objectives: (1) to win a decisive, clean-cut victory in the war, with provisions to insure future peace, and (2) to restore the Republic of France to her rightful place.

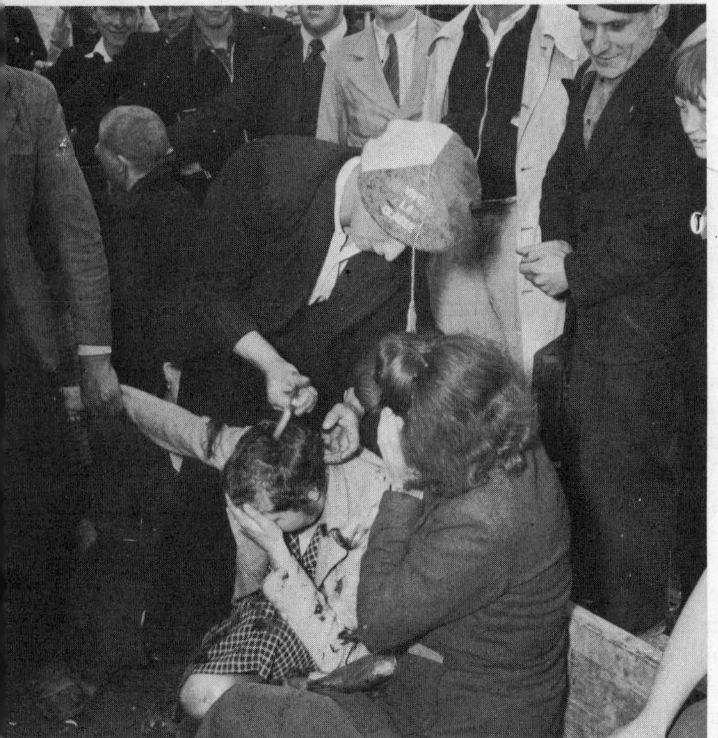

In many parts of Freed France "Axis collaborationists" were shorn of their hair.

REGENERATION

FRANCE, on the day of her liberation, proved that under four years of occupation she had been more truly France than the listless, disillusioned nation of 1940. A people who had feared war so much that they had fallen easy prey to Hitler's diabolically shrewd psychological offensive ("secret weapon") suddenly awoke. It was too late to undo the ravages of Nazi Germany. The armistice was a fact. The Vichy government was a shameful fact. The physical presence of an overwhelming force of occupation was a fact. And there was no French Army because there was no mechanized equipment. The old, fierce pride of France bowed its head in shame and bitter regret, but no longer

FFI MEN AT BRAINE, FRANCE, guard the wreckage of a Nazi train. Loaded with ammunition, it had been captured by American tanks in Sept. 1944. FFI was now part of Allied armies. On and after D-day they had seriously damaged Nazi communications, kept 10 Nazi divisions busy in central France. Their communications, maps, with damages accomplished and planned, were kept at Allied Headquarters. In the month after D-day the FFI had accounted for 3,000 Nazis—dead, wounded, or captured.

OF FRANCE

with the futility or resignation of 1940. From one end of the country to the other, one common impulse surged, drew all classes, all sections together in one common will-to-resist. With every nuance of ingenuity, with every weapon at her command, France threw herself into the business of giving aid and comfort to the Allies who would one day set her free, while her Underground gnawed at Nazi tyranny. The people of France watched, waited and worked as the conquering Axis first tasted the bitter brew of defeat in the ruins of Stalingrad, in the far-away Solomons, on the coasts of Africa. Their own "war effort" doubled, tripled, with each Nazi reprisal. France was herself again!

Tried and found guilty of treason and espionage, they know what to expect from France.

CANADIAN TROOPS IN FRANCE distinguished themselves on many sectors of the front. Soon after the formation of the Canadian 1st Army, Commanded by Lt. Gen. H. D. G. Crerar, it was announced that Canada's entire overseas army was in action in Europe. The first offensive undertaken by the new independent Canadian Army was directed against the Nazi 7th Army entrenched in the Falaise sector. The picture of Vire (*above*), is typical of the destruction wrought in many Norman towns.

IN THE SOUTHERN INVASION OF FRANCE the U. S. 7th Army and the French 1st Army, both under U. S. Gen. Patch, drove disorganized Nazis before them all the way up to St. Etienne and Lyon, which fell on the same day, Sept. 3, 1944. These men of the 7th Army are shown "at ease" in St. Germain Du Bois on Sept. 5, two days after the fall of those cities. From now on, as Gen. Patch swings northward toward junction with the American 3rd Army driving down from Normandy, the Nazi foe will be closed in upon from all sides.

ARGENTAN WAS A BATTERED WRECK (*above*) when one column of Patton's 3rd Army occupied the town Aug. 13 to help British and Canadians draw a noose about a large body of Nazi troops caught in a pocket near Falaise. The taking of Falaise Aug. 18 closed the Nazi escape gap at Trun, opened the way for Allied drives on the Seine. By Sept. the Canadian Army had established 5 bridgeheads over the river, taken Rouen, driven through Lille into Belgium, on toward Holland. Gen. Eisenhower expressed the following verdict: "Elimination of the German 7th Army as a fighting entity has decided the Battle of France."

FORCED BACK from Falaise upon the bridgeless Seine, facing annihilation, thousands of Nazis were killed or captured trying to escape through the narrow opening known as "Coffin Corridor." Note the dazed look on the face of the wounded prisoner above when a U. S. soldier offers to care for his injured arm.

WHEREVER THE AMERICAN SOLDIER GOES you will find American songs. And these American engineers were no exception. In full fighting equipment, it didn't take them long to roll a piano out into the square in a town somewhere in France and settle down to singing some tunes.

EVERY citizen of Paris knew what it meant when the great carillon of Notre Dame de Paris rang out from its ancient lofty tower on Friday, Aug. 25, 1944. Through every side street, every boulevard, surged waves of people who cheered, laughed, shouted, wept. Paris was free! The tricolor blossomed once more against the gray stones of the city. Never before in her long history had Paris known an hour like this. For two days suspense had chilled the city, after her own citizens had fought the Nazi garrison so effectively that the Nazi commander had flashed a false report of surrender to gain time, to call for help. But it was the FFI to whom the help came. Allied tanks roared into the city, each with an American flag or a Cross of Lorraine on its side. Now, the Nazis kissed the white flag, surrendered by the thousands. Their commander turned over his sword to Gen. Jacques LeClerc, Commander of the French Second Armored Division. When Gen. Charles de Gaulle arrived a few hours later Paris roared a welcome, auguring well for unity between the factions which in 1940 had fitted so handily into Hitler's "divide and conquer" scheme. Events moved swiftly now. Nazi-inspired "rebellions" were promptly put down, saboteurs and "Quislings" weeded out. Gen. Pierre Koenig, FFI commander, began incorporating the underground into the new French Army which had been promised new arms and new equipment by the Allies. De Gaulle was made head of a new Provisional Government, and justice was meted out to all traitors. Gradually a strong political coalition emerged from confusion. France was on her way to recognition by the Allies, to resumption of her rightful place among the nations of the world. The war was not over, on that August day when the bells rang out in Paris. But for the Nazis in France it was no longer "beginning of the end" —it was the end. Since D-day they had lost 200,000 prisoners and as many killed or wounded. Thousands of tanks, motor transports, planes, had been destroyed or captured. As Gen. Montgomery declared grimly, "Any enemy units that managed to get away will not be in fit condition to fight again for many, many months."

THE FALL OF PARIS

AFTER THE LIBERATION

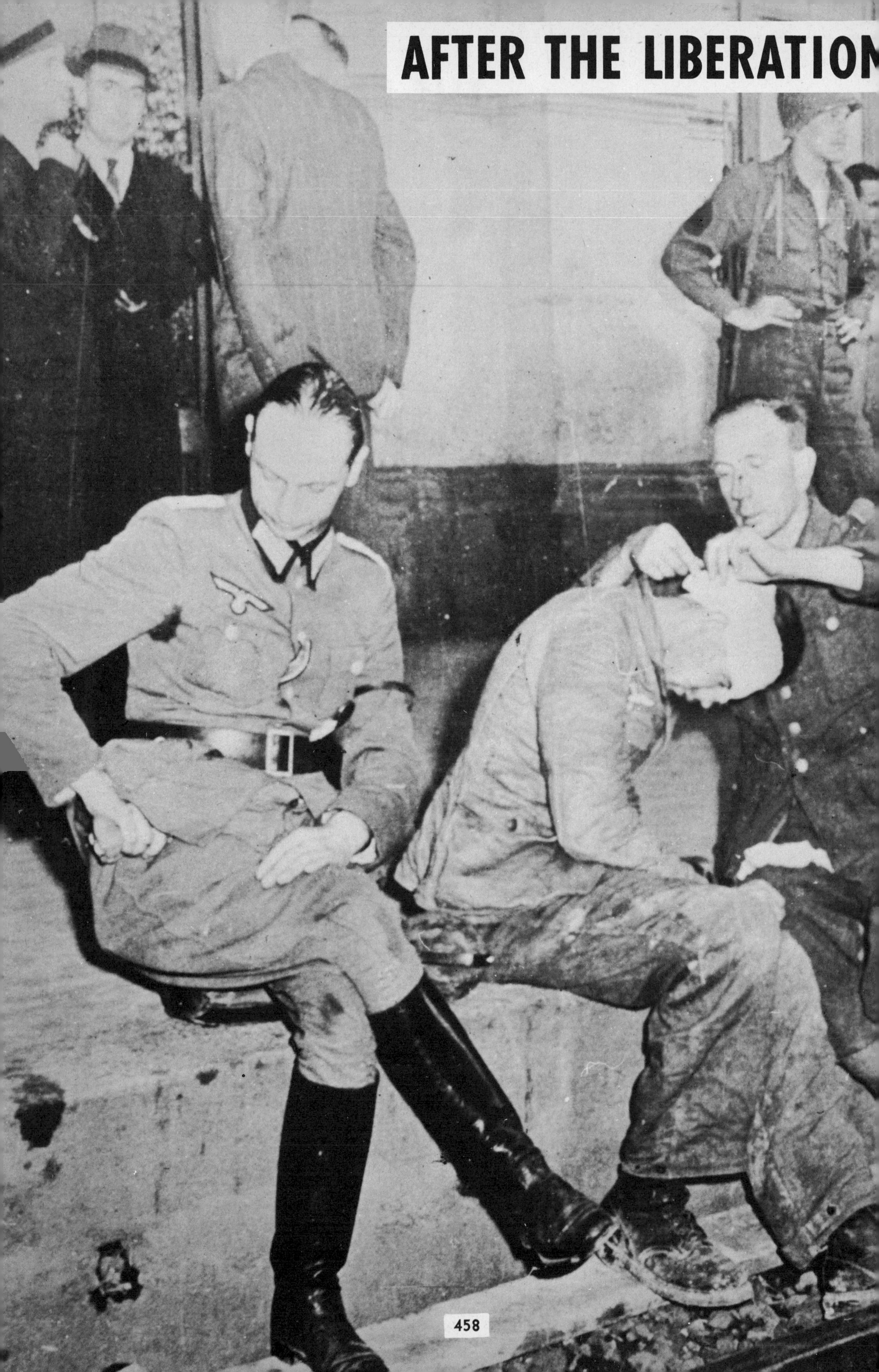

OF PARIS

PARIS BELONGED TO FRANCE AGAIN, but even before the Nazis had known they would be swept out of the city and back to their own troubled borders, they had organized fifth columnists, snipers and spies among those who had collaborated with them. Against these Nazi agents barricades had to be put up in Paris streets even after the Nazis had withdrawn. Above, a sniper is firing from a building on the Place de la Concorde.

FRENCH FORCES OF THE INTERIOR swung into action in Paris to help put down an abortive uprising engineered by Nazi agents soon after the city's fall. Everyone suspected of being involved was rounded up by the FFI, who had instituted a systematic search in all quarters of the city. Known snipers and Axis agents were often beaten by irate citizens from whom they had to be rescued by the police or the FFI.

EVERYWHERE IN OCCUPIED FRANCE, the spirit of Paris was the spirit of the people. More and more frequently Allied fliers shot down over France turned up across the channel, safe. More and more Maquis were armed with Allied weapons drifting down to them from the skies. With bated breath, and a new war-taught gift of patience, the people of France waited for D-day, awaited instructions from London. When at last the blight was lifted, as the Allied armies swept forward in the summer of 1944, the first instinct of dwellers in liberated territory was to clean up, to purge the premises of every trace of the visitors who had made life miserable for four long years. The picture above, taken in Troyes after Gen. Patton's 3rd Army had passed through in August on the heels of retreating Nazis, shows a scene enacted hundreds of times in every town or village where the enemy had left enough buildings standing for community life to go on.

ALLIED ASSAULT recognized no barriers as it rolled back the Nazis and headed toward Germany. Finding no bridges left across the Seine, U.S. soldiers above swam across, towing a 37-mm anti-tank gun.

THE AMERICAN SOLDIER in the picture above looks small beside the massive concrete Nazi gun installation he is examining. Still draped with elaborate camouflage, it was evidently abandoned in a hurry.

While tanks still rumbled toward battle fronts, peace returned to villages along the Seine.

TORTURE CHAMBERS OF THE 20TH CENTURY remained, after Nazis had fled, to bear witness against them. This one in Paris was soundproof, so no one could hear screams of prisoners.

INSTEAD OF THE "BLOODY VENGEANCE" which Herr Goebbels had taught Nazi soldiers to expect from their "barbarous foes," the wounded received excellent care from Allies.

Danger lurks in every doorway of towns abandoned by Nazis. Above Allied soldiers search for snipers and booby traps.

SMOKING RUINS marked Nazi reprisals in all occupie countries. Martincourt, France, paid this price (*above* for harboring FFI members. Brest (*left*), one of the Na "resistance pockets," held out until Sept. 19, 1944, lon after the most parts of France had been cleared of th invaders.

AMERICAN TROOPS are pictured here in ancient Orleans, which had fallen on Aug. 17, 1944. It was "curbstone chow" (*above*) for hurried soldiers racing after the Nazis toward the Low Countries. The picture (*right*) shows how Maxinelle, Belgium, took means to assure the approaching Allies of its sentiments.

Siegfried Line breached Sept. 15, 1944. Here a bulldozer tank and some American Infantry move through a gap at Roetgen.

FIRST ON NAZI SOIL

A WEEK after Paris was free, it was already far behind racing Allied fronts. From the Swiss border to the English Channel, six separate armies moved along parallel routes toward the Low Countries and the Westwall of Germany. Town after town fell; a line reaching from Amiens to Besancon was pushed swiftly forward. By the middle of Sept., 1944, the Canadian 1st Army had taken Ghent in Belgium, crossed into the Netherlands. The British 2nd, occupying Brussels and Antwerp on Sept. 4, had stopped just short of Arnhem, the farthest of any Allied advance at that date. The U.S. 1st Army had divided into two spearheads, one reaching up from Soissons, past Liège (*taken Sept. 9*), to a point before Aachen just across the German border. The second spearhead swerved to the right to take Reims on Aug. 30, Luxembourg on Sept. 11. General Patton's 3rd Army had advanced through Troyes, almost to Metz. One army was left—the U.S. 7th combined with the French 1st. From Lyon, they had taken Besancon on Sept. 8, and were poised before the Belfort gap, just at the Swiss border. Somewhere in the background the mysterious U.S. 9th, the "ghost army," awaited the time to strike. Nazi boasts were loud and long concerning the strength of the Westwall and the Siegfried Line, but in a Cologne newspaper, in September, a new tone had crept into the war news. "The hammer of destiny is striking heavily against us. Leading divisions are retiring and low-flying enemy planes are advancing deep into our territory. There are grounds for fear and the time has come when we are filled with anxiety. The wind has changed in a storm that is sweeping heavily over us." For the first time since Napoleon's day, battles clearly impended which might destroy German cities.

THE SIEGFRIED LINE, though not "impregnable" as Hitler assured his people, proved a formidable barrier to Allied advance. These Nazi soldiers (*above*) were killed defending their trench near the entrance to a pill-box, part of Siegfried Line defense. Roetgen (*right*), just inside the border, was first German town to fall to Americans, in Sept., 1944.

A CASUALTY of the great Allied Airborne Armada which swept over Holland in Sept. 1944.

FLOODS OF WATER —AND BLOOD

Ignoring others' rights, as usual, the Nazis turned Holland's coast into a German defense bastion by flooding lowlands the Dutch had drained and cultivated for centuries. Farms disappeared, whole villages were submerged. Ruined for years to come by sea water, fertile soil became a quagmire interrupted only by Nazi gun emplacements, pill boxes, anti-tank devices. Linked with natural barriers formed by the estuary plain of the Waal and the Neder Rhine—two mouths of the river which are wide, deep and swift—this sector was considered invasion-proof. Without its bridges the plain was impassable, and if the Nazis had to retreat they could blow them up as they went. For the Allies it was necessary to prevent this at all cost. These bridges would be needed in a full-scale invasion of Germany. When Allied leaders decided to by-pass the elaborate Nazi fortification systems by just soaring above them, it was the old El Alamein technique on a vastly enlarged scale. While main Army troops hammered at the Westwall in a frontal attack, the air-borne army would do what the Navy had done in Africa when it swung around the enemy flank at the coast and supplemented flanking ground forces. U.S. Lt. Gen. Brereton planned the multitudinous details of this greatest air-borne expedition. He carried the plans through to successful landing operations—which took the enemy and the rest of the world completely by surprise when troops "dropped" at Eindhoven and Mijnegen and made scheduled contact with the British 2nd Army. But at the farther end of the belt—at Arnhem only a few miles from the German border—the Nazis stood firm.

HOMELESS THOUSANDS, hurled by the catastrophe of modern total war into a world of danger, suffering, and utter hopelessness, constitute one of the most difficult problems civilization has ever had to face. The picture above of evacueés fleeing from the Dutch town of Kerkrade is typical of the tragedy which left no country within the range of Hitler's ambitions untouched. Upon women and children, the very old and the very young, the blows fell with most crushing force. People of the lowlands have twice in a generation known what it was to be swept from their moorings by tides of German aggression. Now, after four years of occupation, they can be released only by armies which pursue the common foe, driving him back the way he came, which once more forces the people to evacuate.

THE VAST SKY-CONVOY launched over Holland in Sept. 1944, dropped parachutists first to clear landing areas, followed with gliders to unload infantry, heavy supplies. At Arnhem the Nazis sent fleets of tanks, cut off and surrounded the troops.

ISOLATED, FIGHTING 11 days in an "island of hell" before British tanks and air-borne units reached them Sept. 23, only 2,000 "Red Devils" were left out of 6,000. Their holding on had given ground troops time to take a vital bridge across the Waal.

FACING THE NAZIS' densest defense system, America's 1st and 9th Armies made slow progress toward the German town of Aachen.

THE 3RD REICH LEARNED what war means when fighting smashed through to rage on Nazi soil. Aachen surrendered Oct. 20, 1944.

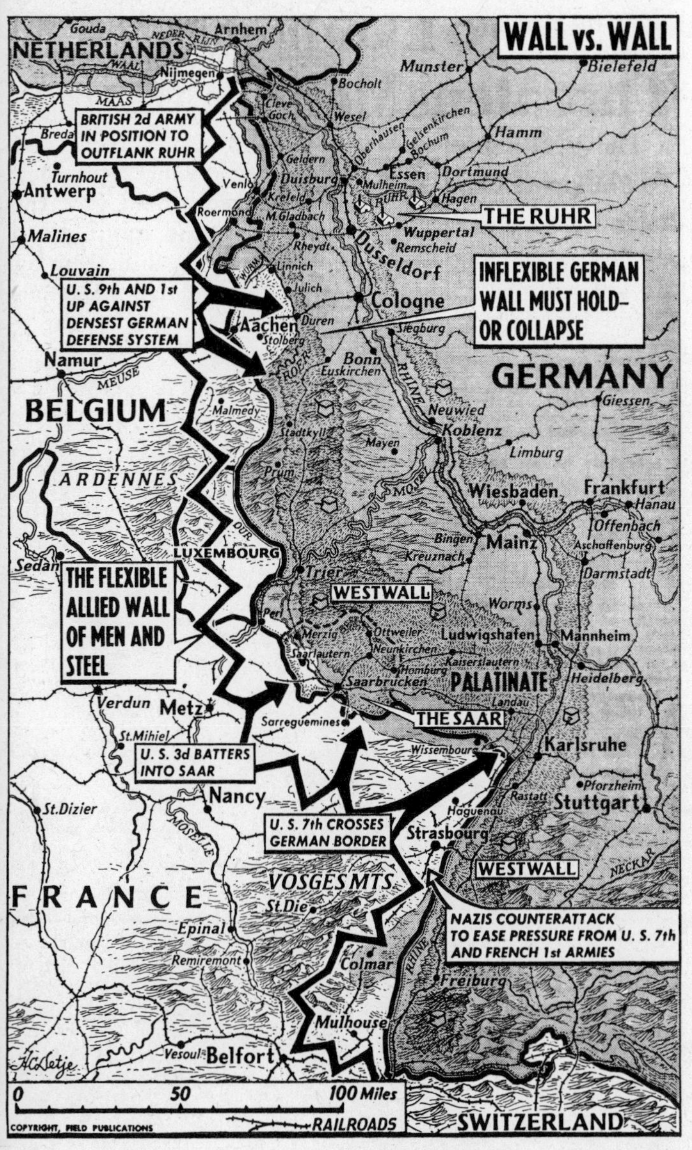

THE APPROACH OF 1945 found powerful Allied armies poised along the borders of Germany from Arnhem down to the Belfort gap, found the Nazis still able to hold, and to fight back. The Westwall breached, but not conquered, still furnished many hazards in the Allies' road to Berlin.

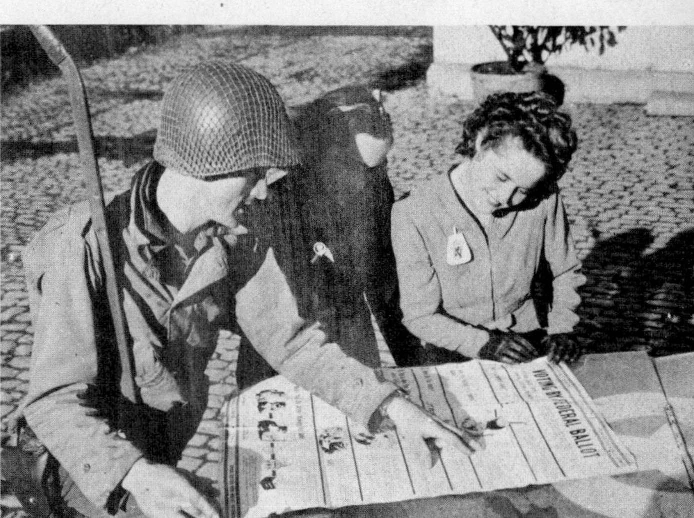

DEMOCRACY FUNCTIONED at the battle front. Every facility for voting in the 1944 election was made available to the United States Armed Forces.

WHEN AACHEN—CHARLEMAGNE'S AIX-LA-CHAPPELLE—refused to yield its centuries' old culture, it had to be blasted to ruins before it capitulated. Here German civilians stop to read the proclamation of the military government authorized by the Allied supreme commander.

THE SALWEEN RIVER FRONT was one of the few bright spots in China's war against Japan. Here a Chinese soldier guards the Hwitung bridge.

CHINA'S DARKEST DAYS

When two of the world's greatest powers became China's Allies in war against Japan, she found herself in a strangely anomalous position. The alliance undoubtedly meant future victory, but what would be its effect upon her immediate fortunes? The answer soon appeared. The war potential of her new Allies was the greatest on earth—when it could be developed. But for some time any large benefits from the partnership must be on the psychological side, where China was strongest, and practically non-existent on the material side, where she was weakest. In fact, the alliance actually plunged her into new dangers. With Japan taking over friendly British Burma and French Indo-China, the foe was on China's flanks, as well as at her throat, cutting her off from the Burma Road, her life-line since Japan had blockaded her coasts. At the Cairo Conference in Nov. 1943 the important position given China by her Allies was gratifying, but again fraught with danger. It served as warning to Japan that concerted Allied effort against her was in the making, even though immediate emphasis might be upon Hitler in the west. For some months, faced with increasing threats from MacArthur in the South Pacific, the Japanese had been content to confine themselves in China to local consolidating actions. But with the conference, and arrival of U. S. heavy, long-range bombers in China, they realized that action much longer delayed would give the Allies time to mobilize China's manpower and equip her to serve as base and nerve center for onslaught against them by land, sea and air. Racing for time, now suddenly precious to her, Japan launched a drive in April, 1944, to knock China, once and for all, out of the war.

SUNGSHAN MOUNTAIN, west of the Salween, was taken by the Chinese on Sept. 7, 1944, after 3 months and 1 day of siege. Capture of this Japanese stronghold commanding the Burma Road meant that supplies for Lungling would no longer have to be shunted around the mountain by pack-horse. The picture above shows Chinese horse-drawn artillery moving over the Burma Road.

RETREATING CHINESE SOLDIERS had blown up the bridge at this point on the Salween River, 2 years before, to keep the Japanese from using it. Now, advancing, they have to cross a precarious impromptu suspension bridge carrying everything they need.

CIVILIAN REFUGEES jammed the trains out of Kweilin as Japanese advanced toward the city. Its fall, on Sept. 17, 1944, was a serious blow. With the loss of this key defense center went also two railroads and an important base for Chennault's 14th Air Force.

The Chinese soldier, having little heavy artillery, became expert at house-to-house fighting and guerrilla type warfare.

THE DRIVE Japan launched in April, 1944, was designed to close the 1,000-mile gap between northern Japanese armies of occupation around Peiping, and those in the south around Canton. This would cut China in two, isolate her from outside help, eliminate her from war before she could be of important use to her Allies, or they to her. By July Japanese troops had battled their way down from Changsha to Henyang, where Chennault's 14th Air Force hung on at its base until the last moment, grimly destroying all installations before its planes moved out and Japanese moved in. Another column was driving up from Canton. By Oct. 1, Lingling, Kweilin, Paoking and Tanchuck had fallen before the converging columns. Reaching Kweilin and Liuchow, the two Japanese armies, 350,000 strong, were less than 100 miles apart. But there were rays of light. The gap was still not closed. All attempts to cripple the 14th Air Force failed. One by one it blew up its bases, retired farther into the interior, operated as devastatingly as before. Success of Allied drives on the Salween front, portending Japanese withdrawal from Burma, had already opened supply routes, among which might soon be the Burma Road. More Superfortresses, of the 20th Bomber Command, were raiding Tokyo from bases in China's interior. If she could hold out, and hold together, until the Allies could establish themselves there to work with MacArthur, moving up from "down under," it would one day no longer be China which was encircled, blockaded, relentlessly bombed. It would be Japan.

CHINESE coolies transport vital military and med

IN THE YANGTSE THEATER OF WAR, Chang
in 1944, but they lacked resources to follow up
shows the devastation its citizens found when th

plies along an old caravan trail from India.

en and retaken, remained in Chinese hands
tory. This picture of Changteh's east gate
uggled back after fighting was over.

Chungking, China's capital, and prime Japanese objective, held out through daily visits from enemy planes.

JAPAN'S April drive found China with her military, economic, and political fortunes at their lowest ebb, while internal dissension between the Chungking government and the so-called "Communists" in the north held many of her best soldiers on her borders, fighting each other instead of uniting against the common foe. Politically these 60,000,000 people, who started out with a "Communist" tag, are actually only social-minded democrats who believe in practicing what they preach. Living where Japan first invaded in 1937—some of them in what is technically "occupied" territory—they had to develop a guerrilla-type fighting which would require only modern arms and armor to turn their "militia" into a real World War weapon. But from Cairo, in Nov. 1943, dispatches stated: "The conference took cognizance of the fact that internal differences between Chiang Kai-shek and the Chinese Communist Army must be overcome before China could be opened as the primary base for direct attack against Japan itself." As 1944 drew toward its eventful end, two new factors appeared in China's situation: (1) Indications that agreement between Chiang Kai-shek and the "Communists" might relieve both regular troops and the military potential of the Partisan Army for the fight against Japan; (2) Announcement of a huge pipeline, 2,000 miles long, to bring oil from Calcutta into China. "A steel link," said the American commander in India, "binding China to her Allies; an artery through which we shall pump a transfusion into the sick body of China."

WITH BURMA PORTS BLOCKED, Calcutta and Bombay became gateways for supplies for Indian troops fighting in Burma beside their Allies from China, Britain, and America. By summer 1944 the Indian Army numbered 2,000,000 men. The picture above shows dock workers fleeing after a ship with munitions for Burma had exploded in the harbor at Bombay, India.

AMERICAN SURGEONS (*below*) saved many lives by operating close behind fighting fronts in the Burma war theater. Under Lord Louis Mountbatten, British, American, Chinese and Indian troops fought on, even through the monsoon period, combating not only the enemy but also the fevers and vermin of the fetid jungle. By fall, 1944, they were gradually pushing the Japanese out of Burma.

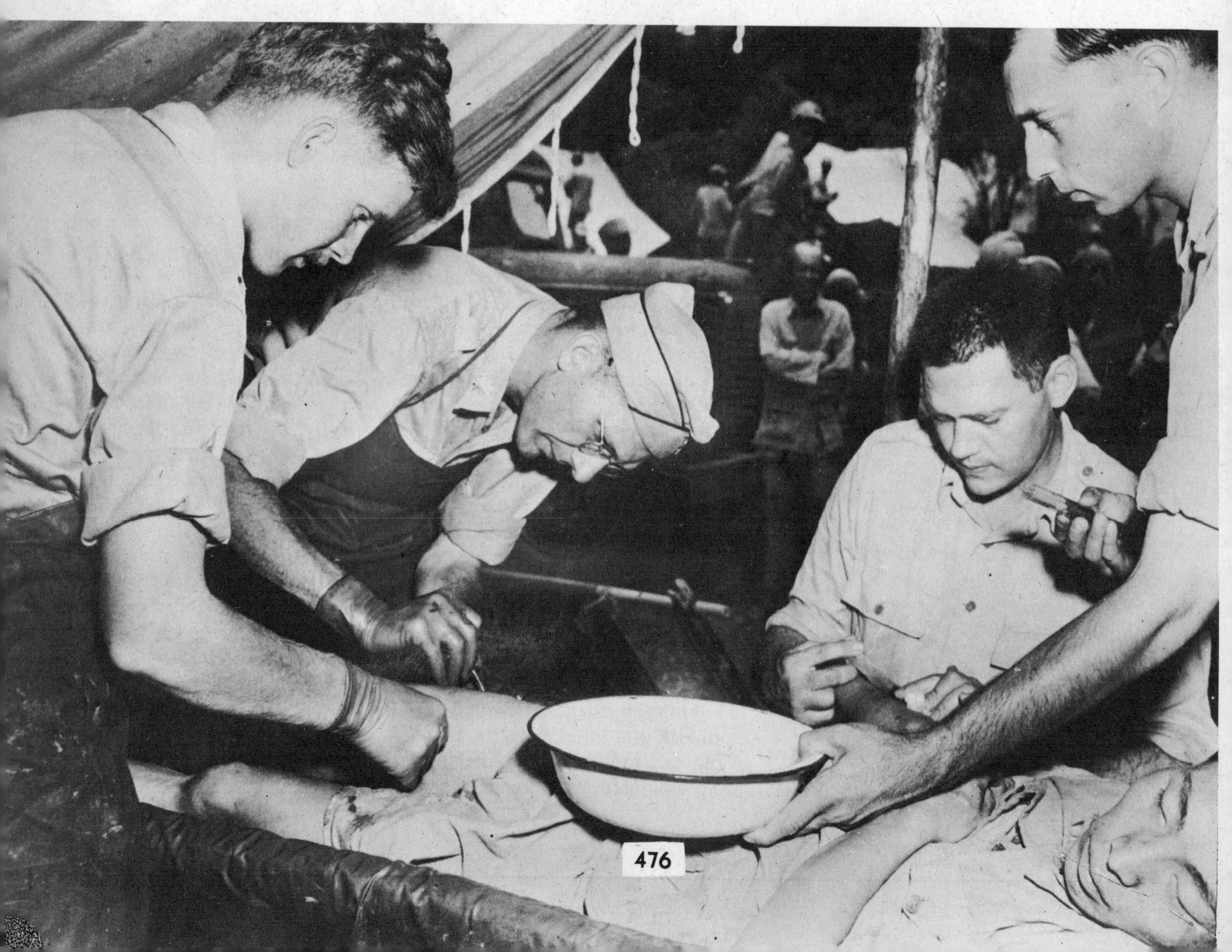

THIS NEW ROAD INTO BURMA was an extraordinary Army engineering feat. Using bulldozers and other up-to-date machinery, and a whole division of troops for digging, uprooting trees, blasting rocks, they put the road through in record-breaking time. The picture above shows troops, with supply mules crossing a jungle stream on this new route for bringing in materiel from India.

"PRAISE THE LORD AND PASS THE AMMUNITION." Ammunition for this American gun crew, firing 1,300 rounds in 8 hours, had to be "passed" all the way from America by sea, shipped across India from Bombay or Calcutta, then flown to the front. To keep them coming, American engineers and Chinese coolies worked feverishly to open new roads behind the Burma-China front.

ALLIGATOR

THE BATTLES of Coral Sea and Midway in June, 1942, served notice upon Japan that she must risk her fleet to establish naval supremacy in the South Pacific, or halt her tide of conquest at the high mark already reached. Even then, she dared not risk her fleet, though each day she held it back added to the odds against her, gave the U. S. time to concentrate her inventive genius and vast resources upon fighting a new kind of war. At the end of six headlong months of conquest, the Japanese-held islands in the Pacific spread along a great arc from the Solomons in the south to the Aleutians in the north. They controlled the resources of the East Indies. They were at Australia's doorstep. To shake them loose from those toe-holds in the Pacific, war must be waged against them on a scale and of a magnitude never known before. Here, island by island, over millions of square miles of sea, stretched a gargantuan theater of war in which the role of overlord must be wrested from Japan. Here the tide of Japanese aggression must be turned back—the Rising Sun must be blotted from the skies. It meant great fleets of ships (*above*)—familiar battleships, transports, supply convoys, destroyers, submarines, carriers. It meant an army, a navy, and an air force of untold, unpredictable strength. But above and beyond all, it called for swift surprise landings of thousands of troops, thousands of miles from home, on any kind of shore, with all the bulky, complicated, delicately adjusted mechanism and supply demanded by modern warfare.

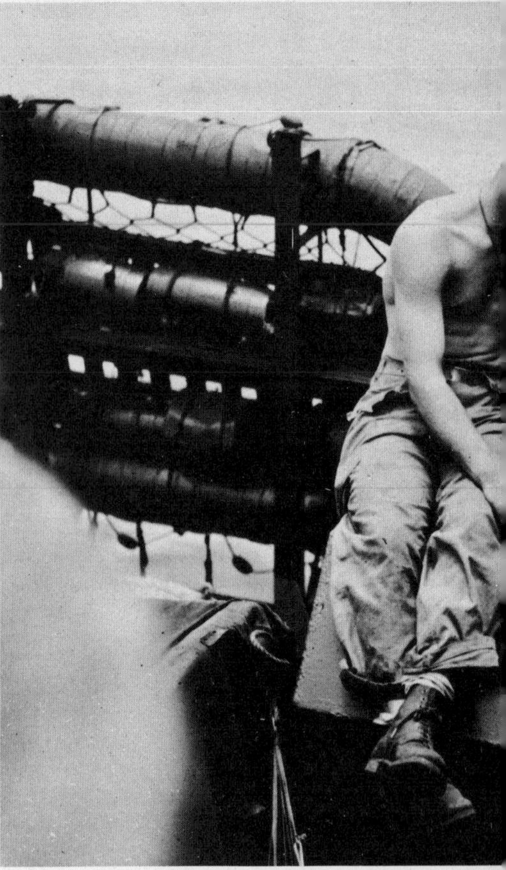

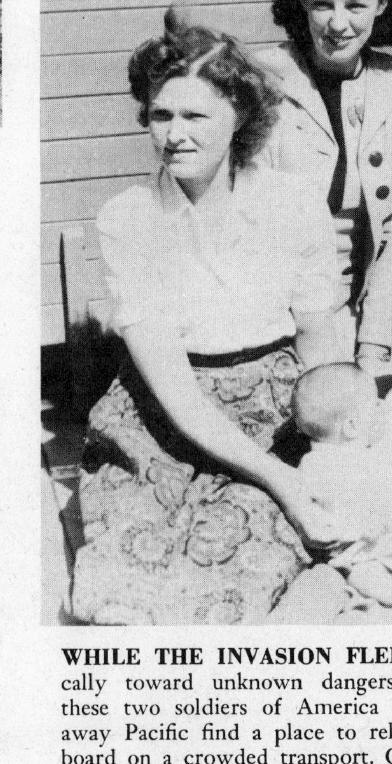

WHILE THE INVASION FLEET sweeps maj cally toward unknown dangers, unknown dr these two soldiers of America (*above*) in the away Pacific find a place to relax with their c board on a crowded transport. Occasionally, on long, hot Pacific journeys, out-door movies are sh at night, but there is little time for anything ex work, and no space for games or sports.

NAVY

HITHER THOU GOEST . . ." Those words the lovely story of Ruth are finding an echo y in many parts of the globe, wherever men of . Armed Forces have won brides from among oung women of our Allies. Above are a few of nore than 1,000 Australian girls who have sailed home to await their service man's return among folks" in America.

It was the gamble the Allies took at Guadalcanal and North Africa, in the months after Midway, which clarified and crystallized the problems they faced, which also suggested the answers. From the moment when those two sea-borne invasions "held," the Allies knew where they still had to go and how to get there in their march to Tokyo and Berlin. Every weakness was checked, every need charted. The result was the most astonishing assemblage of weird-looking craft ever to be classed as "ships," each one to perform a certain highly specialized function, swiftly and smoothly, with deadly efficiency. As naval warfare had been revolutionized after Midway by emergence of the carrier and the land-based heavy bomber to spearhead sea fighting and naval land-attack, so now after Guadalcanal and North Africa, a new type of invasion emerged, never imagined, even by Japanese and Nazi war lords in wild paranoiac dreams of aggression. The core of the new Allied fleets, both in the Pacific and the Atlantic, was the combination of sea-going and shore-landing craft (*above*) in various sizes and of many types, each type designed for maximum loading and unloading speed and efficiency. The ships of that "breed," with mystifying code initials for names, were "specialists" in whatever those initials stood for—there was not one old-style Jack-of-all-trades cargo ship among them. Throwing themselves straight at beaches they struck terror in the hearts of the Axis minion, and even the Nazi "superman" himself.

"LAST STOP, TOKYO"

LST'S, MASSIVE-MOUTHED CARRIERS of war matériel, disgorge their cargoes on a beach, while portable docks move out to meet them.

JAPANESE STRATEGY used Indian technique in jungle fighting. These U. S. Marines follow their example, advancing "Indian file."

PERSIAN hordes of Xerxes attacked Greece by crossing the Hellespont on galley bridges, William the Conqueror's men were ferried across the English Channel, but the "Alligator Navy" is such a complete departure from shipping tradition and precedent that "Amphibs" have been known to refer to their command as the "Ambiguous Navy." The ability to take ships straight up to the shore unhampered by natural conditions, to turn them inside out in a matter of minutes, get away again stripped clean of troops or cargo, is winning this war which for all the Allies except Russia has been largely a war of naval invasion. The Alligator Navy includes huge ships which carry smaller craft on their decks, in their holds, or lashed to their sides, each one fitted to some special cargo. They are known by their initials. In Navy vernacular, "C" stands for craft; a boat small enough to be carried by "S," a ship. "L" is for landing, "T" for tank, "I" for infantry, etc. So "LST" means Landing Ship, Tanks—dubbed by impatient invading troops "Long Slow Target," but changed in the Pacific to "Last Stop Tokyo." When the big ships begin to disgorge their queer amphibious monsters the beach begins to look like a fantastic menagerie.

AGAINST the sinister back-drop of brooding jungles and sultry tropical skies, amphibious warfare becomes a challenge to every ounce of steel in a man's soul. In the jungle war means more than a battle of man against man. It is a battle in which civilized instincts and training are pitted against the timeless savagery of nature in the raw—against the "law of the jungle," in all its most revolting forms. In the South Pacific this war is fought without an audience, without applause; on deadly open beaches, on lonely sun-baked atolls (*above*); on coral reefs that slice hands and legs to ribbons; in reeking jungles, fetid, malaria-infested, loathsome. Jungle fighting means facing a foe you cannot see, a hundred foes you cannot see. It is a war of mud and slime, of nerves and senses, in a land of whispering, eerie sounds, of great crabs crawling past you in the night which cannot be distinguished from the rustling, crawling enemy who slithers into your positions under cover of darkness, whose creed is the jungle creed—"kill or be killed." It is a war of survival in its most primitive forms, ambush and decoy, fighting hand-to-hand. It is not new or loathsome to the soldiers of the Rising Sun. They had been trained to it in Burma, trained in anticipation of the day when they would "infiltrate" the defenses of the globe as they now infiltrated the swamps of Guadalcanal or New Guinea. Their strategists had gone back to savage primitive warfare, gleaned from it every trick which might give an advantage over men used to fighting clean, trained to fight clean, whether in the boxing ring or the battlefield. But for all their cleverness, the Japanese underestimated the "soft" American who was supposed to succumb at once to the combined terrors of jungles and Japanese soldiers, the American who was only one or two or three generations removed from the pioneers who had faced equal hardship, in opening a continent. Grimly American soldiers settled down to learn the ways of this little "yellow belly," to overcome "jungle jitters," to fight fire with fire. They learned fast, turned Japan's own methods against her, surpassed the Japanese soldier at his own tricks, defeated him at every turn.

At Guadalcanal in the Solomons, in August, 1942, was forged the first working pattern of a marvelous invasion machine. This pattern was miniature in scale, dangerously experimental, but it worked. A few flaws which appeared in operations were ironed out. At that time, shock troops in this type of warfare were logically the Marines, who always had been the land arm of the Navy and therefore knew more about ship-to-shore techniques than any other branch of the service. The outnumbered Marines who made the first landing at Guadalcanal had equipment that was like children's toys compared with the equipment of the men who landed on Normandy and Guam some two years later. The men went ashore in wooden ramp boats and tank lighters. Tanks were far too few; so was heavy equipment. But the invasion method proved sound, both in the amphibious landing and in the jungle fighting that followed. Surprise was achieved in the landing. The immediate objective was achieved. Allied experts now had a pattern for invasion which would be enlarged, improved, elaborated, but which has never had be altered drastically. It was Aug. 7, 1942, when Marines, a a Naval task force, launched their attack on the Solomo with two main objectives – Tulagi and Guadalcanal. Guad canal particularly was important because in American han it would insure safety for Allied shipping lanes to Austral and a base from which to start rolling back the tide of Jap nese aggression. On this base, also, was a rich prize for t winner – a fine new airfield which Japan had built. As ways, the first move in the assault was the Navy's. Wh carrier-based planes laid a blanket of fire over the grou defenses (*above*), and the Navy covered the beaches wit heavy bombardment, the Marines stormed ashore, land their supplies, took the airport on the second day before t Japanese had really recovered from their surprise. The a port, renamed Henderson Field, was put into operation, a the Marines had a base for their long-range bombers, in t heart of the enemy's empire.

FRIENDLY NATIVES of a labor battalion helped the Marines unload equipment from landing barges. In the latest invasion pattern, special ships expedite unloading so greatly that it can be done in the early stages of the landing, and the troops go into battle beyond the bridgehead, straight from the shore with all supplies they need to carry on.

MARINES AND THEIR NATIVE HELPERS had to carry supplies through open plains to reach the shelter of the jungle, always alert for snipers in the thick foliage of the trees. By the end of Sept., the Japanese had made several bitterly contested, but partly successful, assaults at Guadalcanal on U.S. forces, who still held the air base and a little territory around it, while the rest of the island was in Jap hands.

T. GEN. THOMAS HOLCOMB, Marine ommandant on inspection tour of the Pa- ific (*left*) looks over a Guadalcanal battle- eld with Marine Commander Maj. Gen. . A. Vandegrift (*right*), and Lt. Col. M. A. dson, Commander of Edson's Raiders, who d the advance at Tulagi in 1942 and fought "Bloody Ridge" on Guadalcanal. For eeks Japanese harassed U. S. defenders of e airport by land, sea and air, slipping in einforcements at night, infiltrating through e jungle, ambushing, sniping, using every ick they knew.

HEAVY GUNS OF A U. S. CRUISER throw a fiery message across dark Pacific waters. Midnight hours were the ones when gallant little Navy PT boats found "good hunting" in the dangerous weird channels winding between the Solomons. Darting through "Lengo" or "the slot," searching through "Iron-bottomed Bay" or "the Sandfly," always on the alert for Japanese landing forces, they turned back many a prowling enemy surface craft, sent to the bottom many a 2,000-ton destroyer of the "Tokyo Express."

The U. S. operation in the Solomons in August, 1942, was the first of many combined ground and naval operations in World War II. Landing on hostile shores from a base 3,600 miles away, in the face of land-based enemy aircraft, was an undertaking fraught with greatest danger. In this case, it was intensified by perils lurking in the waters around the Solomons which were filled with menacing coral reefs and sketchily charted tiny islands. But Adm. Ghormley, to whom Adm. Nimitz had entrusted to strike the first blow, was past master in the art of planning and executing just such an operation. Working in co-operation with Gen. MacArthur in Australia, army planes pounded Japanese air bases at Lae and Salamaua on the coast of New Guinea, Rabaul in New Britain, bases in New Ireland, the Solomons themselves. While the Marines were landing at Guadalcanal, other U. S. forces made other landings in the Solomons—all resisted but all successfully carried through, under cover of bombardment from carrier-based planes and warships of the Pacific Fleet. In the weeks that followed all enemy counterattacks were beaten off. The Japanese drew back from the Tulagi area. U. S. forces consolidated their positions on various islands, and continued to hold the offensive. The Japanese refused to meet U. S. Naval forces in direct action, resorting to "Ding-Dong" fighting—hit and run tactics—while U. S. carrier-based planes joined long-range bombers based at Henderson Field on Guadalcanal to turn back all attacks by land, sea, and air. That fall of 1942 marked growth of Allied air power in the South Pacific under direction of Lt. Gen. Kenney, MacArthur's air chief. In this theater—where vast distances and changing weather conditions set up obstacles unknown in Atlantic waters—problems were faced which developed new techniques of flying and fighting. Here airfields had to be built in teeming, insect-ridden tropical forests. Here skip bombing came into being, sending hundreds of Japanese vessels to the bottom of the sea. Here bombs were developed which "made the jungle an exploding hell for the Japanese, instead of a refuge." More fire power was added to planes. Kenney by initiating parabombing, the carefully guarded "double crisscross" technique of maneuvers, and the use of heavy machine-gun fire power in his attacking planes wrote a new chapter in aerial warfare.

THE TANK IN THIS PICTURE has been destroyed by a land mine, which means "Ambush near." The camouflaged Marines are trying to draw fire in order to locate snipers. Before many months in the jungles, U. S. troops could beat the Japanese at their own game.

GAVATU AND FLORIDA ISLANDS furnish a background, as a Japanese oil dump burns on Tanambogo (*below*) during a barrage preceding landing operations of U. S. Marines in the Solomons on Aug. 7, 1942.

BATTLE OF SANTA CRUZ

HAVING failed, during the fall of 1942, to drive U. S. troops out of the Solomons by harassing tactics, the Japanese settled down in October to concerted assault from land, sea and air. Despite repeated U. S. attacks, they continued to smuggle troops ashore on the tip of Guadalcanal. By Oct. 15, the Japanese had added shelling from ground artillery to bombardment from air and naval units, and on Oct. 23 the real assault on Henderson Field began. Meanwhile two sections of a powerful enemy fleet moved to attack. North of Tulagi, U. S. planes from Guadalcanal swooped down upon one section, while north of the islands of Santa Cruz U. S. carrier-based planes joined in long-range engagement with the 2nd section. In both actions the Japanese were turned back with heavy damage. U. S. losses were only 1 carrier and 1 destroyer—but that carrier was the *Hornet*, immortalized as "Shangri-La," base for the Doolittle air raid on Tokyo in 1942. After Santa Cruz, ground attacks on Guadalcanal died down, though Japanese troops still held out in the island. U. S. reinforcements in Nov. tipped the scale in their favor on Guadalcanal.

IRON MEN AND IRON MACHINES do their part to push the Alaskan-Canadian (Alcan) Military Highway through the wilderness. This project was planned, put under construction by the U.S. Corps of Engineers following Pearl Harbor. Then, it was thought possible Japanese U-boats and planes might endanger traffic in coastal waters and along coast highways. The road—stretching from Fairbanks, Alaska, to Dawson Creek, B.C.—was placed on the eastern side of the mountain ranges both in the U.S. and in Canada but after Allied occupation of the Aleutians and the fading of the submarine menace, there was much agitation about whether it should continue its plotted course or have the unfinished section rerouted between the mountains and the coast.

CAPTAIN EDDIE RICKENBACKER, Ace of World War I, was dramatically rescued Nov. 13, 1942, from a life raft 600 miles north of Samoa, having been lost since Oct. 2 in a plane crash while visiting battlefronts.

"TRAILS" IN GUADALCANAL are traveled at the rate of ¾ mile in two hours. They are muck holes cut out of dense jungle.

VICTORY AT GUADALCANAL

THE BATTLE of Guadalcanal, which raged from Nov. 13 to 15, 1942, was one of the great naval engagements since Jutland in World War I. It began when a small U. S. squadron intercepted a large Japanese transport and convoy fleet with a daring attack which created such havoc that the Japanese ships found themselves firing on each other in the darkness. In confusion, they finally fled but U. S. planes, in hot pursuit, kept up the fight until the whole Japanese armada abandoned the enterprise, retreated toward their bases in the north. It was a costly defeat for them, with 28 Japanese ships lost, 10 damaged, as against U. S. losses of 2 cruisers and 7 destroyers. Air power had played a dominant part, but the major part of the damage had been inflicted by gun crews of U. S. warships. From this victory stemmed fundamental changes in the South Pacific war theater, while in that same Nov. of 1942 dramatic and portentous events were unfolding on another side of the globe. While the great Russian offensive hurled the Nazis back from Stalingrad, the Anglo-American Allies launched their invasion of North Africa applying the many amphibious lessons learned in the Solomons. On Guadalcanal a systematic withdrawal of Japanese forces—constantly harried by U. S. troops on land, U. S. ships and planes at sea—brought the announcement that on Feb. 10, 1943, all resistance in the island had ceased. Japanese losses in troops, transports and battleships had been staggering. Heavy U. S. losses, too, made it a bitter, costly struggle for one small outpost, but that small outpost was a strategic necessity for further offensives, either for Japan or for the U. S. Adm. King paid tribute to its defense by Allied forces: "Because the Japanese through weeks and months were determined that Guadalcanal with its Henderson Field should not be lost to them . . . the world knows by now that the Marines, in their victory at Guadalcanal, completed an ageless epic for American history." Through the spring U. S. air power kept up a continuous assault on Japanese bases and shipping, culminating in sweeping victory on March 4 in the Battle of the Bismark Sea—"a victory of such completeness as to assume the proportions of a major disaster to the enemy," according to official communiqué.

THESE MARINES ON GUADALCANAL celebrated the 167th birthday of the Marine Corps on Nov. 10, 1942, by giving the Japanese a special exhibition of artillery skill. The 75 mm. pack howitzer being used to shell the Japanese position is a favorite Marine weapon because of its mobility.

THIS JAPANESE SOLDIER chose death by sneaking back into positions lost 3 days before, hoping to kill 1 American before his own certain end should overtake him.

A SOLDIER'S MAIL is usually the most important thing in his life. Despite valiant efforts to keep it coming through, it is necessarily often delayed. This was especially true in outposts widely separated by the far spaces of the Pacific, and whenever mail-day came to Guadalcanal it came in thousand-bag lots—all at once.

CLEANLINESS IS NEXT TO IMPOSSIBLE, but this "September Morner" carries on a Marine tradition in a stream at the edge of a Guadalcanal jungle, with excellent light for his mirror.

Rendova, in the central Solomons, fell June 30, 1943 to U. S. Marines who began to lay log roads through jungle muck.

SHELL CASES LITTERED the deck of a U.S. ship, as day dawned off the coast of New Georgia Island. All night, guns had thundered over Munda and its airfield, stepping-stone from central Solomons to northernmost Bougainville, thence toward major Japanese defense lines. On July 4th, 1943, U.S. troops from north and south alike sang "Marching through *New Georgia*" as they settled in to besiege Munda.

JAPANESE PRISONERS, almost unknown early in the war, were taken in increasing numbers during 1943. Creed of fanatical individual or mass suicide, "for the honor of the Emperor," had lost some of its appeal when soldiers learned U.S. did not torture and murder prisoners.

U. S. forces, May 11, 1943, landed on bleak Attu in the Aleutians occupied by Japanese since May, 1942.

FIGHTING FANATICALLY, Japanese held out three weeks on Attu, then were killed or committed "hara kiri." When the U.S. took over, only 11 were left out of 3,000. But when U.S. and Canadian troops landed, Aug. 15 at Kiska after heavy bombardments, the entire garrison (10,000) had run out under cover of fog. Perhaps the "Son of Heaven" in Tokyo had decided live soldiers were more useful than "honor."

EVEN IN ICE-BOUND ALEUTIANS, the new invasion technique was helpful, as when the caterpillar tractor above backed into a barge to pull out a 105 howitzer. Aleutian occupation by Allied forces made the Japanese-built seaplane and U-boat bases available to them for raids on the Kuriles, a long string of islands leading from Japan toward Alaska.

MUNDA AIRFIELD was battered day and night with artillery and bombs (*above*), but the Japanese garrison refused to surrender. U.S. ground forces struggled through the jungle to surround it. Still it held out, until last remnants of the garrison were killed or scattered in the fury of the fighting. It fell to the U.S. on Aug. 14, 1943. By Aug. 27 most key positions in the central Solomons were freed of Japanese occ tion, while those they still held were rendered useless by constan raids and ever-growing U.S. sea power in the Pacific. The slow pro of "island hopping" was still necessary, but a few more steps wo establish a firm base for bolder plans of the South Pacific comm

:US ISLAND, only 4 air hours from Tokyo, was in Sept., 1943, by carrier-based Grumman Hellcats ir combat début. Score: 7 Japanese bombers de- d on the ground, with 85% of all installations—bar- runways, fuel tanks, radio station. Fires were still g the next day.

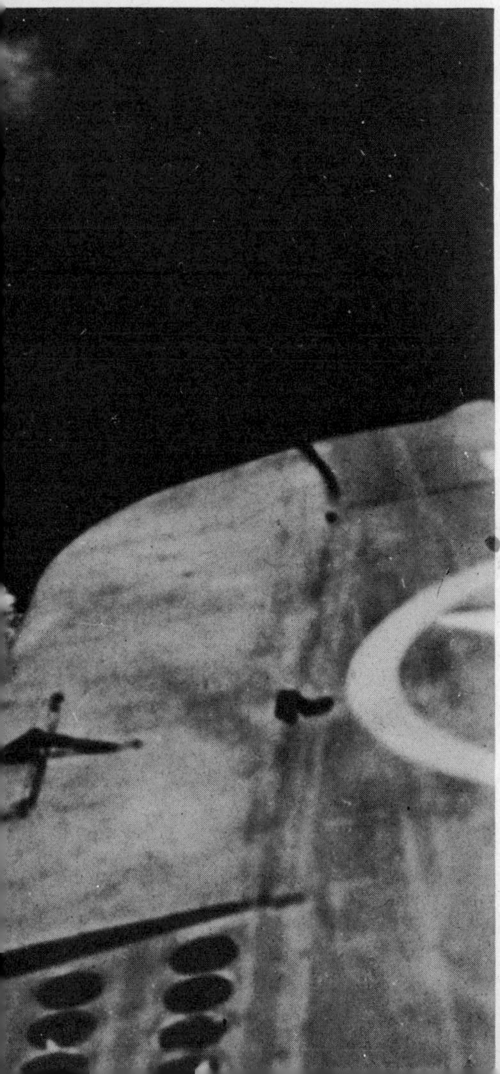

MARCHING THROUGH NEW GEORGIA

TWELVE DAYS AT THE FRONT in New Georgia made welcome a furlough from the jungle, where life was reduced to barest necessities, with days and nights alike a horror of fatigue, danger, and slime.

MUNDA WAS A GRAVEYARD of Japanese planes when U.S. forces took over the airstrip. Junk was collected in piles for sorting, all engines and metal parts loaded on a landing craft for salvage.

BOUGAINVILLE WAS THE LAST large Solomon's island remaining in Japanese hands after Allied occupation of New Georgia. On Nov. 1, 1943, U.S. Marines opened the campaign for Bougainville by landing in shallow waters on Empress Augusta Bay (*above*). Since the first invasion a year before at Guadalcanal the Allied nations had been work on problems of amphibious landing on hostile shores, and man of the newly designed craft were already in use in the Pacific theate Above: Water vehicles released from LST's scuttle ashore.

FLAME THROWERS, developed by U.S., proved their value in breaking the siege of Munda and again at Bougainville, where the portable one-man model in the picture was used to clean out Japanese pillboxes. A new strategy was tried in this island—attack was concentrated on a vital point which undoubtedly could be held, while the rest of the island was "by-passed." Here, a defense perimeter about the airfield, firmly established, kept the enemy out.

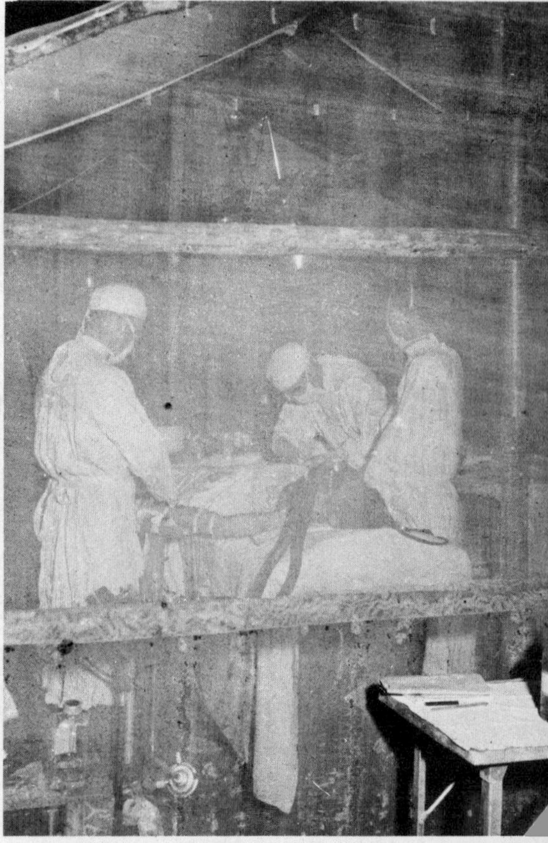

FIELD SURGERY is one of the miracles of modern war fare. Closer and closer to fighting fronts doctors and nurse have gone, with portable operating rooms, and all equip ment for emergency operations. This, plus developmen of life-saving drugs such as sulfa and penicillin, has cut th death rate among wounded to less than 3%.

THE GILBERT ISLANDS came next in the Allied "counter-expansion" in the South Pacific. Critics who complained that "island hopping" would take hundreds of years, at Guadalcanal speed, to reach the Philippines got their answer. For months U.S. forces were still weak, as well as far from home base. Japan still had more matériel for war, in each area; and the entire surrounding territory about each base had to be cleared of the enemy to make it secure from counterattack. By the end of 1943 balance of power was shifting.

TARAWA WAS THE FOCUS of resistance in the Gilberts. The Japanese knew its importance, on the direct line of Allied communications to Guadalcanal and Australia. They had turned the coral island into a "total" fortress, and dug in to stay. Rock was reinforced by concrete and steel. Every defense device they knew was installed. Guns raked the narrow beach, razor-edged with coral reefs. There was no cover. There was no escaping those entrenched guns. But there was no retreat for the defender on the stony atoll, either. He had to beat off the invasion, or die. It took 3 days of incredibly bloody fighting on the beach to make an opening in the fortress wall. Tarawa fell on Nov. 20, 1943, having become the costliest single action in Marine Corps history. The pictures on this page tell the story of the Battle of Tarawa.

MAKIN ATOLL

Already visited in the summer by the Marine force called "Carlson's Raiders," Makin fell on Nov. 20, 1943, to U. S. Army troops under Maj. Gen. Ralph C. Smith, just before Tarawa capitulated; thus began a long series of victories which the U. S. Navy-Marines-Army team has since strung across the Pacific. The August raid had been a foray of "Carlson's Raiders" in the best Commando tradition, under spectacular Col. Evans Carlson, with Maj. James Roosevelt second in command. In their lightning visit they had disposed of a small Japanese garrison, destroyed 2 seaplanes and a radio station, then stood by while Japanese bombers from a neighboring island poured destruction upon their own men and equipment, in the mistaken belief that they were wiping out the invaders. For the "Raiders" it meant another step in their development as "specialists" in the hit-and-run brand of amphibious warfare—for America's widening offensive it meant Makin had been "softened up" for the knock-out blow to come in November. With two bases in the Gilberts, the Allies were now ready to take on the Marshalls.

Jeeps go ashore at Cape Gloucester, New Britain, Dec. 17, 1943.

The South Pacific Empire, which Japan had so confidently planned and so nearly achieved, had reached the limits of its expansion at the moment when her naval and air power were no longer strong enough to protect the widely separated bases she had seized and fortified. When Allied forces called a halt at Coral Sea and Midway, in the summer of 1942, turning Japan's fleet back before she had reached Australia on her scheduled list of conquests, a new phase in the conflict had been reached. The steady increase of Allied sea and air power since Dec. 1941 had soared to such proportions by the end of 1943 that the naval balance of power had definitely shifted, even without counting Japan's catastrophic losses. The U. S. fleet had been growing at an incredible rate, and guns from British ships had spoken again in Far Eastern waters. The spectre of Japanese naval supremacy had been finally destroyed. Meanwhile, without risking itself in a major battle, the Japanese Navy had been nibbled at so constantly in its desperate efforts to convoy troops and supplies over the staggering distances "between stops" in the Pacific, that it was in no condition to attempt the further expansion planned there. By spring of 1944, American task forces striking deep into the once closed Japanese "Sphere" encountered no opposition from her fleet. Her far-flung island bases, cut off from the mother plant, without reinforcement or supplies, had been left to wither on the vine, or be plucked whenever and wherever MacArthur and Halsey spoke the word. Before the Japanese bases had reached this unhappy state, Rabaul in New Britain had been cast for the role of key supply base and nerve center for Japanese expansion in the Solomons, New Guinea, and the Bismark Archipelago, and the air fields and harbor there had been subject to repeated air and sea attacks. But when U. S. Marines and Gen. Krueger's 6th Army invaded New Britain on Dec. 15, 1943, they chose Arawe peninsula, at the opposite end, directly across the straits from New Guinea where Australians had gained positions on the Huon peninsula. Establishment of the Arawe beachhead, two days after landing, linked Allied forces across the straits, while it severed Japanese communications with their base on the north shore of New Britain. On Dec. 26, after a prelude of bombardment from air and sea, landings were made on either side of New Britain's Cape Gloucester, from which the Japanese launched strong counterattacks, clinging stubbornly to key hill positions. It was Jan. 14, 1944, before the last defense post fell, giving the Allies control both of southern New Britain and the Vitias Strait. This was important. It blocked the path of any attempted thrust to the south by the Japanese, it pierced their outer defense ring, and it gave the Allies a connecting link with other operations simultaneously under way in the South and Central Pacific.

Bulldozers have become important invasion weapons.

Having been initiated in the peculiar dangers of atoll warfare by the blood bath at Tarawa, the Allied Command checked the picture, revised methods, worked out improved tactics, with more amphibious landing craft, more attention to preliminary softening up. They also made sure of the element of surprise, even though they could not conceal the fact that, due to geographical logic, a blow at the Marshalls must follow fairly soon after the taking of the Gilberts. When Japan's path had been blocked in 1942, Australia, New Zealand, New Hebrides, New Caledonia, Samoa, Hawaii, having remained outside the ring of conquest, stood as guardians of Allied shipping lanes, and as bases from which a wide counter-offensive might be launched. The Marshalls belonged to the rim of the power-circle Japan had reached, in 1942, when she expected to go right on pushing that circle out still farther. But now, in 1944, there was no "conquering Japan" expanding to include that outer circle under her sinister shadow. Now there were only hostile forces closing in on her, first from one point in the perimeter, then another. Japan's circle of empire was slowly but inexorably shrinking. And her mighty fleet was hiding somewhere in home waters, or licking its wounds in dry dock. Preliminary bombing of the Marshalls by the Allies had begun as early as Nov., 1943, and continued with such harassing frequency that air bases there were in very bad working order most of the time. When the moment came to strike, the Allies achieved a tactical surprise by sweeping in behind the outer islands, which had been heavily prepared for surprise attacks, and hurling their landing craft at inner islands which had been regarded as safely sheltered. Most important of these was Kwajalein, considered the finest naval base east of Truk. The plan of attack followed the classic pattern. For two days probably one of the greatest naval striking powers ever assembled stood offshore, carrier raids alternating with terrific naval shelling. When the vast amphibious armada arrived on Jan. 3, 1944, from various bases, it was the new type of combined Army-Navy-Marine team which stormed onto the designated beaches under cover of bombardment from air and sea. To prevent such carnage as on Tarawa's beaches, orders had been given that by the time Allied troops made their landing, no shelter must be left on the island for the defending garrison. Mighty Kwajalein staggered under the blows, and resistance ended Feb. 4. The lessons learned at Tarawa had brought complete victory, with loss of life in reverse ratio—8,000 Japanese killed as against an Allied death list of 286. The fall of Kwajalein opened the door to Truk, after a few more of the Marshall bases had been isolated. But by Feb. 16, when *Task Force 58* steamed up to Truk, long considered impregnable, it found there only what was virtually an empty coral shell.

BEACHHEAD AT

EARLY in 1944, while arm-chair strategists were still coldly critical of "island-hopping," three dramatic events were shaping, all destined to confound critics by injecting into the Pacific war qualities of speed and drive such as no other war theater had ever known. (1) Reorganization of the Pacific Naval Command, in Jan., 1944, created *Task Force 58*, which was to startle the world with its unprecedented mobility, power, and striking force. (2) Organization of the *20th Air Force* in April, 1944, added another new weapon to the Allied arsenal—a special "global task force," under direct control of the Chiefs of Staff, to be assigned to any area in any theater of war, and made up entirely of Superfortress (B-29) bombers, half as large again as the Flying Fortress, twice as powerful, unique in combination of range, speed, and bomb-load. (3) A new "island-maneuvering" strategy was worked out to synchronize all branches of Allied Pacific force into a closely co-ordinated, fast-moving, hard-hitting, almost irresistible weapon of defense. With MacArthur's occupation of the Green Islands, Feb. 16, 1944, completing a ring of conquest above Bougainville, cutting off 22,000 Japanese still hiding on that island, the new tactical pattern began to emerge. When MacArthur stabbed next to the north, through the Bismark Sea, to make a landing on Los Negros Island in the Admiralties on Feb. 29, it was evident that at last the strategy which had swept the Japanese, in six months, from Manila to the Solomons was about to be reversed—just as the Nazis' *blitzkrieg* had been reversed in Europe. With 100,000 "sons of heaven" scattered through the islands below the Bismark Archipelago, cut off from communications and supplies, left in isolated garrisons to tremble and starve, MacArthur could take off the clumsy, cautious galoshes in which he had waded through the Solomons, to New Britain, to Los Negros. Now he could pull on those seven-leagued boots which were to carry him, in a few tremendous strides, back to the shores and the people of the Philippines, to whom he had made his famous pledge: "I shall return!"

GREEN ISLANDS

THE JAPANESE GARRISON in the Green Islands had resisted, to the last man, Americans and New Zealanders who now went to work with "cat" tractors to clean up the terrain and establish a garrison while Allied forces continued their triumphal progress northward. In the Admiralties (*left*) U. S. soldiers took flags and Samurai swords from Japanese officers who had led waves of screaming, crazed soldiers to certain death in front of the invaders' guns.

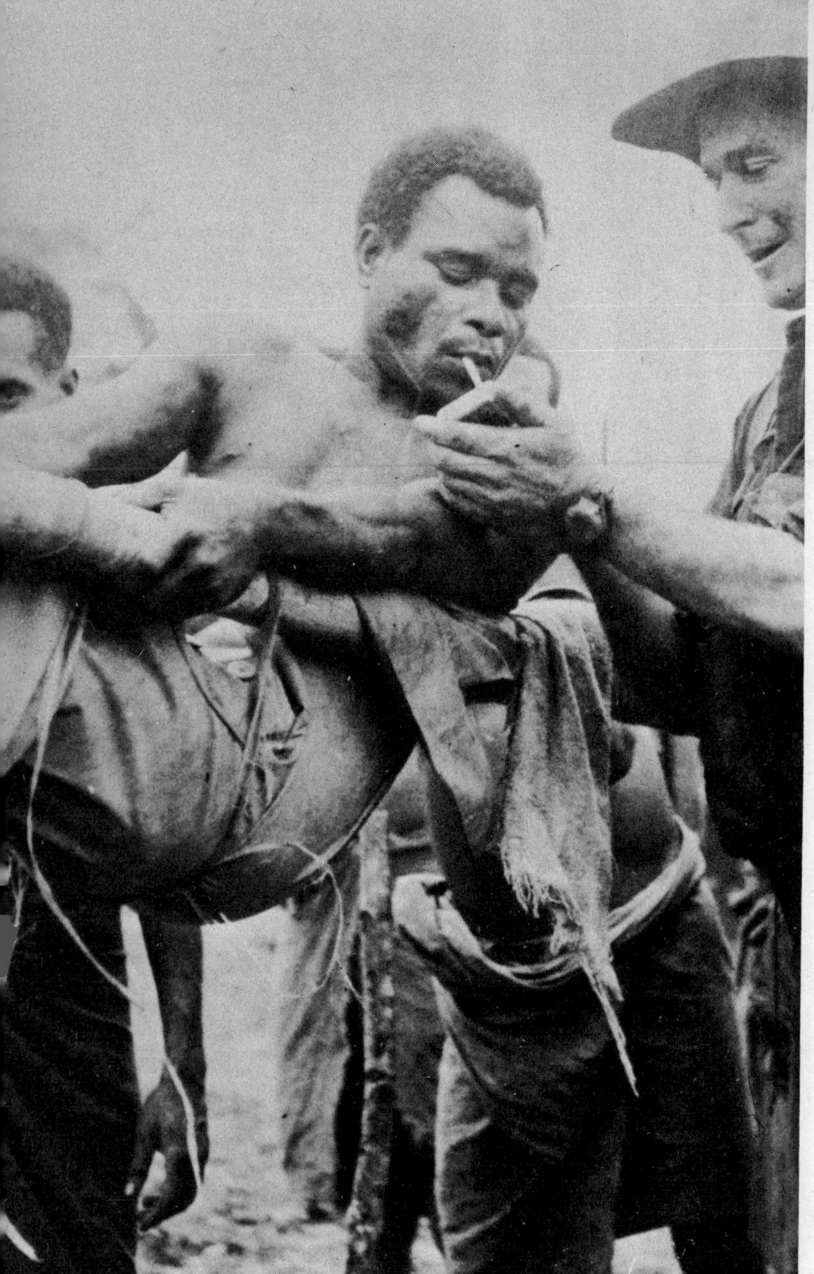

Natives of New Guinea joined Aussies in war against Japs.

NEW GUINEA—AUSTRALIA'S

Kokoda, in the Owen Stanley foothills, captured by

Sombre Milne Bay, graveyard for the Japanese who Guinea's southern tip. Jumping-off place for Australia,

In the Japanese plan for conquest, New Guinea and the Solomons were bases from which Japan was to strike at Australia, cut shipping anes from the U. S., then sweep forward around her island circle of ggression. Even with the intensive "simulated-jungle" training U. S. oldiers had received in Southern swamps, the actuality of New Guinea's jungles was an experience interesting, exciting, horrible, all t once. Yet the green mold, steaming heat and loathsome luxuriance of poisonous-looking vegetable and animal life were no more sinister han the gnome-like little yellow men who slipped dangerously in and out of jungle-shadows, at home in the murk as if they too had been pawned in its slimy depths. In the summer of 1942, at the peak of apan's aggression, these men of Nippon had been in New Guinea ong enough to have dug themselves in to stay. The coastal areas they occupied were surrounded by close networks of bunkers and pill-boxes, solid with concrete and steel, deeply hidden in dense jungle. Bombs had little effect on them. Each separate fortification had to be educed by land assault; each lurking sniper had to be run down and inished hand-to-hand. Early in the spring of 1942, Japan had pounced upon Lae, Salamaua, and Finschhafen, harbor cities on the New Guinea coast, facing New Britain where she had also seized Rabaul and Kavieng with their valuable air bases. From these points the Japanese attempted one attack after another by land, sea, or air, at Port Moresby, Milne Bay, near-by islands, various points on the Australian coast. Time after ime they were thrown back, their planes shot down, their convoys unk. But new convoys kept arriving, new men, new equipment. They

FIRST LINE OF DEFENSE

Japanese early in the war, was recovered Nov. 1942.

tried more than once to take it, is at New
it held irresistible lure for Japanese strategists.

Aussies in the Ramu Valley remove traces of Japanese occupation.

tried hacking a path inland across the narrow part of the island to Port Moresby which they wanted because, like Milne Bay, it was a gateway to Australia. But not even their jungle-wise Japanese cunning was able to "infiltrate" the towering Owen Stanley mountains, thick forests and terrible swamps. Once, by squirming their way through a small gap in the range, they came within 12 miles of Port Moresby, but they were promptly thrown back. So the struggle went on, a test of endurance, on one of the world's worst battlefields. Gen. MacArthur and Australian Gen. Blamey came to look over the ground, brought in more guns, light tanks, reinforcements. While the Japanese contested every foot of earth—mud, rather—Buna and Gona were retaken, the enemy was pushed slowly out of Papua. Then for months the stalemate was broken only by air and sea raids in a campaign of attrition. On June 30, 1943, U. S. ground reinforcements landed, drove inland for junction with Aussies, July 10. Early in Sept. more Allied troops landed to help in the campaign for Salamaua and Lae. Parachutists were dropped in Markham valley to the rear. Dec. 12, 1943, Salamaua fell, Lae on the 16th. Still the same slow, weary, bitter fighting went on. With new Aussie reinforcements, Finschhafen, on the tip of the Huon peninsula, had been occupied by the Allies Oct. 2, 1943. It took the next 2 months to advance 12 miles, to break Japanese resistance at Sattelberg, Nov. 26, and Wareo, Dec. 8. But now the Huon peninsula commanding the straits between New Guinea and New Britain was in Allied hands. Taking of Arawe and Cape Gloucester meant control of the water-way linking central and southern Pacific waters.

VICTORY at Salamaua and Lae, held by Japanese since their first sweep south in 1942 until Sept. 12, 1943, revealed a shaft 30 ft. deep under the hut of the Japanese commander leading to an elaborate underground shelter. At Lae, Sept. 16, Aussies celebrated their victory at the ice plant the Japanese left in operation. Dogs of the Army K-9 Corps (*upper rt.*) and the Marines' War Dogs Division, used on many battlefronts, proved especially useful in the jungles. They do their best work as messengers, scouts, spotters of wounded and snipers, and discoverers of land mines, especially the plastic kind which defy mechanical detectors. Bulldozers and tractors (*rt. center*) do a giant's job clearing out reeking jungle vegetation.

AFTER THE CAPTURE OF FINSCHHAFEN (*above*) in Oct., 1943, by Aussie troops, and occupation of New Britain's coast across the straits by U. S. forces, American engineers began preparing coastal harbors for Allied use. With sea and air control in Allied hands, the new strategy of neutralizing and by-passing enemy strongpoints, without wasting men or time on complete conquest, was applied to the Allied march up the Pacific toward Tokyo. By a combination of amphibious landings, air-borne landings back of enemy lines and surprise sea and air raids, key points along the New Guinea coast were taken, with Aussies later continuing the same tactics along New Britain's coast toward Rabaul. Saidor fell to the Allies Jan. 2, 1944, while Madang was threatened by an air-borne Australian force.

ALLIED TROOPS made an amphibious landing, May 18, 1944, on Wadke Island, off the New Guinea coast 110 miles north of Hollandia. Pinned down at first on the beach by machine-gun fire, they forged ahead to put down a suicidal defense by the Japanese garrison and take over the airfield. In the New Guinea mainland opposite, it was May 24 before the Maffin airstrip was won. During the entire spring MacArthur's planes had battered airfields from Wewak to Hollandia, ranged as far afield as Truk and the Carolines. In April U. S. troops had taken Madang, landed at Hollandia and Aitape. All Japanese left now in New Guinea or New Britain were cut off, pounded from the air, rendered incapable of anything more than suicidal resistance, while the Allies broke through to the open sea.

THE U. S. ARMY SENT VETERAN FIGHTERS ashore at Saipan in June, 1944, to join Marine and Naval forces. One factor in the pattern for victory now emerging in the South Pacific lay in increased co-ordination and co-operation on the part of Army, Navy and Air arms of the service. All shadows of peace-time rivalries were cast aside. They were a team now, all U. S. Forces, in a new kind of game —amphibious warfare, on an unimagined scale, where every operation meant unified action, split-second timing, all the way through.

Marine flame-throwing tanks wiped out many Jap pillboxes.

SAIPAN—GATEWAY

SAIPAN, in the Marianas, offers a clear picture of the whole new pattern in the Pacific war—combined operations in which land, sea and air forces attack, outflank, neutralize, and attack again. By preliminary raids on air bases within plane-flight of Saipan, the enemy's air power was put out of commission, at least for a time. By moving the powerful *Task Force 58* into the area, control of the sea was insured, at least within range of her guns. Keyed entirely to offense, this new unit of the fleet corresponded to the "armored fist" of the *blitzkrieg* on land. Made up of new fast battleships and their complement of smaller ships, it was centered around 20 or more of the newest and biggest carriers, accompanied by its own supply train from which it could be refueled and supplied in mid-ocean. Large enough to divide into spearheads, or in full strength to take on a major engagement, it was a naval weapon of surpassing mobility and power. The Marianas, next U. S. objective after the Gilberts, had been in Japan's possession twenty years, and the fight put up by its 20,000-man garrison was evidence that Japan appreciated the island's strategic value to her. But the Jap-

S. PARATROOPS PLAYED A GALLANT PART in many a hard-ıght campaign, both in the Pacific and in Europe. Their job was rticularly hazardous on an atoll like Saipan, where flat plains pro-ded little cover, and a hill section, infiltrated with caves, was made to order for snipers. On Saipan in a ravine called "Hell's Pocket," with limestone cliffs towering hundreds of feet, and honeycombed with caves, thousands of Japanese waited with mortars and machine guns, had to be cleaned out with flame-throwers.

TO TOKYO

nese had depended upon hazardous off-shore reef forma-ions to protect much of their coast from landings, and when he tracked landing vehicles carried surprise waves of assault roops right over those reefs, instead of coming up on the at sandy beaches where sentries' guns were waiting, the irst stage of successful invasion had been accomplished. The ext step—seizing ground with infantry and tanks—was aken at the cost of bitter fighting and many lives, but it vas taken. July 8, 1944, when U. S. forces were in complete ontrol, the battle for Saipan had been the costliest yet ought in the Pacific. The present measure of Japan's des-eration was the measure of the suicidal zeal of Saipan's lefenders, but not even the importance of Saipan induced apan to risk a major naval engagement. A strong fleet came ut of hiding, for the first time in a year, but it only came lose enough to lose many carrier planes and several ships efore it scuttled back to home waters, pursued by a swarm f Allied planes until contact was lost in darkness. After J. S. forces finished burying the 25,000 Japanese dead they ound on the island, they began converting it to an airbase.

Over 700 Japanese planes were turned into junk at Saipan.

FROM GUAM TO NEW GUINEA—PRELUDE TO INVASION

GUAM rejoiced when the Japanese capitulated on Aug. 9, 1944, to American forces after a 3-week siege of the island. Trooping down from the hills, singing, praying, shouting their thanks to U.S. soldiers and Marines who had set them free, the people of Guam poured into their little capital, hysterical with relief from the long nightmare of Japanese occupation. Guam had belonged to the U.S. from 1899 until the Japanese seized it in the early days of the war, and it was the first U.S. possession to be retaken. The strategic importance of Guam to Japan is apparent on any map. It is literally a hub from which lines of approach radiate to every part of the circle of islands and coastline bordering the Pacific. Powerfully fortified—by Japan, unfortunately, after Dec. 1941, instead of by America before that date—Guam was necessary to the Allied offensive. After the fall of Kwajalein in Jan. 1944, the Allies had established garrisons at strategic points in the Marshalls. In Feb., Enewitok was taken—and its wide air control—while at the other end of a downward arc, Allied seizure of the Admiralties isolated Japanese positions on New Britain and in the Solomons. In April, many Japanese garrisons in New Guinea were bypassed when troops landed at Aitape, Hollandia, and Madang. Wadke, an island off the coast, and Biak, marked 2 forward leaps in May. At the same time, at the upper end of the arc, Marcus and Wake were being pounded, their installations neutralized. In June, invasion of Saipan permanently outflanked Truk, and capture of Guam neutralized all Japanese holdings on islands to the south. Guam also opened sea and air invasion doors to any coastal point, from Japan down to the Philippines. Operating from captured bases, Allied air power ranged far and wide over an ocean very little disturbed now by Japanese sea power. Potential trouble spots were knocked out by shelling or isolation, while the enemy was kept in a state of confusion by softening-up raids, from the Bonins down to the Carolines.

ɪ GUAM, TO CAPE SANSAPOR at the western tip of New a, the way was open by Aug., 1944, for a great Allied offensive would retrieve all Japan's purloined Pacific possessions. At the view from a Navy plane far overhead shows a fleet of amphibi-nks racing toward the beach at Guam. In the background picture, ibious tanks are lined up at a U.S. Pacific base, ready to roll into elly" of the LST waiting to take them to the invasion of Sansapor, 0, 1944.

IN A SUDDEN DRAMATIC MOVE, mid-Sept., 1944, MacArthur staged one of the most important actions of the Pacific offensive. Striking simultaneously almost 500 miles apart, U.S. troops landed on enemy-held islands directly in sea routes to the Philippines. From bases in New Guinea, one invasion armada swept upon Morotai island in the Halmahera group beyond New Guinea and only 300 miles from Mi- danao. Here Gen. MacArthur led his troops ashore in a landing almo unopposed, so well had the softening-up been done. In the pictu above, the bobbing heads and packs belong to U.S. Infantrymen wh are wading from ship to shore, to take over Morotai.

LANDING AT PELELIU in mid-Sept. was in grim contrast to Morotai. The Palau Island group, with Peleliu its strategic defense hub, lay at the rim of the Carolines, only 500 miles from Davao. Despite the most terrific softening-up campaign and preliminary bombardment yet staged in the Pacific, the Japanese offered such desperate resistance that weeks of bitter fighting were required to subdue the fanatical de- fenders. In the above picture, amphibious tanks churn toward beache at Palau.

GENERAL DOUGLAS MACARTHUR came back to the Philippines without fanfare, as he had left two and a half years before. Wading ashore, in the greatest amphibian landing ever made at such a distance from bases and supplies, he greeted his men with a wave of the same battered leaf-encrusted cap he had worn at Corregidor. In this October of 1944 Field Marshal MacArthur of the Philippine Army had returned to his command. Speaking to them the next day over the radio, the few words he had to say were weighty words. "I have returned," he said to them, and the whole world knew what that simple statement meant. It was the fulfillment of one of the most famous pledges in history. The American flag went up on the beaches Oct. 1944, while machine guns and mortars still raked the area.

Graphic Picture of Our Philippines Victory

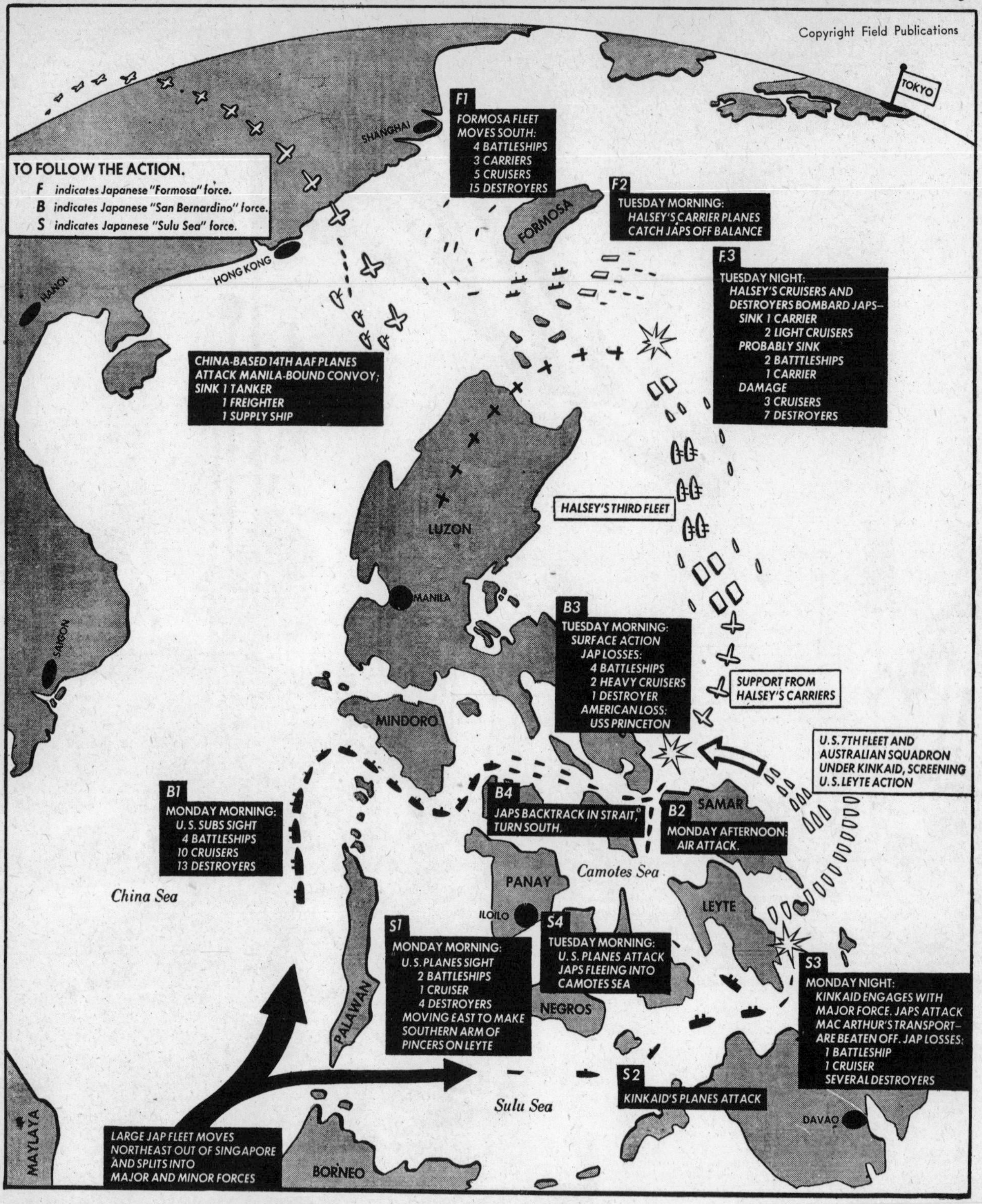

TOKYO

SHANGHAI

F1
FORMOSA FLEET MOVES SOUTH:
4 BATTLESHIPS
3 CARRIERS
5 CRUISERS
15 DESTROYERS

TO FOLLOW THE ACTION.
F indicates Japanese "Formosa" force.
B indicates Japanese "San Bernardino" force.
S indicates Japanese "Sulu Sea" force.

FORMOSA

F2
TUESDAY MORNING:
HALSEY'S CARRIER PLANES CATCH JAPS OFF BALANCE

HONG KONG

HANOI

F3
TUESDAY NIGHT:
HALSEY'S CRUISERS AND DESTROYERS BOMBARD JAPS–
SINK 1 CARRIER
2 LIGHT CRUISERS
PROBABLY SINK
2 BATTLESHIPS
1 CARRIER
DAMAGE
3 CRUISERS
7 DESTROYERS

CHINA-BASED 14TH AAF PLANES ATTACK MANILA-BOUND CONVOY;
SINK 1 TANKER
1 FREIGHTER
1 SUPPLY SHIP

HALSEY'S THIRD FLEET

LUZON

MANILA

SAIGON

B3
TUESDAY MORNING:
SURFACE ACTION
JAP LOSSES:
4 BATTLESHIPS
2 HEAVY CRUISERS
1 DESTROYER
AMERICAN LOSS:
USS PRINCETON

SUPPORT FROM HALSEY'S CARRIERS

MINDORO

U.S. 7TH FLEET AND AUSTRALIAN SQUADRON UNDER KINKAID, SCREENING U.S. LEYTE ACTION

B1
MONDAY MORNING:
U.S. SUBS SIGHT
4 BATTLESHIPS
10 CRUISERS
13 DESTROYERS

B4
JAPS BACKTRACK IN STRAIT, TURN SOUTH.

SAMAR

B2
MONDAY AFTERNOON:
AIR ATTACK.

China Sea

PANAY

Camotes Sea

LEYTE

ILOILO

S1
MONDAY MORNING:
U.S. PLANES SIGHT
2 BATTLESHIPS
1 CRUISER
4 DESTROYERS
MOVING EAST TO MAKE SOUTHERN ARM OF PINCERS ON LEYTE

S4
TUESDAY MORNING:
U.S. PLANES ATTACK JAPS FLEEING INTO CAMOTES SEA

S3
MONDAY NIGHT:
KINKAID ENGAGES WITH MAJOR FORCE. JAPS ATTACK MAC ARTHUR'S TRANSPORT– ARE BEATEN OFF. JAP LOSSES:
1 BATTLESHIP
1 CRUISER
SEVERAL DESTROYERS

PALAWAN

NEGROS

S2
KINKAID'S PLANES ATTACK

Sulu Sea

DAVAO

MAYLAYA

LARGE JAP FLEET MOVES NORTHEAST OUT OF SINGAPORE AND SPLITS INTO MAJOR AND MINOR FORCES

BORNEO

THE SECOND BATTLE OF THE PHILIPPINES was the climax to all that had gone before in the Pacific. The great Allied sweep northward from the Solomons, with latest victories at Morotai and Palau, had opened a straight clear road to the Philippines through which Nimitz's Navy and MacArthur's Army swept to a landing at Leyte on Oct. 20, 1944. For 3 days they poured ashore, the harbor in the heart of the island filled with shipping. Now at last Japan must throw her hoarded navy into the balance. These Philippines were the keystone to her arch of Pacific empire. In Allied hands, they would be a two-edged sword to cut her life lines. On Oct. 23, 1944, Japan accepted the challenge. The ensuing battle, greatest in our naval history, resulted for Japan in one of the "worst naval defeats ever inflicted." In 3 days she lost 69 ships—ships she would need most desperately when the Battle of the Pacific became the Battle of Japan. In the insert, *right*, is Adm. Ernest J. King, Commander in Chief, U. S. Fleet and Chief of Naval Operations; at the left is Adm. Chester W. Nimitz, in Supreme Naval Command in the Pacific.